Manna in the Morning

Charles E. Fuller & J. Elwin Wright

"He . . . commanded the clouds from above, and opened the doors of heaven, and . . . rained down manna upon them to eat." PSALM 78:23, 24.

✠

THE FELLOWSHIP PRESS
9 PARK STREET, BOSTON, MASS.

PRINTED AND BOUND IN THE U. S. A. BY
KINGSPORT PRESS, INC., KINGSPORT, TENN.

Dedicated to

the millions of listeners in every country

on the globe who are a part of

THE OLD FASHIONED REVIVAL HOUR FAMILY.

ACKNOWLEDGMENTS

WE ACKNOWLEDGE with deepest appreciation the courtesies which have been extended to us by more than one hundred publishers and authors, who have allowed us to use material for this volume. The names of the authors are given in connection with the quotations used. The publishers and books include the following: Abingdon Press, extracts from *The Glory of Going On*, by R. L. Gautrey; poem by John Oxenham in *Bees in Amber*, copyright by the American Tract Society and used by permission; *The Alliance Weekly*, for extracts from sermons; Augsburg Publishing House, for extracts from *Prayer*, by O. Hallesby; William Ward Ayer, for excerpts from sermons; Bible Institute Colportage Association, for extracts from *The Prayer Life*, by Andrew Murray, *Light on Life's Duties* and *Christ Life*, by F. B. Meyer, *In His Presence*, by Anna Lindgren, *The Doctor's Best Love Story* and *The Sure Remedy*, by Walter L. Wilson; Concordia Publishing House, for excerpts from *The Cross from Coast to Coast*, by Walter A. Maier; The Society for Promoting Christian Knowledge, for extracts from *Gold Cord*, by Amy Carmichael; William B. Eerdmann Publishing Company, for excerpts from *A Philosopher's Love for Christ*, by William H. Wrighton; copyright poems of Annie Johnson Flint, used by permission of Evangelical Publishers, Toronto and New York; Grosset and Dunlap, for extracts from *The Silver Lining*, by J. H. Jowett; Harper and Brothers, for poem by Grace Noll Crowell; Norman B. Harrison, for extracts from *Living Without Worry*; Houghton, Mifflin Company, for poem by Caroline Atherton Mason; Japanese Evangelistic Band, for extracts from *The Dynamic of Service*, by Paget Wilkes; Louizeaux Brothers, for extracts from *We Beheld His Glory*, by Northcote Deck and from *Restoration*, by C. H. Mackintosh; Marshall, Morgan and Scott, for extracts from *Texts That Have Touched Me*, by W. S. Bruce, and *The Work God Blesses*, by Oswald J. Smith; *The Moody Monthly*, for poems by Beatrice Cleland, Edith Dunn Bolar, Bessie Patton Gilmore, Mary Stoner, and T. O. Chisholm; Fleming H. Revell Company, for extracts from *The Wealth, Walk and Warfare of the Christian*, by Ruth Paxson, *Quiet Talks on Personal Problems* and *Quiet Talks on Power*, by S. D. Gordon, *Road to Revival*, by Vance Havner, *God's Perfect Will*, by G. Campbell Morgan, *You Must Go Right On*, by A. Z. Conrad, *Living Above*, by Howard W. Ferrin; Silver Publishing Company, for extracts from *The Three-fold Secret of the Happy Life*, by James McConkey; *The Sunday School Times*, for extracts from editorial and for poems by T. O. Chisholm, F. W. Pitt, and Agnes Barden Dustin; *The Watchman-Examiner*, for extracts from sermons and poems by Clarence Edwin Flynn; and Zondervan Publishing House, for extracts from *The Gospel of the Cross*, by Karl Heim. In a few instances we have been unable to discover the sources. If we have inadvertently omitted any acknowledgment which should have been made we crave the indulgence of author or publisher and will gladly make acknowledgment in future editions.

We are grateful to Mrs. J. Elwin Wright for her untiring work in preparing the manuscript and to Miss Elizabeth M. Evans for valuable editorial assistance.

INTRODUCTION

IN THE SPRING of 1940, a book entitled *The Old Fashioned Revival Hour and the Broadcasters* was published, giving the story of the remarkable world-wide broadcast originated by Rev. and Mrs. Charles E. Fuller. Nearly 100,000 copies have been sold and the demand continues unabated.

During this time there have been many requests for other books. After much prayer and consultation it was decided that the author should collaborate with Mr. Fuller in the preparation of a volume which it is hoped will bring comfort, inspiration and spiritual instruction to the members of the great and ever-growing family who listen eagerly for the broadcasts of the Pilgrim Hour and the Old Fashioned Revival Hour, now being released over 777 stations.

This book has taken the form of devotional readings for every day of the year. The "cream" of the writings of many authors is included. Mr. Fuller has provided a regular weekly message. Also, at bi-weekly intervals, there appears an interesting letter from one of his listeners. These letters are reproduced for the purpose of stimulating prayer and active effort in soul-winning on the part of the reader.

Many of the messages are addressed to the unsaved or to those who need to come into a more vital experience of companionship with Christ. Others have a definite appeal to Christians to become intercessors and soul-winners. By including messages of these types we have frequently departed from the stereotyped form of devotional readings. We trust that this depature will serve its purpose in bringing conviction to those who need to lose themselves in the joy of Christian service.

Mr. Fuller has arranged for the Fuller Evangelistic Foundation to receive all of his profits from the book, without deduction. This money will be used exclusively for missionary work at home and abroad.

J. ELWIN WRIGHT

Boston, Mass.

THE OLD FASHIONED REVIVAL HOUR

FROM the city auditorium in Long Beach every Sunday morning, in the presence of a large audience, and again in the late afternoon from the Don Lee Studios in Hollywood, there goes out to all the world a broadcast that is unique in its arrangement, unexcelled in its sincerity, and unparalleled in its far-reaching spiritual effect upon its hearers. This broadcast is having a more profound influence upon religious thought than has been produced by any revivalist since the days of Moody and Sankey, two generations ago.

Little did the scientists who pioneered in radio broadcasting realize that, although it would be used extensively by great artists to bring the best music within reach of all, by politicians to advance their ambitions, by newscasters to tell the world what is happening from moment to moment, and by advertisers to sell their products, the greatest broadcast of them all, in coverage, as well as in the intrinsic value of its message, would be a simple presentation of the Gospel conceived and carried on by a business man who became a preacher because he couldn't help it. And yet that is what has happened.

There is no spot on the surface of the globe today where a person with a reasonably good receiving set may not hear The Old Fashioned Revival Hour. There is no area of any considerable extent, inhabited by civilized people, where it is not actually being heard from week to week.

Charles Edward Fuller, God's instrument for a twentieth century revival of unprecedented character, was born in Los Angles on April 25, 1887, and has lived in or near there ever since. His father was a successful business man and a great benefactor of missionary work. During most of Charles' boyhood his parents lived on a ranch near Redlands. He attended school in that city and later Pomona College, from which he graduated in 1910.

For a time Mr. Fuller was engaged by his father, working in his orange groves, and also, at one period, in a mine in northern California in which the family had an interest.

A year after his graduation from college he married a schoolmate, the attractive and talented Grace Payton. She was the daughter of a successful physician residing in Redlands. The young couple commenced their life together in their home city, where Charles engaged in business as an orange grower and also as chemist for the Agricultural Chemical Works.

There were several years of ups and downs in business before they finally settled in Placentia, California, where Mr. Fuller rose to a responsible position with a large packing firm. During all this time he was uninterested in spiritual things, although Mrs. Fuller had been brought to Christ through the personal ministry of a godly woman, Mrs. Leonora Barnhill, who became a very dear and intimate friend of them both.

Several years elapsed, bringing something of financial success and also of sorrow and anxiety. A little one was lost. Mrs. Fuller's health became seriously impaired. Then, one day, Mr. Fuller attended a service in Los Angeles, out of curiosity, at which the speaker was a former amateur wrestler and boxer whom he had known years before. The text that day was, "The eyes of your understanding being enlightened that you may know what is the hope of His calling and what the riches of the glory of His inheritance in the saints" (Eph. 1:18).

As he listened, Mr. Fuller became convicted of sin and his need of a Saviour. Leaving the service he drove out to a quiet spot in Hollywood, near Franklin Park. There he knelt in the back of his car and, after a long struggle, yielded to God. It was the beginning of a new era in his life.

For some time he continued in business while giving more and more time to the study of the Word. He became the teacher, in the Presbyterian Church at Placentia, of a Bible class with a most unusual name. It was called "The Unearthly Hour Bible Class" because it was held at 8 o'clock on Sunday morning.

After some months the conviction came to him that he must preach the Gospel. There were many problems and a great struggle in his soul, but in the end he said, "Yes," to the Spirit of God and resigned his position to attend school in preparation for the ministry. In a remarkable way his financial need was met during these years of study at the Bible Institute of Los Angeles. He graduated in 1922.

In the spring of 1925 Mr. Fuller was ordained as a Baptist minister and in the autumn of the same year the Lord blessed their home with a baby boy, Daniel Payton. That winter a very nice edifice in Placentia, known as Calvary Church, was dedicated and he became its pastor. From then until 1932 he ministered to the people there with great blessing. He not only accepted no salary but was able to help materially with the financial needs of the church from his investments in grove properties. Like Paul he had great joy in preaching the Gospel while he "made tents" for a living.

Then came the dark days of the depression. Real estate values dropped; bank loans were called; there was no sale for crops. Millions were out of work. Multitudes were ruined financially. Mr. Fuller, in the providence of God, was caught like many others. He was soon fighting with his back to the wall to avoid insolvency. All this was hard to understand, but God was working out a better plan for his life and the severe testing was a necessary part of the preparation for a wider ministry.

In the midst of all the financial trouble and anxiety little Danny became very ill with pneumonia. Word came to Mr. Fuller at the office of his attorney that the child was near death and that oxygen was being used in an effort to save his life. This stroke was almost too much. With a rebellious heart he drove toward home with little regard for speed limits, praying as he went, "O Lord, I have tried to serve you but if you take our little boy, I'm through! This is one thing I just can't endure. Lord, I can't give him up. I can't go on if you take him."

But gradually the rebellion in his heart melted as he drove on, and he

said, "Yes, Lord, Thy ways are best—I yield to Thee; I want Thy will done."
And he found himself singing that sweet old song:

> *"I will say, 'Yes,' to Jesus,*
> *'Yes, Lord, forever Yes':*
> *I'll welcome all Thy blessed will,*
> *And sweetly answer, 'Yes.'"*

How God wrought deliverance and brought the child back from the jaws of death is told in the book, *The Old Fashioned Revival Hour*. During those terrific days of suspense and trial they found comfort in God's Word, particularly in Psalm 37:5 "Commit thy way unto the Lord, trust also in Him and He shall bring it to pass."

While attending a Bible conference in Indianapolis in 1927, Mr. Fuller was invited to "pinch hit" on a gospel radio program in place of the regular speaker. This was the beginning of his interest in radio as a means of giving out the gospel message. A great burden was laid upon his heart as the vision of its possibilities came to him. This resulted in an arrangement being made for broadcasting the morning and evening services from his church in Placentia over KGER, Long Beach. Later the Thursday evening service also was broadcast. This proved to be a great spiritual blessing and was continued until he resigned from the church in 1933.

He now felt led to give his entire time to broadcasting. There could scarcely have been a more unpropitious time. He had no money, times were hard, the big earthquake came on March 10, 1933, and on March 13 every bank in the country was closed. But he believed God had spoken so he kept courageously on and the money came in from week to week in a marvelous way, although there were many testings.

In May, 1933, the Gospel Broadcasting Association was incorporated. Mr. Fuller wished to put the broadcasts on a sound financial basis so that there could be no possible basis for criticism regarding the disposition of funds. A group of well-known business men and clergymen were elected to the directorate. Mr. Fuller was made Chairman and Director and was given a modest salary.

About this time arrangements were made for the half hour weekly broadcast over KFI in Los Angeles. Soon KNX in Hollywood was added. Both of these were 50,000 watt stations. In 1935 he attempted successfully a full hour over the latter. That was the beginning of the Old Fashioned Revival Hour.

In January, 1937, he signed a contract with the Mutual Broadcasting System for programs over thirteen stations, reaching as far east as Gary, Indiana. Many were saved and the offerings received were sufficient to enable him to continue until August, 1937, when a bombshell burst which seemed about to bring his work to an end. An eastern firm wanted his time over the coast-to-coast network. His agent, Mr. Alber, brought him the bad news that he would have to give up his program.

Mr. Fuller could not believe that his work on radio was finished. After a few minutes of prayer and meditation he rose to his feet and said to

Mr. Alber, "Rudy, you tell the Mutual Broadcasting System that the Old Fashioned Revival Hour will take the coast-to-coast network."

The agent looked at him aghast. "Can you make it, Charlie?"

"No," replied Mr. Fuller, "but GOD CAN."

It meant a jump from thirteen to sixty-five stations and an increase in cost from $1441 to $4500 a week. There was little time to notify his audience of the great step of faith he was taking. However, when the day came for the first payment, the money was in hand and there was a balance of $4.29 left over!

Later, the number of stations was increased to eighty, then to one hundred seventeen, then to over two hundred. Today the message goes out over seven hundred seventy-seven outlets each Sunday. The weekly cost is $35,-000. Every cent of it comes from the voluntary gifts of the listeners. There are no wealthy sponsors or underwriters. Most of the gifts are in small sums.

Thirty-five people are employed in the office, taking care of the printing and mailing of the "Heart-to-Heart Talks" that have been so helpful, and looking after the innumerable details of the work.

Between 1937 and 1942, Mr. Fuller accepted many calls for services in the principal cities of the United States. The largest auditoriums in Detroit, San Francisco, Denver, St. Louis, Buffalo, Cleveland, Flint, Grand Rapids, Boston, Washington, and other cities were scarcely able to hold the crowds which came to hear him. In every city there were many conversions. These great mass demonstrations of revival interest have necessarily been discontinued for the present because of war conditions.

The Fullers are the same warmhearted, approachable, humble-spirited people that they were in the days when the broadcast was over one station and they faced the weekly problem of being able to continue it. Dan has grown to young manhood, still in school but an earnest student of the Bible, a real soul winner, and shows signs of becoming a capable assistant to his devoted parents in Christian service.

Who shall say what the future holds for this gospel broadcast? Its influence is universal. Its effect on all evangelical work is tremendous. Perhaps when the war clouds pass away there may be an even wider ministry. Radio sets will doubtless multiply. Television is soon to come into general use. We may be entering the greatest period of missionary activity and revival that the world has ever known. It is not beyond the bounds of possibility that invitations to visit foreign mission fields may be accepted by Mr. and Mrs. Fuller. Wouldn't it be thrilling to hear the Old Fashioned Revival Hour some Sunday evening coming from Calcutta, Shanghai, Quito, Jerusalem or Addis Ababa!

And remember, I am with you always, day by day,
until the close of the age.

Matthew 28:20 (Weymouth).

WHAT promise of our Lord could be more pertinent for the New Year than this last word recorded in Matthew's Gospel? Having His presence with us continually we are endowed with every spiritual and material blessing which life's journey, and its emergencies, in the coming year may require. Our ticket, our passport, our baggage, and every accessory are in His possession for our benefit. He looks after all changes in schedule, all departures and arrivals. All we have to do is heed His instructions, stay near His side, and confidently trust Him to bring us to our destination.

J. ELWIN WRIGHT

Standing at the portal of the opening year,
Words of comfort meet us, hushing every fear;
Spoken through the silence by our Father's voice,
Tender, strong, and faithful, making us rejoice.
Onward then, and fear not, Children of the day!
For His word shall never, never pass away!

For the year before us, Oh, what rich supplies!
For the poor and needy living streams shall rise;
For the sad and sinful shall His grace abound;
For the faint and feeble, perfect strength be found.
Onward then, and fear not, Children of the day!
For His word shall never, never pass away.

FRANCES RIDLEY HAVERGAL

Draw me, we will run after Thee.

Song of Solomon 1:4.

CHRISTIAN experience may be compared to a suite of royal apartments, of which the first opens into the second, and that again into the third, and so on. It is, of course, true that believers enter on a possession of all so soon as they are born into the royal, divine household. But, as a matter of fact, certain truths stand out more clearly to them at different stages of their history, and thus their successive experiences may be compared to the chambers of a palace, through which they pass into the throne-room and presence-chamber of their King.

And the King Himself is waiting at the threshold to act as a guide. The key is in His hand, which opens, and no man shuts; which shuts, and no man opens. Have you entered the first of those chambers? If not, He waits to unlock the first door of all to you at this moment, and to lead you forward from stage to stage, till you have realized all that can be enjoyed by saintly hearts on this side the gates of pearl. Only be sure to follow where Jesus leads the way.

F. B. MEYER

My soul is transported with Jesus,
My heart is a heaven of love;
Earth seems like a vanishing bubble,
I seem to be dwelling above;
In the depths of my bosom is springing
A chorus of glory divine,
And this is the song it is singing,
My beloved forever is mine.

I stand on the mountains of vision,
I look o'er the land far and wide, . . .
I gaze on my King in His beauty,
I know He has made me His bride;
To His banqueting house He has brought me,
I am drinking of heavenly wine,
I am singing the song of the ransomed,
My beloved forever is mine.

Beloved, Redeemer, and Master,
Oh, how can I tell what Thou art, . . .
Thou gavest Thy life for my ransom,
Thou givest Thyself to my heart;
On Thy bosom, oh, keep me abiding,
Oh, let me forever be Thine,
Still singing with rapture unceasing,
My beloved forever is mine.

A. B. SIMPSON

JANUARY 3

And the man believed the word that Jesus had spoken unto him, and he went his way.

John 4:50.

THE narrative of the nobleman and his sick son beautifully illustrates the beginning of faith and its rapid progress in a human soul. It is one thing to hear about the conversion of someone else but it is another to experience this great salvation personally, and to appropriate it by saving faith. This same living Christ is ever ready to help in time of great need, as He helped this nobleman.

Trouble led this man to Jesus. Had it not been for this severe trial he might have lived on, never knowing the Saviour. Listen! trouble will do one of two things for you. It will either drive you to the place of refuge, shelter, and safety or it will cause your heart to become hard and rebellious. Pharaoh was made bitter, stiff-necked and hard.

When the nobleman heard that Jesus was passing that way he went to Him. That was the evidence that there was within his heart a spark of faith. Faith without works is dead. He "went and besought Him." And he continued to beseech until the assurance of the answer was given him. That is your privilege and mine, also.

CHARLES E. FULLER

Just one touch as He moves along,
Push'd and press'd by the jostling throng;
Just one touch and the weak was strong,
Cured by the Healer divine.

Just one touch and He makes me whole,
Speaks sweet peace to my sin-sick soul;
At His feet all my burdens roll,—
Cured by the Healer divine.

Just one touch! and He turns to me,
O the love in His eyes I see!
I am His for He hears my plea,
Cured by the Healer divine.

BIRDIE BELL

JANUARY 4

I exhort therefore, that, first of all, supplications, prayers, intercessions, and giving of thanks, be made for all men. *1 Timothy 2:1.*

OUR prayer for a spiritual awakening will without question be most effective if we take up the work of interceding for certain individuals in particular.

We find that most of us who have been converted have had some one praying for us, some one who carried us personally to the throne of God while we were unconverted. It seems to me that no one is so poor as he for whom not a single soul is praying, he who has no one who takes him personally and persistently to God in prayer.

We should enter into this work and become personal and regular interceders for certain definite individuals. Ask the Spirit of prayer to assign to you the individuals for whom you should pray. If every be-

3

liever would do this, the Spirit would distribute the unconverted in every community among the believing men and women of prayer; and ultimately there would not be a single soul but what some consecrated and faithful believer would be praying for him.

Then it would not be easy for the unconverted to continue to live in sin! Holy spiritual explosive materials would be planted into their souls daily, and the ground blasted from beneath their unrepentant lives.

O. HALLESBY

There is a place where thou canst touch the eyes
    Of blinded men to instant, perfect sight;
There is a place where thou canst say "Arise!"
    To dying captives, bound in chains of night.
There is a place where thou canst reach the store
    Of hoarded gold, and free it for the Lord;
There is a place here, or on a distant shore,
    Where thou canst send the worker and the Word.
There is a place where Heaven's resistless power
    Responsive moves to thine insistent plea;
There is a place, a silent holy hour,
    Where God Himself descends and works for thee.
Where is that secret place?—dost thou ask "where?"
    O soul, it is the secret place of prayer!

A. A. POLLARD

JANUARY 5

And hast made us unto our God kings and priests: and we shall reign on the earth.   *Revelation 5:10.*

SUCH a thought seems incredible. Perhaps at this moment we are feeling like spiritual weaklings and cowards, not able to face courageously even the burdens and tasks of the day that lies before us. The thought of such a position and such power is preposterous! Dare we believe that any such inheritance is really ours? Let God answer the question and silence our doubt.

"Being predestinated according to the purpose of Him who worketh all things after the counsel of His own will." In the eternity of the past God marked us out for that son-place in His family which relationship puts us in line for heirship. Our redemption in Christ was the first step in the outworking of the counsel of His own will. Can God's eternal purpose be thwarted half-way? Can His sovereign will be stalemated? What God has sovereignly purposed will He not sovereignly perform? In God's eternal purpose and His sovereign will we have an all-sufficient ground for assurance that we shall obtain our inheritance in full.

Then stop just here for one moment of silent praise for such an inheritance as you have in Christ. That act of praise will double your assurance of obtaining it and increase your appreciation of its value. If you are not in the royal line of inheritors because you are not a child, will you not this moment become a child and heir by opening your heart to receive the Lord Jesus Christ as your personal Saviour?

RUTH PAXSON

JANUARY 6

If any man thirst, let him come unto Me, and drink. He that believeth on Me, . . . from within him (his innermost being) shall flow rivers of living water. *John 7:37, 38 (R. V.).*

WHILE there is in my heart an unsatisfied longing, there is available a corresponding "fullness." As long as my innermost being is not an effervescent spring, I have not received all that God has for me.

"But this spake He of the Spirit, which they that believe on Him should receive." Thank God, then, there is a way! There is an ocean of God's fullness into which I may "launch out!" There is a new venture, an experience more revolutionizing and satisfying than any I have ever known!

ANNA J. LINDGREN

> Ho! ev'ry one that is thirsty in spirit,
> Ho! ev'ry one that is weary and sad,
> Come to the fountain, there's fullness in Jesus,
> All that you're longing for, come and be glad.
>
> Child of the world, are you tired of your bondage?
> Weary of earth-joys, so false, so untrue;
> Thirsting for God, and His fullness of blessing?
> List to the promise—a message for you.
>
> Child of the kingdom, be filled with the Spirit,
> Nothing but fullness thy longing can meet,
> 'Tis the enduement for life and for service;
> Thine is the promise, so certain, so sweet.
>
> "I will pour water on him that is thirsty,
> I will pour floods upon the dry ground;
> Open your heart for the gift I am bringing,
> While ye are seeking me, I will be found."

LUCY J. RIDER

5

JANUARY 7

A sower went out to sow his seed: and as he sowed,
some fell by the way side; and it was trodden
down, and the fowls of the air devoured it . . . and
other fell on good ground and sprang up, and bare
fruit an hundredfold.   *Luke 8:5, 8.*

ON ALTERNATE weeks throughout the year we shall share
with you striking letters which have come to Mr. and Mrs.
Fuller of the Old Fashioned Revival Hour. The purpose is
threefold.

First, that you may rejoice because of the power of the Gospel
in this day to melt and move hearts God-ward.

Secondly, that you may be convicted of your responsibility to become a winner of souls as you are made to realize how many need
a Saviour.

Thirdly, that you may become a prayer-warrior, joining on this
day especially with thousands of others who will be interceding for
the lost as the messages go out again over the Pilgrim Hour and the
Old Fashioned Revival Hour.

Here is the story of one who was born again in North Carolina as
a result of these prayers and messages:

"Dear Brother Fuller: I am writing a few lines just to let you
hear the good news. As you were preaching last night about the
Sower (Luke 8:5) some of those seed fell into the heart of our
oldest boy and he surrendered his heart to Christ. You had already preached him under conviction before this. We had retired
and he was seated at the foot of my bed. Just in the last part of
your service he came to my side with tears and said, 'Daddy, I
couldn't wait any longer.'

"He is married and has one child. I have another unsaved boy.
Pray for him."

JANUARY 8

And immediately she arose and ministered unto
them.   *Luke 4:39.*

THIS woman used her new strength to return to her old duties.
She employed her divinely restored health in homely ministries
about the house. The first evidence of her restoration was found
in her own home. "Immediately she arose and ministered unto them."

6

She did not even make her way to the synagogue to offer public praise to the Lord. Nor did she retire to her chamber, that she might place upon the altar some secret thanksgiving to the King. She just took up her duties with a new strength, and found her joy in immediate ministration to those who were round about her.

It is beautiful to think that one of those to whom she ministered was the Lord Himself. The Lord of all glory sat down to her table, and the once helpless and fever-stricken woman used her new-found strength in ministering to His needs. The mother went on with her motherly work.

J. H. JOWETT

Teach me that harder lesson—how to live;
To serve Thee in the darkest paths of life;
Arm me for conflict now, fresh vigor give,
And make me more than conqueror in the strife.

Teach me to live Thy purpose to fulfill;
Bright for Thy glory let my taper shine;
Each day renew, remold this stubborn will;
Closer round Thee my heart's affections twine.

Teach me to live for self and sin no more;
But use the time remaining to me yet;
Not mine own pleasure seeking as before,
Wasting no precious hours in vain regret.

Teach me to live; no idler let me be,
But in Thy service hand and heart employ.
Prepared to do Thy bidding cheerfully—
Be this my highest and my holiest joy.

AUTHOR UNKNOWN

JANUARY 9

But when he saw the wind boisterous, he was afraid; and beginning to sink, he cried, saying, Lord, save me. And immediately Jesus stretched forth His hand, and caught him. *Matthew 14:30, 31.*

BEGINNING to sink . . . immediately . . ." But even so, for we are all weakness in ourselves, there are times when nothing comes to mind but these words. They assure us of so much more than they seem to say. . . . Chiefly they bring the certainty that there will be no sinking, for Peter never sank. ("When I said, My foot slippeth,"—in that moment—"Thy mercy, O Lord, held me up.")

7

They come underneath the feeling of sinking; they say, "This shall never be." It was Christ's sorely tried prisoner, Samuel Rutherford, who wrote that the parings and crumbs of glory, a shower like the thin May-mist of his Lord's love was enough to make him green and sappy and joyful. Such a word, even such a little word as this, if only we open our hearts to its healing power, may be a crumb of glory enlightening the soul, a thin May-mist of His love making green and sappy (or glowing and golden) what was so dull and dry before. "And immediately Jesus stretched forth His hand, and caught him." How many seconds lie between a man's beginning to sink and his sinking? A second or less, I suppose, sees one who is beginning to sink under water. How swift, then, was the movement of love! And as He was, so He is.

AMY CARMICHAEL

Oh, how sweet to walk in this pilgrim way,
Leaning on the everlasting arms;
Oh, how bright the path grows from day to day,
Leaning on the everlasting arms.

What have I to dread, what have I to fear,
Leaning on the everlasting arms?
I have blessed peace with my Lord so near,
Leaning on the everlasting arms.

E. A. HOFFMAN

JANUARY 10

Therefore if any man be in Christ, he is a new creature: old things are passed away; behold, all things are become new.　　*2 Corinthians 5:17.*

SALVATION is not an improvement of the old nature. God doesn't take the old nature and fix it up by reforming it. No, the old nature is dead in trespasses and sins. When you become a new creature in Christ Jesus you have the new nature, God's nature, imparted to you. Old things pass away and ALL THINGS become new. As you once loved the things of the world, now you will turn away from them because you have different affections. Once you had no taste for the church or prayer meetings. Now you love the brethren; you love times of spiritual fellowship. Once you had no interest in God's Word. Now it is meat and drink to your soul. Once you craved sinful pleasures. Now it is your highest pleasure to do His will. Once your time was occupied with scheming and working for money and success. Now you have found eternal riches in Him.

Why? Because you have the very nature of God transplanted into your heart.

CHARLES E. FULLER

Search me, O God, search me and know my heart,
Try me and prove me in the hidden part;
Cleanse me and make me holy as Thou art,
And lead me in the way everlasting.

Thou art the same today and yesterday,
O make Thy life in me the same alway,
Take from my heart the things that pass away;
Lead, lead me in the way everlasting.

Give me the heart that naught can change nor chill,
The love that loves unchanged through good or ill,
The joy that through all trials triumphs still,
And lead me in the way everlasting.

Take my poor heart and only let me love
The things that always shall abiding prove;
Bind all my heart-strings to the world above,
And lead me in the way everlasting.

A. B. SIMPSON

JANUARY 11

Always bearing about in the body of the dying of the Lord Jesus, that the life also of Jesus might be made manifest in our body. *2 Corinthians 4:10.*

THE emergency that the whole world is in through sin calls for sacrifices that bring great pain of spirit. A young man in a small church college in the Middle West was stirred by the needs of the foreign mission fields. He determined to offer his life and service to help meet that need. But before committing himself actively with his church authorities he wrote to her who had given him life, telling her of the burning desire in his heart, and asking her consent. By and by the answering letter came. It was blotted with tears. Its pages brought up a vivid picture of that mother's face and heart. She replied, in effect giving her consent, and then writing down these words: "I never knew until now how much it cost God to give His Son."

S. D. GORDON

Some feet must bleed,
Bruised and torn by rocks and thorns
Which in their path unbidden lie.
If any mortal can with grace endure
Those things for which earth has no cure,
Why should not I?

Some backs are bent
'Neath loads of never-ending care,
Yet all is fair as they go by.
If others then can bear their load
And smile and sing along life's road,
Why should not I?

Some eyes are dim—
Each tear speaks silently of pain
Known only to their God on high.
If weeping ones can still be bold
And carry sorrows never told,
Why should not I?

Some souls are large—
They have for grief but little heed;
Brave souls are they; souls that are high;
If they can pass 'neath chastening rod,
Keep hope undimmed, and faith in God,
Why should not I?

Through strength divine,
Come gain or loss, each one may win,
For will not God His help supply?
'Tis written, Grace for every need
Sufficient IS—you then may plead.
Why should not I?

GRANT COLFAX TULLAR

JANUARY 12

O Nebuchadnezzar, we are not careful to answer
thee in this matter . . . our God whom we serve is
able to deliver us from the burning fiery furnace,
and He will deliver us out of thine hand, O King.
But if not, be it known unto thee, O King, that we
will not serve thy gods, nor worship thy golden
image which thou hast set up.   *Daniel 3:16–18.*

THERE ought to be about every Christian a sense of power and
triumph. He ought to impress the world as being charged with
a divine electricity, drunk on heavenly wine. He has no right
to cringe through this world and talk in an apologetic tone. If we have

the only answer to the world's problem, the only cure for its ills, we have a right to speak with authority and not be cowed by the fear of man. The world had better cringe, and cringe it will if we call its bluff and meet its bravado with the courage of God.

We are persuaded that many precious testimonies are being lost today because of enervating fear. Often a supersensitiveness and over-conscientiousness becomes so fixed in the heart of a well-meaning and sincere Christian that he mistakes it for a mark of piety and confuses it with true humility. To distrust self is indeed proper, but when we have committed all to God, then to go on doubting is to doubt God. So Jeremiah needs to be braced up and bidden not to be afraid of rebellious faces. Ezekiel is given an adamant face, and Timothy is exhorted not to despise his youth. For ours is the spirit of power and Satan dreads that power, so he tricks us with ruses so clever that we fancy we please God, while in reality we possess a cowardice that is not humility.

VANCE HAVNER

JANUARY
13

This Child is set for the . . . rising again of many.
Luke 2:34.

You can rise with Christ, particularly when your hopes are lowest and when you understand His ways, though not your ways, are always the best. Sir Henry M. Stanley, searching for Livingstone in the heart of Africa, had to be led through a siege of tropical fevers that kept his temperature constantly at 105 degrees before his hardened attitude toward life turned to the joy of his salvation. His sick-bed became his school for Christ, and having read the warnings and promises of Scripture, he wrote: "I flung myself on my knees and poured out my soul utterly in secret prayer to Him from whom I had been so long estranged, to Him who had led me here mysteriously into Africa, there to reveal Himself and His will." Perhaps God has been leading some of you through the jungles of life, through the wastes of illness and loneliness, to have you find Christ and with Him this uplifting grace which Simeon proclaimed as his voice rang through the Temple, "This Child is set for the . . . rising again of many."

WALTER A. MAIER

Lonely! The very word can start the tears
And chill the heart as with the sun's eclipse;
It used to fall so sadly from my lips,
It used to sound so mournful to my ears.

Then, like Naomi in an alien land,
  I found the One who loved and guided her;
And, like Elijah by the juniper,
I tasted meat and drink from God's own hand.

Lonely? The knell fades on the brightening air,
  And melts into a happy carillon.
Is the road rough? I have a Friend to share
  Its brave adventure till the journey's done.
Come, lonely heart, will you not join us there?
Who walk with Christ can never walk alone.
                                    RUBY WEYBURN TOBIAS

JANUARY 14

And it came to pass, as He sat at meat with them,
He took bread, and blessed it, and brake, and gave
to them. And their eyes were opened, and they
knew Him.   *Luke 24:30, 31.*

HE Old Masters did not understand that God does not call men
away from the commonplaces of the busy days, but conditions
their life within them, until the meanest thing flashes and
gleams with the glory of the heavens. The monastic system was the
outcome of a pure and holy desire, but it was based upon a mis-
conception of God. Men desired to serve their age by prayer; and to
do so, retired from the hurry and rush of life, turning their back upon
marriage, parenthood, home and friendship. It was a fatal mistake.
When men retire from the conflict to pray, they cut the nerves of
prayer. Men only pray with prevailing power who do so amid the
sobs and sighing of the race. If the genesis of monasticism was a pure
desire, its history proves that it ended in lewd and awful corruption.

These illustrations are given to show that any conception of God
that makes it necessary for man to depart from the commonplaces of
life to find Him are wrong. The Old Masters saw no possibility of the
identity of an actual fisherman and an apostle. The monks went
alone to pray, because they thought that God was out of the midst
of the strife.

                              G. CAMPBELL MORGAN

The parish priest, of austerity,
  Climbed up in the high church-steeple,
To be nearer God, so that he might
  Hand His word down to the people.

12

And in sermon script he daily wrote
What he thought was sent from heaven;
And he dropped it down on the people's heads
Two times one day in seven.

In his age God said, "Come down and die";
And he cried out from the steeple,
"Where art Thou, Lord?" and the Lord replied,
"Down here among My people."

AUTHOR UNKNOWN

JANUARY
15

He that giveth, let him do it with simplicity.
Romans 12:8.

THE Apostle Paul calls Christian giving a GRACE which he wished the Corinthian Christians to learn and in which they might abound. This expression is quite contrary, I am sure, to the common conception among Christians of this day in regard to the matter of material giving. All too many think of giving as a sort of painful but necessary duty, resenting appeals for financial support of the Church, and trying to get along with giving as little as they possibly can. But Paul says, "Wherefore as ye abound in everything, in faith, and utterance, and knowledge, and in all diligence, and in your love to us, see that ye ABOUND IN THIS GRACE also."

MARTIN DeHAAN

Share thy handful with the stranger;
Bid the Prophet to thy board;
No resources are in danger
Whose exchequer is the Lord.
Daily new demands await thee,
Daily new supplies are sent;
He alone who doth create thee
Can secure thy nourishment.

Trust! the Lord will not deny thee,
Ev'ry longing shall be stilled;
Trust! the cruse will yet supply thee,
Never empty, never filled.
Should the lilies lack apparel?
Should the ravens cry in vain?
Even then the widow's barrel
Shall its handful still retain.

Why shouldst thou forecast the morrow?
Take with gladness while you may;

Why, dismayed, forebodings borrow?
See! thou hast enough today.
'Tis by loving that thou livest,
Spending doth not waste thy store,
Tho' it seem the last thou givest,
There is, aye, one handful more.

LUCY A. BENNETT

JANUARY 16

Know ye not that they which run in a race run all,
but one receiveth the prize? So run, that ye may
obtain.   *1 Corinthians 9:24.*

THE deepest misery is that which a man has when his life possesses no ultimate purpose, when he has nothing to take him beyond himself. A man who knows of no pearl so costly that he would gladly sell all others to gain it, is a miserable man. There are many such people today. That is the fundamental ailment of our generation.

We have, in our day, accomplished great things in many different fields of activity. Nevertheless, there are thousands who have not achieved genuine and thankful joy in life because they have seen no other goal before them than a week of labor, a week-end of lethargy and then another round on the treadmill of life. What does it all mean? What purpose does it all have? To these questions there is no answer. That is why the number of neurotics increases daily and the number of suicides rises to such tragic heights. One does not turn open the gas-jets merely because his wages are insufficient to provide for his needs or because of unrequited love. There is a more basic cause. It is the nothingness—the darkness of futility—that seems to stand behind all of life.

If we read the words of the Apostle which form our text with eyes open to the need of our day, we shall be impressed with the glory of them. At first reading, they seem to be a series of difficult dramas, of whiplashes that drive us forward unmercifully: "So run, that ye may attain! . . . I keep under my body!" But when we penetrate a bit deeper, we can hear the entire Gospel in this text. Here is no hard and cruel "must," but a blessed "may." God has released us from the nothingness in which we formerly lived. He has redeemed us from the futility of life. He has given us a goal, in the achievement of which we can forget ourselves, a goal which gives an eternal glow to even the poorest of human lives. Let us stand quietly before this gift of God and meditate upon the two truths to which the Apostle testifies:

14

1. There is an indestructible crown for which we may strive.
2. This gives an immeasurable value to even the most pitiful human life.

KARL HEIM

From *The Gospel in the Cross*

Christian, dost thou see them
On the holy ground,
How the hosts of darkness
Rage thy steps around?
Christian, up and smite them,
Counting gain but loss;
In the strength that cometh
By the holy cross.

JOHN M. NEALE

JANUARY
17

That we henceforth be no more children, tossed to and fro, and carried about with every wind of doctrine. *Ephesians 4:14.*

IT IS dangerous for a Christian to lose interest in the great foundational truths of our faith because they have become familiar. This is one of the reasons for the many exhortations in the Word to "hold fast," "be stedfast," "watch and pray." And let me say this to you, that one of the outstanding essential marks of a true, growing, deepening Christian life is to be stedfast, unmovable, "not carried about by every wind of doctrine." Such a Christian becomes strong because he is rooted and grounded, like a tree planted by the rivers of water, not merely set out for decorative purposes, but deeply rooted. We need warning against the peril of drifting.

CHARLES E. FULLER

"What think ye of Christ?" is the test,
To try both your state and your scheme:
You cannot be right in the rest,
Unless you think rightly of Him:
As Jesus appears in your view—
As He is beloved or not,
So God is disposed to you,
And mercy or wrath is your lot.

Some call Him a Saviour, in word,
But mix their own works with His plan;
And hope He His help will afford,
When they have done all that they can:

If doings prove rather too light
  (A little they own they may fail),
They purpose to make up full weight,
  By casting His name in the scale.

Some style Him, "the Pearl of great price,"
  And say, He's the fountain of joys;
Yet feed upon folly and vice,
  And cleave to the world and its toys:
Like Judas, the Saviour they kiss,
  And while they salute Him, betray:
Oh! what will profession like this
  Avail in His terrible day?

AUTHOR UNKNOWN

JANUARY 18

**I have glorified Thee on the earth: I have finished
the work which Thou gavest Me to do.** *John 17:4.*

EACH one of us should be in a state where we can say this in the day when an account must be given of all our works. I should look upon the work I have to do each day as ordered by God, as the work God entrusts me with, and devote myself to it in a worthy manner, that is to say, with exactness and in peace. I will neglect nothing, I will be hurried about nothing. To do God's will with negligence, or when self-love appropriates it, is dangerous, and it is then done with a false zeal. The work is accomplished in the spirit of the one who does it: one does it badly; another gets heated over it; each wishes to succeed. And the glory of God is the pretext that hides each illusion. Self-love disguises itself in a zeal that worries and annoys and makes success an impossibility. O God, give me the grace to be faithful in action and indifferent in success. My one work is to do Thy will and to remain hidden in Thee in the midst of all activity; and Thine is to give me the fruit of my feeble efforts, if Thou art so pleased; or if it is Thy will to give me nothing, let me still remain hidden in Thee.

FENELON

Dwell deep, my soul! Forbid thou shouldst stay shallow!
  Dwell deep in thought, in purpose, wish, and will!
Dwell deep in God, let His own presence hallow;
  Thy inner being let His presence fill.

Dwell deep, my soul! for human hearts are breaking
  With sorrow, sin, and sadness, and despair;
And thou, if thou wouldst help to heal the aching,
  Must learn to dwell more deep for them in prayer.

Dwell deep, my soul! God's purposes are waiting;
  The tasks of His appointing lie undone:
Full many hearts, in folly, are debating
  Should His or their will be the chosen one!

J. Danson Smith

JANUARY 19

**For if ye live after the flesh, ye shall die: but if ye
through the Spirit do mortify the deeds of the body,
ye shall live.**   *Romans 8:13.*

IT IS a fact that our old man has been crucified with Christ, but it
must be remembered that we are still living in our old bodies
subject to habits and appetites which were formed by the old
man. All of these are to be dealt with, and each one must be put to
death. There is still a vast field in which we are to win victories. We
can add nothing to that which the Lord Jesus did on the cross for us,
that is a finished work into which we are to enter by faith, but in the
realm of habits which we formed before we became Christians, there
is without doubt much land to be possessed. These habits must never
be confused with the old man which was crucified.

We are to put away falsehood, to stop stealing, to cease the habit
of corrupt speech of every sort, to cease from bitterness and anger
and wrath and clamor; all of these are old practices and habits which
must be put away (Eph. 4:24–31). These with many other habits
and customs and practices must be put to death. "Put to death therefore your members which are upon the earth: fornication, uncleanness,
passion, evil desire, and covetousness, which is idolatry; for which
things' sake cometh the wrath of God upon the sons of disobedience:
wherein ye also once walked, when ye lived in these things" (Col.
3:5–7). Some of these things became habitual, habits which had
fastened themselves upon the body and mind, and because they were
habits we thought nothing of them. When later the conscience became awakened to them, we were not able to throw them off nor to
lay them aside, because they had become part of the mind and of
the physical life. All these things are to be put to death. "But if by
the Spirit ye put to death the deeds of the body, ye shall live" (Rom.
8:13).

L. L. Legters

But I keep under my body, and bring it into sub-
jection.   *1 Corinthians 9:27.*

THE habitual cultivation of the friendly mastery of Jesus draws
out most the mastery of self and of circumstances. The keeping
of the body pure and sound and under the thumb of the will;
the keeping of the mind clear and quiet and alert and ever bending
towards a keener discipline; the keeping of the social contacts simple
and warm and cheery; the keeping of the spirit ruggedly strong and
softly gentle; the keeping of the heart pure in its loves and motives;
the meeting of all difficulties and disappointments with the cheeriness
which regards these as mere subways through to places farther up the
road; and with all this, under and through, above and around all, a
simple, confiding trust in God that sings most when the subway
lights all go out—this is the roadway to self-mastery.

S. D. GORDON

I am saved, but is self buried?
Is my one, my only aim
Just to honor Christ my Saviour,
Just to glorify His Name?

I am saved, but is my home life
What the Lord would have it be?
Is it seen in every action,
Jesus has control of me?

I am saved, but am I doing,
Everything that I can do
That the dying souls around me,
May be brought to Jesus too?

I am saved, but could I gladly,
Lord, leave all and follow Thee;
If Thou callest can I answer,
Here am I, send me, send me?

AUTHOR UNKNOWN

Him that cometh to Me I will in no wise cast out.
John 6:37.

SOMETIMES it takes only a few words, spoken at the right time and place, to bring a soul to Jesus. A listener in Michigan wrote of such an experience.

"*Dear Mr. Fuller*: I was at home last Sunday morning, so I tuned in on the Pilgrim Hour. Just as Mr. Fuller started to preach an old man came over to see me. He is 76 years old and many times I had testified to him with no visible results. This time when Mr. Fuller gave the invitation I urged him to surrender to Jesus and he did. When he said he would accept Christ I felt very weak-kneed. You see this is the first time I ever led anyone to the Lord. We both knelt by the radio and he said he was willing to let Christ come in. He promised to trust Him for his salvation."

Pray for courage to speak to sinners of their need of Christ. Pray for a passion for the lost. Pray for a world-wide revival.

There was no room in Bethlehem
For Him who left His throne,
To seek the lost at countless cost
And make their griefs His own.

But there was room on Calvary
Upon the cross of shame,
For Him to die uplifted high
To bear the sinner's blame.

There was no room in Bethlehem,
And in the world today
Men will not give Him room to live,
And bid Him turn away.

But there is room on Calvary,
And there He stands to give
A home to all who heed His call
And look to Him and live.

There was no room in Bethlehem
For Christ, the Prince of Kings,
From throne and crown to earth come down
With healing in His wings.

19

JANUARY
22

Walk about Zion, and go round about her: tell the towers thereof. Mark ye well her bulwarks, consider her palaces; that ye may tell it to the generation following. For this God is our God for ever and ever. *Psalm 48:12–14.*

EVERYTHING depends upon our point of view. I stood a short time ago in a room which was furnished with wealthy pictures, and I fixed my gaze upon a Highland scene of great strength and glory. The owner of the picture found me gazing at this particular work, and he immediately said, "I am afraid you won't get the light on the hill." And, sure enough, he was right. From my point of view I was contemplating a dark and storm-swept landscape, and I did not get the light on the hill. He moved me to another part of the room, and, standing there, I found that the scene was lit up with wonderful light from above.

Yes, everything depends upon our point of view. If you are going to look upon your trouble, the primary question will be, "Where do you stand?" See where the Apostle Paul plants his feet. "Blessed be God!" That is the view-point in the life of faith! Standing there, we shall get the light on the hill. Paul takes his stand on the grace of God, and he gazes upon the ministry of mercies and comfort in the otherwise midnight wastes of affliction and pain. He begins, I say, in doxology. He sings a paean over his mercies and comfort, and lifts his soul in adoration to God.

J. H. JOWETT

I would not lose the sense of Majesty;
Nor cease to worship at the Throne Divine:
But fear and trembling should not dwell within me;
Since God's forgiveness through His Son is mine.

Therefore, throughout the day, God in His Glory;
God in His Word; and God within my soul;
Should be the central thought in all Life's story:
Making not a part of living but the whole.

WILLIAM OLNEY

Thou therefore endure hardness, as a good soldier
of Jesus Christ.   *2 Timothy 2:3.*

PAUL was one of those men you can neither bend nor break. Principle was the rock upon which he stood secure. Faith was the shield which his tormentors could not shatter. Great convictions, tested and tempered in many a fire of affliction, kept his heart from bitterness and his spirit from repining. Jerusalem had excommunicated him, but God had given him a place among them that are sanctified. Rome had made a jail-bird of him, but Jesus had made him God's freedman and wrapped his soul in the peace which passeth all understanding. He speaks of himself as "an ambassador in bonds." What a startling paradox! Ambassadors live in kings' palaces. They clothe themselves in purple and fine linen, and fare sumptuously every day. Who ever heard of an ambassador in jail? Everywhere he describes himself as "the prisoner of Christ at Rome." Note the splendor of that conjunction. He was not Nero's prisoner. Had he been merely Nero's prisoner he would have fretted his heart away. He was "the prisoner of Christ," and it makes a world of difference if you take Jesus into jail with you. Jesus can turn a prison into a paradise, a prisoner's bench into a pulpit, a felon's bonds into a silent exposition of his gospel. That was why Paul rejoiced in his afflictions. "I would have you know, brethren, that the things which happened unto me have fallen out rather unto the progress of the gospel; so that my bonds became manifest in Christ throughout the whole praetorian guard." The household troops became his audience, and furnished fresh recruits for the great campaign. Nero might drink himself blind drunk, murder his mother, play the mountebank at Corinth, set fire to Rome, and eventually slay himself in the vain endeavor to escape the ghosts which haunted him day and night; but in all his brutal reign of terror there was one man whom he could never terrify—the little tent-maker out of Tarsus.

R. Moffat Gautrey

Must I be carried to the skies
On flowery beds of ease,
While others fought to win the prize,
And sailed through bloody seas?

Since I must fight if I would reign
Increase my courage, Lord;
I'll bear the toil, endure the pain,
Supported by Thy Word.

Isaac Watts

Behold the Lamb of God!   *John 1:36.*

T HE Bible makes very clear this outstanding fact, that there is universal condemnation of the human race before God, for "all have sinned," high and low, rich and poor, bond and free. All have broken God's commandments and are guilty, worthy of death. For anyone to say that he has not sinned is to make God a liar. This is God's camera-shot of the human heart, which is deceitful above all things and desperately wicked. Since all have sinned, all are condemned.

But here is the good news, and I like to dwell on this side of it. It is welcome and comforting news. Listen to these words, "He that believeth on Me," (that is, on Christ) "is not condemned," but is pardoned. What a wonderful truth we have to proclaim that all guilty sinners can be pardoned and have their sins put away. They can stand in the sight of God as though they had never been guilty. Listen carefully. There is not one sin in the Book of God against one of those who are "in Him," for "the Lamb of God . . . taketh away the sins of the world." Believe it, O friend, accept God's Word, and become a new creation in Christ Jesus.

CHARLES E. FULLER

O solemn hour! O hour alone,
  In solitary night;
When God the Father's only Son
As man for sinners to atone
  Expires—amazing sight!
The Lord of glory crucified!
The Lord of life has bled, and died!

O mystery of mysteries!
  Of life and death the tree;
Center of two eternities,
Which look with rapt adoring eyes,
  Onward and back to Thee—
O cross of Christ, where all His pain
And death is our eternal gain.

AUTHOR UNKNOWN

Seeing then that we have a great high priest . . .
For we have not an high priest which cannot be
touched with the feeling of our infirmities.

Hebrews 4:14, 15.

THE other day I heard a woman recite a beautiful poem written
by herself. And the substance of it was that I may know God
through my five senses. I may see Him in the starry heavens,
touch Him with the tips of my fingers in the petal of a lily, hear
Him in the song of the nightingale and meadow lark, smell Him in
the perfume of the rose, and taste Him in the luscious fruit He made.
It was fine poetry about our great God, but it left my heart untouched.
A little later I turned the dial of my radio to catch the broadcast of
a devotional service. The minister spoke of music and its great influence over the soul, how it dispels gloom and fear and lifts the
spirit on golden wings to higher worship and nobler service. It was
true, but it did not touch my heart.

I opened the old Book and read the great text above. It unveiled
before me a picture that made my heart like wax within me. Great?
Oh, yes! He flings the stars into space and speaks in thunder and
lightning. He paints the sunset with a brush dipped in flaming light.
He stoops to put the perfume in the rose and the sheen on the lily,
but His greatest greatness is love. So deep is the tenderness of His
infinite love that as I gaze up into His face I find that He is touched,
and His face is even as the face of a mother whose whole heart goes
out in compassion to her suffering child.

Ah, that is the kind of God I need! For I am like the woman who
came into the pastor's study and asked, "Is there any one here who
has a broken heart who can talk to me?" Thank God, there is! As I
look at the cross I know that He cares.

ANNA J. LINDGREN

I have redeemed thee . . . thou art mine.

Isaiah 43:1.

CONSECRATION is giving Jesus His own. We are His by right,
because He bought us with His blood. But, alas! He has not
had His money's worth! He paid for all, and He has had but a
fragment of our energy, time and earnings. By an act of consecration,
let us ask Him to forgive the robbery of the past, and let us profess

23

our desire to be henceforth utterly and only for Him; His slaves, His chattels, owning no master other than Himself.

As soon as we say this, He will test our sincerity, as He did the young ruler's, by asking something of us. He will lay His finger on something within us which He wants us to alter, obeying some command, or abstaining from some indulgence. If we instantly give up our will and way to Him, we pass the narrow doorway into the Chamber of Surrender, which has a southern aspect, and is ever warm and radiant with His presence, because obedience is the condition of manifested love (John 14:23).

F. B. MEYER

Set apart for Jesus!
  Is not this enough,
Though the desert prospect
  Open wild and rough?

Set apart to love Him,
  And His love to know,
Not to waste affection
  On a passing show;
Called to give Him life and heart,
  Called to pour the hidden treasure
  That none other claims to measure,
Into His beloved hand! thrice blessed, "set apart!"
  Set apart forever,
  For Himself alone!

Now we see our calling
  Gloriously shown;
Owning, with no secret dread,
  This our holy separation,
  Now the crown of consecration
Of the Lord our God shall rest upon our willing head.

ELLA M. PARKS

JANUARY 27

Behold, I stand at the door, and knock: if any man hear my voice, and open the door, I will come in to him, and will sup with him, and he with Me.
Revelation 3:20.

I DOUBT that I know of a passage in the whole Bible which throws greater light upon prayer than this one does. It is, it seems to me, the key which opens the door into the holy and blessed realm of prayer.

To pray is to let Jesus come into our hearts.

This teaches us, in the first place, that it is not our prayer which moves the Lord Jesus. It is Jesus who moves us to pray. He knocks. Thereby He makes known His desire to come in to us. Our prayers are always a result of Jesus' knocking at our hearts' doors.

This throws new light upon the old prophetic passage: "Before they call, I will answer; and while they are yet speaking, I will hear" (Isaiah 65:24). Yea, verily, before we call, He graciously makes known to us what gift He has decided to impart to us. He knocks in order to move us by prayer to open the door and accept the gift which He has already appointed for us.

From time immemorial prayer has been spoken of as the breath of the soul. And the figure is an excellent one indeed.

The air which our body requires envelopes us on every hand. The air of itself seeks to enter our bodies and, for this reason, exerts pressure upon us. It is well known that it is more difficult to hold one's breath than it is to breathe. We need but exercise our organs of respiration, and air will enter forthwith into our lungs and perform its life-giving function to the entire body.

The air which our souls need also envelopes all of us at all times and on all sides. God is round about us in Christ on every hand, with His many-sided and all-sufficient grace. All we need to do is to open our hearts.

Prayer is the breath of the soul, the organ by which we receive Christ into our parched and withered hearts.

He says, "If any man open the door, I will come in to him." Notice carefully every word here. It is not our prayer which draws Jesus into our hearts. Nor is it our prayer which moves Jesus to come in to us. All He needs is access. He enters in wherever He is not denied admittance.

O. HALLESBY

JANUARY 28

My little children, these things write I unto you, that ye sin not. And if any man sin, we have an advocate with the Father, Jesus Christ the right-eous.   *1 John 2:1.*

I WONDER if any of you, this morning, are out of fellowship with the Lord because of disobedience, neglect to read His Word, or lack of prayer. Here is the way back to justification and right-eousness. He says, "If any man sin, we have an Advocate with the Father, Jesus Christ, the Righteous." That word "advocate," of course, means lawyer, the pleader of our case, or one who can represent us before the Father.

25

Now this is exactly what takes place when you disobey God and then come to Him in contrition and repentance asking His forgiveness for Christ's sake. Our Lord Jesus Christ, who loved us well enough to die for us in order that we might be freed from sin, appears before the Father representing that He, Himself, bore this very sin of which we have been guilty, in His own body on the tree. He, then, as our Advocate, pleads that because of the efficacy of His cleansing blood, shed upon the cross, we shall be judged guiltless and restored to fellowship with God the Father.

It is wonderful to think about! No matter how grievously you may have failed in your life yesterday, you may look up to Him this morning, repent of your failure, cry to Him for mercy, and in a moment of time receive the witness of the Holy Spirit that He has met your need, and know that your sin stain has been washed away. How wonderful it is that there is a fountain filled with blood to which we may come. Nothing else in all the world can wash away sin stains but the blood of the Lord Jesus Christ.

J. ELWIN WRIGHT

JANUARY
29

Knowing this, that our old man is crucified with Him, that the body of sin might be destroyed, that henceforth we should not serve sin. For he that is dead is freed from sin. *Romans 6:6, 7.*

THE journey to the upper room of Pentecost must needs be by a place called Calvary; God has the self-same place for self as for sins—the cross of Christ. The man who cried, "It is no longer I but Christ that liveth in me," first cried, "I have been crucified with Christ." But it hurts to be crucified even with Christ! And so there is darkness, and struggle, and agony, and suffering. Nevertheless, "fear not, only believe," for "if we have been united with Him by the likeness of His death, we shall be also by the likeness of His resurrection," and out of it all will come God's own rest, peace and power.

JAMES H. McCONKEY

Jesus, I my cross have taken,
All to leave, and follow Thee;
Naked, poor, despised, forsaken,
Thou, from hence, my all shalt be!
Perish, every fond ambition,
All I've sought, or hoped, or known,
Yet how rich is my condition,
God and heaven are still my own!

26

Let the world despise and leave me,
They have left my Saviour, too;
Human hearts and looks deceive me—
Thou art not, like them, untrue;
Oh, while Thou dost smile upon me
God of wisdom, love, and might,
Foes may hate, and friends disown me,
Show Thy face, and all is bright.

HENRY F. LYTE

JANUARY
30

The grass withereth, the flower fadeth; because the Spirit of the Lord bloweth upon it: surely the people is grass.   *Isaiah 40:7.*

WHAT! the Spirit a destroyer! I thought it was the source of life. I would have expected it to have been written, "The grass withereth because the Spirit of the Lord does not blow upon it." Here for the first time the breath of the Spirit is said to give not life but death. Yes, but is not death the prelude to life? "That which thou sowest is not quickened except it die." . . . The flowering of the flesh is killing the Word of the Lord within me; if that Word is to endure forever, the flowering of the flesh must fade. What power shall make it fade, what but the Spirit divine? . . . Shall it not blow upon the flesh that impedes the immortal life? Shall it not breathe upon the grass that buries the Word of the Lord? O Thou divine Destroyer, . . . blow upon our deadness that it may die. Wither all in my heart that would wither Thy Word. Wither its pride, its self-seeking, its vanity. Wither its malice, its hatred, its envy, its all uncharitableness. Wither its preference for the seen and temporal, its estimation of the dross above the gold. . . . Wither the gourd that shuts out the larger view, that prevents me from seeing the woes of Nineveh. When Thou blowest upon the grass, mortality shall be swallowed up of life.

GEORGE MATHESON

Lord, when I cannot understand
Thy silence in the hour,
When I most need Thy helping hand,
And Thy delivering power;
This shall my joy and comfort be,
That it so seemeth good to Thee.

When things on which my heart is set
    Thy sovereign will denies;
If I am tempted to forget
    That Thou art just and wise,
Let this my joy and comfort be
That so it seemeth good to Thee.

F. W. PITT

JANUARY 31

Believe . . . and thou shalt be saved. *Acts 16:31.*

BUT you say to me, "The devil believes and he is not saved." Listen! To believe (in a saving sense) means to trust, to repose, to commit, to lean, to have faith in—a heart assent. It is not merely a "head" knowledge. The Scripture says, "If thou shalt confess with thy mouth the Lord Jesus, and shalt believe IN THINE HEART that God hath raised Him from the dead, thou shalt be saved" (Romans 10:9). It is not a "head" belief but a "heart" belief.

CHARLES E. FULLER

I am trusting Thee, Lord Jesus,
    Trusting only Thee!
Trusting Thee for full salvation,
    Great and free.

I am trusting Thee for pardon,
    At Thy feet I bow;
For Thy grace and tender mercy,
    Trusting now.

I am trusting Thee for cleansing,
    In the crimson flood;
Trusting Thee to make me holy,
    By Thy blood.

I am trusting Thee to guide me,
    Thou alone shalt lead,
Every day and hour supplying
    All my need.

I am trusting Thee for power,
    Thine can never fail;
Words which Thou Thyself shalt give me,
    Must prevail.

I am trusting Thee, Lord Jesus,
    Never let me fall!
I am trusting Thee for ever,
    And for all.

FRANCES RIDLEY HAVERGAL

28

I have learned, in whatsoever state I am, therewith to be content. *Philippians 4:11.*

YOUR position is in CHRIST. You are standing today in Christ. Never forget to distinguish between your standing and your experience. Your standing is in Christ, your experience is in your emotion. John Bunyan says that our emotion is like our spending money, the money we have in our pocket: it is sometimes more, but generally less; but our standing in our Forerunner is like the money we have in the bank, which is not affected by our daily expenses. I am sometimes happy, sometimes worn, overtired, inclined to be nervous; but I never mind, because it does not matter to me whether I pass through the dark and the valley of sorrow and all transient depression. My position is unaffected because it is settled in my Forerunner, my Priest, my Saviour, my Head, in whom I stand before God. Oh, blessed be God for that! Do not look, therefore, for evidence in your emotions, but look for your title deeds in Christ the Forerunner.

F. B. MEYER

My life is but a weaving
  Between my Lord and me,
I cannot choose the colors
  He worketh steadily.

Ofttimes He weaveth sorrow
  And I in foolish pride
Forget He sees the upper
  And I, the under side.

Not till the loom is silent
  And the shuttles cease to fly
Shall God unroll the canvas
  And explain the reason why.

The dark threads are as needful
  In the Weaver's skilful hand
As the threads of gold and silver
  In the pattern He has planned.

AUTHOR UNKNOWN

By the power of the Spirit of God . . . I have fully
preached the gospel. *Romans 15:19.*

IT TAKES power for the man of God in the pulpit to speak
plainly about particular sins before the faces of those who are
living in them; and still more power to do it with the rare tact-
fulness and tenderness of the Galilean preacher. It takes power to
stick to the gospel story and the old book, when literature and
philosophy present such fine opportunities for the essays that are so
enjoyable and that bring such flattering notice. It takes power to
leave out the finely woven rhetoric that you are disposed to put in
for the sake of the compliment it will bring from that literary woman
down yonder, or that bright, brainy young lawyer in the fifth pew on
the left aisle. It takes power to see that the lips that speak for God
are thoroughly clean lips, and the life that stands before that audience
is a pure life.

It takes power to keep sweet in the home, where, if anywhere,
the seamy side is apt to stick out. Of how many wooden oaths could
kicked chairs and slammed doors tell! After all the home-life comes
close to being the real test of power, does it not? It takes power to be
gracious and strong, and patient and tender, and cheery, in the commonplace things, and the commonplace places, does it not?

Now, I have something to tell you that to me is very wonderful,
and constantly growing in wonder. It is this—the Master has thought
of all that! He has thought into your life. Yes, I mean your particular
life, and made an arrangement to fully cover all your need of power.
He stands anew in our midst today, and putting His pierced hand
gently upon your arm, His low, loving, clear voice says quietly, but
very distinctly, "You—you shall have power." For every subtle, strong
temptation, for every cry of need, for every low moan of disappointment, for every locking of the jaws in the resolution of despair, for
every disheartened look out into the morrow, for every yearningly
ambitious heart there comes that unmistakable ringing promise of His
—ye shall have power.

S. D. GORDON

Spirit of burning! quick descend,
Like mighty rushing wind;
Thy strength unto my weakness lend,
My all in Christ to find.

Consume, O Lord! my tin and dross,
With holy love inspire;
Nail my affections to the cross,
And set me all on fire.

R. KELSO CARTER

And the Lord said, Simon, Simon, behold, Satan
hath desired to have you, that he may sift you as
wheat.   *Luke 22:31.*

THE Apostle Peter is a living example how living faith may fall,
and yet not utterly be cast down. He was bold, energetic, ardent, and generous. When called, he immediately relinquished
all. When assured that it was Jesus, he volunteered to walk the stormy
waters. When asked his judgment about his Master, he gave that
noble, unreserved confession which "flesh and blood" had not "revealed" to him. Were it not for the fidelity of Scripture we might
have thought nothing could have shaken the constancy of his devotion. And yet, how read we? He who alone of men ever "walked
upon the water," took his eye off Jesus, saw the boisterous waves, and
began to sink. Immediately after his glorious confession, he was
stumbled at the thought of his Master's crucifixion, and began to rebuke Him. Then came his last awful denial. He did not fall all at
once. . . . Self-confidence led to slumber. He slept when Jesus was
in an agony of prayer; nor even awoke to watchfulness at the piercing
question, "Simon, sleepest thou?" We will not pursue his mournful
fall. He fell lower and lower till there was but one thing between
him and destruction, and that was the omnipotent prayer of Jesus:
"I have prayed for thee, that thy faith fail not." That plank saved him.
O trembling believer, though your faith in time past has faltered and
fallen even like Peter's, do not despair. You, too, have "an advocate
with the Father."

BICKERSTETH

. . . to give unto them beauty for ashes, the oil of
joy for mourning, the garment of praise for the
spirit of heaviness; that they might be called trees
of righteousness, the planting of the Lord, that He
might be glorified.   *Isaiah 61:3.*

HERE is a letter from a Kentucky farmer. He has made a sanctuary of his hayloft and found it a place of such blessing that
it fairly "hurts" his heart, he is so bursting with joy.

"*Brother Fuller,* do you mind if I ask you a question? Does
God's love come so strong that your heart hurts with joy and

31

you feel so full that you run over and begin to shout, 'Glory, glory, glory to God,' when you are alone with the Lord? I do.

"I am a farmer, and the Lord is my Shepherd. Sometimes as I am working around on the farm I feel His presence. Truly He watches over His flock. He was with me this afternoon when I went to the barn loft to pray, (I go there morning and evening for secret prayer). He blest me until my cup was running over. I love Him."

Is it that way with you, this morning? God wants you to be a fully satisfied, joyful Christian. You will be if you meet Him in the morning in the secret place of prayer and then share your joy with others.

> *Did you ever hear the story*
> *Of the man who searched so hard*
> *For the flower of happiness, and*
> *Found it in his own back yard?*
>
> *Seems to me we're like that often,*
> *When we're so dissatisfied*
> *With our homes and friends and neighbors,*
> *And the towns where we abide.*
>
> *When we've tried new friends and places,*
> *And have sought in every part,*
> *Don't we always find contentment,*
> *After all, is in the heart?*
>
> *For we haven't different natures,*
> *Though we're in surroundings strange;*
> *'Tis our hearts that need adjusting,*
> *'Tis ourselves we need to change.*
>
> NINA WILLIS WALTER

FEBRUARY 5

And Elisha prayed, and said, Lord, I pray Thee, open his eyes that he may see. And the Lord opened the eyes of the young man; and he saw: and, behold, the mountain was full of horses and chariots of fire round about Elisha. *2 Kings 6:17.*

How we do let circumstances blind us to the all-sufficiency of God! I think of the morning when Elisha's servant must have walked out on the back porch and discovered an army sent to capture the great prophet. (In those days God's preachers were such troublemakers that they sent the militia after them.) The servant was horrified to see soldiers to the right of him, soldiers to the left of him, soldiers before him, soldiers everywhere. But Elisha came out calmly, and instead of bothering to look around him, he looked higher and saw angels to the right of him, angels to the left of him, angels before him, angels everywhere, for the angels of the Lord were encamping round about him who feared God to deliver him. No wonder Elisha could pray for this frightened servant's eyes to be opened that he might see! And we need such an eye opener today.

VANCE HAVNER

HIS PRESENCE

"My presence shall go with thee." Exodus 33:14.

> *Cherish no doubt of it,*
> *Ever abide in it,*
> *Travel about in it,*
> *Rest and reside in it,*
> *Walk in the midst of it,*
> *Work in the might of it,*
> *Let your whole life be lived*
> *Full in the light of it.*

BEATRICE CLELAND

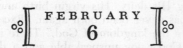

FEBRUARY 6

And Joshua blessed him, and gave unto Caleb the son of Jephunneh Hebron for an inheritance.

Joshua 14:13.

AN INTERESTING incident is told of a soldier wounded in the last great World War. As a result of fierce battle, it was found necessary to amputate both arms and legs. Although life was despaired of, by careful surgery it was spared, but his courage failed. He faced the future as a helpless cripple and often begged the attending physician to put an end to it all. "I am of no use to any one; no one wants me," he exclaimed one day in utter desperation. The word was carried to the king in whose service he had enlisted and for whose cause he had suffered. Quickly came the return message, "Your king has need of you," and the helpless man, who felt life was worthless, is today a member of the royal household.

Many a servant of Christ, bruised and battered from service in the royal ranks, with the best of life behind him, may feel as this private felt, that he is of no use to any one, even the King Himself. But God has need of the weakest saint in His household and ranks. The step may be feeble and the hands shaky; the hair may be white and the

natural strength spent, but God has said—and His word is true—
"Even to your old age I am He" Jehovah-Ja (the Lord, my Strength),
and "They shall bring forth fruit in old age." God knows no age limit
and has no superannuated or retired servants. The kind of service
may be changed, but the challenge to service is never revoked. Caleb
asked for and was given Hebron long after, humanly speaking, he
should have retired. "Is there anything too hard for me?" asks our
strength-giving Father.

PAMEII

FEBRUARY 7

Concerning His Son Jesus Christ our Lord . . . declared to be the Son of God with power . . . by
whom we have received grace and apostleship.
Romans 1:3-5.

WHEN you are truly born again the glory of Christ will flood
your soul. There will be no doubt in your mind about His
deity and sonship. When I hear a man begin to talk about
Jesus Christ as simply a human teacher, a moral leader on a level with
other men, denying His deity, His virgin birth and His resurrection,
I know that man has never been born again. "Except a man be born
again he cannot see the kingdom of God." There is within the heart
of a real child of God a joy unspeakable and a desire to exalt and
crown Christ Lord of all. Social gospel sermonettes about morality
which leave out the cross and the blood atonement for sin make my
heart sick.

CHARLES E. FULLER

Poor? No, of course not! Why, how could I be,
When Christ, the King, is taking care of me?

Tired? Sometimes;—yes, more than tired; but then,
I know a place where I can rest again!

Lonely? Ah, well I know the aching blight;
But now—I've Jesus with me day and night!

Burdens? I have them; oft they press me sore,
And then—I lean the harder, trust the more.

Worthy? Oh, no! The marvel of it is
That I should know such boundless love as His!

And so, I'm rich; with Christ I am "joint heir,"
Since He once stooped my poverty to share.

EDITH LILLIAN YOUNG

34

I am persuaded, that neither death, nor life, nor angels, nor principalities, nor powers, nor things present, nor things to come, nor height, nor depth, nor any other creature, shall be able to separate us from the love of God, which is in Christ Jesus, our Lord. *Romans 8:38, 39.*

JUST as beholding the glare of the sun, men lose their power of vision, so raising our eyes to the brilliance of Jesus, the Sun of of Righteousness, we are blinded by the splendor of the greatest gift that God Himself could bestow. Christ came to save—blessed assurance! But more: He came to "save . . . to the uttermost," so that no sin is too great, no sinner too vile, to be blessed, when penitent and believing, by this Gift. Christ came to save; but more: He came to save freely. No conditions are attached to this gift of God in Christ; nor is it offered to those who have earned or deserved it. It is the free, gracious, unearned, unmerited gift of God to those who with the humility of the shepherds and the reverence of the Magi believe with a personal and trusting faith that Jesus is the Ransom of their souls and that He "shall save His people from their sins." Christ came to save; but more: He came to bring with His salvation positive, doubt-destroying conviction. The gift of His grace is not a matter of speculation, not a theory of conjecture. It is the absolute and final truth, which does not leave men in suspense, in question, or doubt as to their salvation. It does more than teach men to yearn and pray and hope for their deliverance from sin; it gives them that exultant conviction by which nothing in life or death itself "shall be able to separate us from the love of God which is in Christ Jesus."

WALTER A. MAIER

Yea, they turned back and tempted God, and limited the Holy One of Israel. *Psalm 78:41.*

THEY limited the Holy One." Is it not true that God is limited because of the lack of purpose in the lives and labors of His own? Think of the Apostle Paul who was the means of linking himself to the Almighty, and who became a channel of great blessing! He was a man of purpose. "This one thing I do" was his life motto. But we have no such concentration.

Quite recently, it was my privilege to browse among some of the unpublished letters of D. L. Moody, and I found that a favorite word of his was the word "push." It characterized that honored man of God. It seems to me that D. L. Moody stood before doors of opportunity and on his side of those doors he read the word "Push." On the other side of the door, hidden from his gaze, was the word "Pull." There was divine attraction, God pulling him, God urging him, and Moody pushed where God pulled. They called him a man of one Book. He was also a man of one purpose. He had one supreme mission in life, and that was to glorify God in and through the salvation and sanctification of souls.

HERBERT LOCKYER

Did we in our own strength confide,
Our striving would be losing;
Were not the right man on our side,
The man of God's own choosing.
Dost ask who that may be?
Christ Jesus, it is He;
Lord Sabaoth in His name,
From age to age the same,
And He must win the battle.

That word above all earthly powers—
No thanks to them—abideth;
The Spirit and the gifts are ours
Through Him who with us sideth.
Let goods and kindred go,
This mortal life also;
The body they may kill:
God's truth abideth still,
His kingdom is forever.

MARTIN LUTHER

FEBRUARY 10

If thou canst believe, all things are possible to him that believeth.   *Mark 9:23.*

ALL difficulties and dangers must give way before the omnipotence of faith. "By faith the walls of Jericho fell down, after they were compassed about seven days," and still the mightiest citadels of the adversary must give way before the steadfast and victorious march of faith. By faith Daniel stopped the mouths of lions and was delivered, we are expressly told, because he believed in his God. It was not his uprightness of life, or courageous fidelity that saved him, but his confidence in Jehovah. Such faith carried the intrepid Arnot through the jungles of Africa, delivered the heroic Paton from the murderous fury of the savages of Tanna, and held back the stroke of death and the threatened disaster from many of us in the humbler experiences of our providential lives. Still the God of faith is as near, as mighty, and as true as when He walked with the Hebrew children through the fire, and guarded the heroic Paul through all the perils of his changeful life. There is no difficulty too small for its exercise, and there is no crisis too terrible for its triumph. Shall we go forth with this shield and buckler, and prove all the possibilities of faith? Then indeed shall we carry a charmed life even through the very hosts of hell, and know that we are immortal till our work is done.

A. B. SIMPSON

> Keep up the song of faith,
>   However dark the night;
> And, as you praise, the Lord will work
>   To change your faith to sight.
>
> Keep up the song of faith,
>   And let your heart be strong,—
> For God delights when faith can praise
>   Though dark the night and long.

M. E. BARBER

FEBRUARY 11

A friend loveth at all times, and a brother is born for adversity. *Proverbs 17:17.*

THE Shadow once said to the Body: "Who is a friend like me? I follow you wherever you go. In sunlight or in moonlight I never forsake you." "True," answered the Body, "you go with me in sunlight and in moonlight. But where are you when neither sun nor moon shines upon me?" The true friend is one who is faithful in adversity and who abides with us in the darkness of the night.

A man in adversity is like a ship which has been driven on the shore and wrecked. The ship needs extensive overhauling and repair before it will be ready for sea again. So it is with the friend who has met with trouble and disaster. He needs the ministry of his friends. There is a beautiful example of that in the Old Testament. When David's fortunes were at the lowest ebb, when he was pursued day and night by the relentless hatred and jealousy of Saul, and when, apparently, his own hope was sinking and his faith in God declining, then that faithful friend, Jonathan, whose love David said to him was "wonderful, passing the love of women," went to him at night in the Wood of Ziph and strengthened his hand in God.

In *Great Expectations,* Charles Dickens tells how Pip went to visit for the last time his benefactor, Magwitch, the dying ex-convict, who had been condemned to be hanged. The convict took Pip's hand and said, "You have never deserted me, boy; and what's the best of all, you have been more comfortable alonger me since I was under a dark cloud than when the sun shone. That's the best of all." Yes; it is not when the sun is shining, but when the clouds gather, and darkness comes down, that friendship has its real test.

CLARENCE EDWARD MACARTNEY

FEBRUARY 12

For we are members of His body, of His flesh, and of His bones. *Ephesians 5:30.*

A S N O man can come to God except through Jesus Christ, so no one can hope for victory over sin and the devil except through Him; and that not as an abstract theory or thought, but as a personal living union with the Son of God. "Nay, in all these things we are more than conquerors through Him that loved us" (Romans 8:37). We have peace with God through Him; we have access through Him; we come to the Father through Him; we have victory through Him; in reality all that we have is through our union with Christ Jesus, the Lord.

God has given us five illustrations of this union, among them that of marriage. "Wherefore, my brethren, ye also are become dead to the law by the body of Christ; that ye should be married to another, even to him who is raised from the dead, that we should bring forth fruit unto God" (Romans 7:4, A. V.). We are now married to Christ by God. The trouble is that most Christians neither know this nor have even heard of it. The result of this ignorance is that they live like a young woman who is married, but who has never realized what it means to be married. She goes to the home of the husband, but most of her time is given to her old lovers, and she is careless and thoughtless of her lover-husband who is waiting for her. May the Holy Spirit open the understanding of each of us to the fact that we are vitally united to Jesus Christ, the Lord.

L. L. LEGTERS

None but Christ; His merit hides me,
He was faultless—I am fair:
None but Christ, His wisdom guides me,
He was out-cast—I'm His care.

None but Christ: His life sustains me,
Strength and song to me He is;
None but Christ, His love constrains me,
He is mine, and I am His.

ANNE R. COUSIN

FEBRUARY 13

Adorn the doctrine of God our Saviour in all things.
Titus 2:10.

IT IS good to be well and beautifully dressed. It gives a sense of freedom and self-assurance, but the woman who would make herself a reproduction of the fashion plate must pay for that pleasure with great realities; perhaps the sacred joys of self-effacing wife and motherhood, perhaps the development of some inherent gift that would enrich other lives.

Popularity, public acclaim, is an intoxicating thing, much desired, but the applause of men is often the price a messenger of God must pay for the infilling of the Spirit's power. Culture, broadness, knowledge are good things, but often a man must pay for them with an impoverished prayer life. He must decide on the things he wants most.

ANNA J. LINDGREN

Call Thy people back, O Lord,
As in the early days,
When love was warm, and fresh, and bright,
When first we knew Thy grace;
When first Thy light broke through our night,
And set our hearts ablaze.
Lord, call us back!

Call Thy people back, O Lord,
To that simplicity
Which marked Thy servants long ago;
Our yearning hearts would be
Full satisfied with Thee, although
The world against us be.
Lord, call us back!

H. McD.

If we say that we have fellowship with Him, and walk in darkness, we lie, . . . but if we walk in the light . . . we have fellowship. . . . *1 John 1:6, 7.*

SOME people have the mistaken notion that the moment they have become spiritually cold and lost their fellowship with God they have lost their relationship to Him as well. This is not the case. Let me give you an illustration. In the fifteenth chapter of Luke is the story of the Prodigal Son. You remember how he asked for his portion of the inheritance and then went into a far country. He spent all his money, then a famine came. Now listen carefully. He did not lose his relationship. He was simply a son out of fellowship. When he finally came to himself, he said, "I will arise and go to my father." When he went back home he was restored to fellowship.

And so David, after his sin, did not say, "Restore unto me my salvation," but, "Restore unto me the JOY of Thy salvation."

CHARLES E. FULLER

At cool of day with God I walk
My garden's grateful shade;
I hear His voice among the trees,
And I am not afraid.

I see His presence in the night—
And though my heart is awed
I do not quail before the sight
Or nearness of my God.

He speaks to me in every wind,
He smiles from every star;
He is not deaf to me, nor blind,
Nor absent, nor afar.

He is my stay and my defense;
How shall I fail or fall?
My helper is Omnipotence!
My ruler ruleth all!

Thus dowered, and guarded thus, with Him
I walk this peaceful shade,
I hear His voice among the trees,
And I am not afraid.

CAROLINE ATHERTON MASON

All things are yours. *1 Corinthians 3:21.*

EVERY Christian is the potential possessor of every spiritual blessing by virtue of being in Christ. But how spiritually poverty-stricken the average Christian seems. How few of us give any adequate impression to the worldlings among whom we live of our incalculable wealth in Christ! Why is it so?

Perhaps our desire for spiritual treasures is at a low ebb. To claim effectually we must covet eagerly. There are even among reborn Christians those who would quickly reach out for a bit of earth's filthy lucre, who would not raise a finger to get the golden coins of heavenly riches. To some, two hours at a movie seems no longer than ten minutes, while ten minutes of Bible study drags on like an hour. To others a weekly prayer-meeting would be intolerable, but a weekly dance which debilitates spirit, soul and body and destroys one's effectual witness for Christ would be keenly enjoyed.

"To put on the new man" will mean an eager seeking after spiritual riches and setting the affections primarily and pre-eminently upon heavenly things, rather than earthly. For co-resurrection with Christ lifts one into a sphere where only Christ and the things of Christ can ever satisfy or suffice.

RUTH PAXSON

Let us come in full assurance,
We whose hearts are purified
By the Precious Blood of Jesus
And in whom His words abide:
Great things let us ask, undoubting,
Through our faith in Him made bold;
He is faithful, who has promised—
He will nothing good withhold!

There is One whose love unbounded
Gave His Son that we might live;
How shall He not with Him, also,
All things else as "freely give"?
"Thou shalt call, and I WILL ANSWER."
Such the assurance given of old;
And He's faithful who has promised—
He will nothing good withhold!

MABEL JOHNSTON CAMP

Thou hast beset me behind and before.

Psalm 139:5.

ow perfectly complete is the suggestion of an all-encircling presence, round about me on every side. The ramparts are built up all about me, and the ring of defence is complete. Perhaps there is no experience in human life which more perfectly develops the thought of the Psalmist than the guardianship offered by a mother to her baby-child when the little one is just learning to walk. The mother literally encircles the child with protection, spreading out her arms into almost a complete ring, so that in whatever way the child may happen to stumble she falls into the waiting ministry of love. Such is the idea of "besetment."

J. H. JOWETT

*In the secret of His presence
    I am kept from strife of tongues;
His pavilion is around me,
    And within are ceaseless songs!
Stormy winds, His word fulfilling,
    Beat without, but cannot harm,
For the Master's voice is stilling
    Storm and tempest to a calm.*

*In the secret of His presence
    All the darkness disappears;
For a sun that knows no setting,
    Throws a rainbow on my tears.
So the day grows ever lighter,
    Broadening to the perfect noon;
So the day grows ever brighter,
    Heaven is coming, near and soon.*

*In the secret of His presence
    Never more can foes alarm;
In the shadow of the Highest,
    I can meet them with a psalm;
For the strong pavilion hides me,
    Turns their fiery darts aside,
And I know, whate'er betides me,
    I shall live because He died!*

HENRY BURTON

Your Father knows what things you need before
ever you ask Him.   *Matthew 6:8 (Weymouth)*.

WHY does God say "No"? Because of our shortsightedness and His omniscience. He sees "the distant scene" and He knows how the next step should be taken that the "distant scene" may be made clear to us.

What we mistake for God's denials are often God's wise and providential delays, which are not denials at all. He sees the peril lying ahead which we cannot see. It is only after long years have passed that we gain a true vision and say: "Well, if I had taken the road I had expected to take it would not have resulted as I had hoped it would." Many an individual thanks God that he did not have his way, that things were taken from him, that difficulties were put in his way to block his advance in order that he might have the delight of overcoming, or the delight of awaiting God's time. How often that is true in the ordinary events of life, when we use our ability to the utmost and things do not seem to turn out as we had expected them. If we are children of God, they have turned out as He had expected them and it will be wonderfully beneficial and blessed to us just a little later on. He sees the perils that are in our path that we cannot see. He speaks to us in mercy and grace and He builds us up to meet the dangers and be prepared to receive the things we could not wisely use today. There are many things which we can employ tomorrow that we cannot wisely use today.

A. Z. CONRAD

> *When I cannot understand my Father's leading,*
> *And it seems to be but hard and cruel fate,*
> *Still I hear that gentle whisper ever pleading,*
> *God is working, God is faithful—Only wait.*
>
> *When the promise seems to linger, long delaying,*
> *And I tremble, lest, perhaps, it come too late,*
> *Still I hear that sweet-voiced angel ever saying,*
> *Though it tarry, it is coming—Only wait.*

A. B. SIMPSON

How then shall they call on Him in whom they
have not believed? and how shall they believe in
Him of whom they have not heard? and how shall
they hear without a preacher? *Romans 10:14.*

No one can understand the hunger of those who are isolated
and unable to hear the Gospel in church regularly unless they
themselves have passed through the same experience. This letter from a shut-in will be of interest to you, we are sure. It is from
a little town in Tennessee.

"Dear Brother Fuller: Sometime before we got our radio my
cousins came to spend the night with us. They are an old couple
in their sixties. They said, 'We hear the Old Fashioned Revival
Hour from Los Angeles.' Their eyes just sparkled as they told us
how they enjoyed it. In a few days mother sold her turkeys and
we bought the radio. I have been sick for two years and Mother
and Daddy have no car to go to church, so you can imagine how
glad we were to hear a sermon.

"We didn't know what station you were on or what time in
the day so each Sunday I would get up, turn the radio on and
turn the dial back and forth every fifteen minutes when the
programs changed, trying to find you. After two or three Sundays
I finally found you over a Louisville station. When I heard your
voice I said, "That sounds just like him," although I had never
heard you before.

"We have listened now for three years. Our batteries are worn
out but we are going to sell a ham and get some new ones. We
would rather hear you than eat ham.

"I haven't been saved yet. Every day I think of my unsaved
neighbors and wish I was saved so I could pray for them and
speak a word to them about their souls. I ask God every day to
save me, but it don't look like I'll ever be saved."

We somehow believe the Lord is hearing this young woman's
prayers and that she is accepted in the Beloved. How can her love
for the Word and desire to be a soul-winner be accounted for otherwise? She needs instruction so the assurance may come to her heart.
Suppose we pray for her and others like her today.

So the Spirit lifted me up, and took me away, and
I went in bitterness, in the heat of my spirit; but
the hand of the Lord was strong upon me.

Ezekiel 3:14.

GOD's Spirit often leads me against the will of my spirit; I go in
bitterness in obedience to the pressure of a mightier Hand.
How often do I say, "A sense of duty compels me." It is a
wonderful confession that there is something in me which is higher
than myself, something which uses me as an instrument, which commands me as a servant. How many places have I visited as a sacrifice
just because I ought to go; and how many times have I reaped from
the sacrifice an unlooked-for harvest! I went in bitterness, in the
heat of the spirit, in enforced submission to the call of right, and I
found in the scene of my expected torment the turning point of my
destiny; under the dust-heap was gold. Spirit of Christ, I thank Thee
that Thy love constraineth me. I thank Thee that in the great labyrinth
of life Thou waitest not for my consent to lead me. I thank Thee that
Thou leadest me by a way which I know not, by a way which is
above the level of my poor understanding. . . . There is no force in
this universe so glorious as the force of Thy love . . . It binds me
with golden fetters, it draws me with silver cords. O divine servitude,
O slavery that makes me free, O love that imprisons me only to set
my feet in a larger room, enclose me more and more within thy
folds.

GEORGE MATHESON

Darkest night will always come before the dawning;
Silver linings shine on God's side of the cloud;
All your journey He has promised to be with you,
Naught has come to you but what His love allowed.

Have faith in God, the sun will shine,
Though dark the clouds may be today,
His heart has planned your path and mine,
Have faith in God, have faith always.

MAY AGNEW STEPHENS

FEBRUARY
20

If ye shall ask anything in My name, I will do it.
John 14:14.

W E N E E D do but one thing: tell God about our condition, about our faith, our solicitude, and our worldly and prayer-weary heart; and then pray in the name of Jesus.

We can come before God and say to Him, "I do not have a right to pray because I do not have a truly prayerful heart. Much less do I have any right to receive what I ask for. Everything which Thou seest in my heart, O Lord, is of such a nature that it must close Thy heart to me and all my supplications. But hear me, not for my sake, nor for the sake of my prayer, and not even because of my distress, for it is a result of my own sinfulness. But hear me for Jesus' sake."

Such souls as these have from time immemorial rejoiced to sing:

"Thy name, O Jesus, beckons me,
That trusting I shall come to Thee,
In faith and love on Thee lay hold
And deep within my heart enfold.

"I call upon Thy name each day,
Where'er on earth I wander may,
It is for me a house of peace,
Where from all grief I find release."

We have learned that to pray in the name of Jesus is the real element of prayer in our prayers.

It is the helpless soul's helpless look unto a gracious Friend. The wonderful results which attend prayer of this kind can be accounted for only by the fact that we have opened the door unto Jesus and given Him access to our helplessness.

O. HALLESBY

FEBRUARY
21

Rend your heart, and not your garments, and turn
unto the Lord your God: for He is gracious and
merciful, slow to anger, and of great kindness, and
repenteth Him of the evil.   *Joel 2:13.*

T HE history of man is a record of his repeated failures to save himself. Time and again in the story of Israel we read of the apostasy of the nation. Even the House of God was polluted. Do you recall the story of Eli and his sons? Even the priests and those in high places were evil. The child Samuel ministered unto the Lord before Eli. But this was the condition when God's time of visitation came. We read that Eli's eyes had begun to grow dim. His sons were evil. Today, those who should be ministering the Word have eyes that are dim. No love for souls. No vision for revival. I wish to say to you that the Holy Ghost cannot bring conviction to the people unless the Word of God is preached.

We read further in the story of Eli that "the lamp of God went out in the temple of the Lord where the ark was and Samuel was laid down to sleep." It does seem that God's lamp has gone out in His own House and that the leaders are asleep. The night is far spent, and the Word exhorts us, "Awake, thou that sleepest."

But even in that dark hour of Israel's history it pleased God to reveal Himself to His people. What brought the revival then? "All the house of Israel lamented before the Lord." How will it come again today? When God's people become troubled enough to lament and call on Him.

Charles E. Fuller

Redeem the time, for the days are evil!
It rings o'er the earth with its notes sublime;
'Tis the voice of God to His slumbering people;
Redeem, redeem the time.

Redeem the time, for the Lord is working,
By His mighty power in every land;
Let us follow on as He leads His armies;
With strong and mighty hand.

Redeem the time, let us send the Gospel
To the farthest bounds of the human race;
Over all the world let us spread the tidings,
While lasts our day of grace.

A. B. Simpson

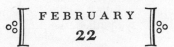

FEBRUARY 22

I know thy . . . poverty (but thou art rich).
Revelation 2:9.

A MISSIONARY reported the following true reminiscence of work in China. Among those who came regularly to worship were a couple of poor country people named Wang. The man had been baptized, and his wife was interested in the Gospel. They lived nearly ten miles from the city, and earned a very scanty living by the hardest of toil, but they were always regular in their attendance at the services, whether it was wet or fine. On one occasion I said to Mrs. Wang, "Don't you get very hungry before you reach home at night?"

"No," she replied; "not when I have a meal of rice before I start in the morning."

"What!" I said, "are there any times when you cannot get that?"

"Yes. When our rice is gone, and we have no money to get more, we have only the chaff mixed with water into a kind of porridge."

"How do you manage to walk on such poor food?" I asked.

"Well," continued Mrs. Wang, "there was one day when I was so faint and tired on my way home that I sat down by the roadside and cried. My husband said weeping would do no good, and that we had better get away from the main road and go behind the hills, where the passers-by would not interrupt us in prayer. We did this, and my husband prayed that God would make the hunger of soul more real than the hunger of body."

"Well, Tang-ma, what then?" I asked.

"Why, of course," she said, "we were not hungry after that; I got up and walked the rest of the way home, prepared a supper of rice husks, and after eating this, we went to bed feeling quite happy."

Sunday School Times

FEBRUARY 23

There was given to me a thorn in the flesh.

2 Corinthians 12:7.

P A I N has a great mission. While God does not send pain, He lets it stay, though He might intervene and take it away. While as a rule, with possibly rare exceptions, it comes through sin, it remains through the deliberate purpose of God. God has a great purpose of love in pain. He uses it as His teacher. It is the greatest of all His great teachers. It charges the very highest rates, insists upon the severest discipline, will tolerate nothing short of the highest ideal, needs our sympathetic help in working, and produces the very finest results.

S. D. Gordon

O Christ of Calvary, this Lent
Has brought Thee strangely near;
Perhaps it is because I too
Have borne a cross this year.

I did not climb Golgotha's brow
Nor in Thy sufferings share;

But knowing Thee has made my cross
Much easier to bear.

It somehow granted me a part
In Thy great sacrifice;
Thus sorrow has its recompense
Where joy cannot suffice.

O Christ, dear Christ of Calvary,
In gratitude I bow;
Thy resurrection day will dawn
With deeper meaning now.

ALICE HANSCHE MORTENSON

FEBRUARY 24

And He . . . shewed me that great city, the holy
Jerusalem, descending out of heaven from God,
having the glory of God: and her light was like
unto a stone most precious, even like a jasper
stone, clear as crystal.   *Revelation 21:10, 11.*

THERE is something in the heart of every believer in the Lord
Jesus Christ that responds to the suggestion that we are some
day to live in a city prepared by God Himself: a city of wonderful beauty and architecture; a city without slums, ward politics,
areas of poverty, filth and ramshackle buildings; a city without a
cemetery, hospital, or a jail. It is a city without a fire department, an
insane asylum, a home for the aged, or an orphanage. There never
has been a city like this in all the world. How can this great city get
along without all these things? There is but one answer. There is no
sin there.

This city has gates made of jewels. Even its foundations are
precious stones. The principal structural material is pure gold. The
streets are not merely paved with it, they are entirely built of it. In
fact, the cheapest material used in any part of the city is gold of a
purity beyond description, for God's Word tells us that this gold of
which the city is made is transparent, like glass.

If there is no sin in this wonderful city it is apparent that those
who live there must get rid of sin before they go there to reside, for
God will allow no taint of sin ever to spoil its perfection. God knew
all about this problem of sinful man and a sinless city, and made adequate provision for it. He sent His Son to meet the hosts of hell and
death in mortal combat. As a result of His victory, man may be
cleansed of every defilement through faith in Christ our Saviour and
may thus be made fit for the city. Paul tells us about this in Colossians

2:13 (Weymouth): "And to you—dead as you once were in your transgressions and in the uncircumcision of your natural state—He has nevertheless given you Life with Him, having forgiven us all our transgressions."

Friend, let me ask you a question. Are you prepared for the city which God has prepared for you? Do you have friends who are asleep in Jesus whom you wish to see again some day? Do you realize that your only hope of ultimate reunion with that godly mother or father, that precious wife or husband whose chair is vacant in the family circle, that child whose memory is one of your greatest treasures, is to prepare now by a complete surrender of your heart to God?

J. ELWIN WRIGHT

FEBRUARY
25

For our gospel came not unto you in word only,
but also in power, and in the Holy Ghost.
1 Thessalonians 1:5.

CHARLES G. FINNEY, entering a mill, was so filled with the power of the Spirit that the operatives fell upon their knees in tears before the mere presence of the evangelist, ere he uttered a word. At a camp-meeting where the most learned and eloquent sermons had utterly failed to move men to repentance, the whole congregation broke down in tears of conviction and penitence under the quiet words of an unassuming man who spoke manifestly filled with the Spirit. A word, a prayer, an earnest appeal, a song that would fall otherwise unheeded, goes home to the heart, filled with some subtle power when issuing from a Spirit-filled life. Moody testifies that never until he knew the fullness of the Spirit did he know the fullness of God's power in his preaching, but after that his preached words never failed of some fruitage. Neither is the power of the abundant life confined to the preaching of God's Word. God gives to some power in prayer; to others power in testimony; to others power in song; to others power in suffering and affliction. Every soul that knows the Spirit's abounding life is touching other lives with power whose full scope and intensity he will never know until the Lord comes to reward.

JAMES H. McCONKEY

There's a battle raging in the heavenly places,
Sin and death and sickness with Satan leading on:
With the hosts of earth and hell arrayed against us,
How in all our weakness shall the fight be won?

Faith can hear our Captain calling from the heavens,
"Courage, brother, I have overcome for you,
Fear not, I am with you, I will never fail you,
Trusting in My promise, you shall conquer too."

A. B. SIMPSON

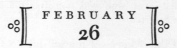

FEBRUARY 26

My word . . . shall not return unto Me void, but
it shall accomplish that which I please, and it shall
prosper in the thing whereto I sent it.

Isaiah 55:11.

IN ALL things God's ways are higher than our ways, and His thoughts, higher than our thoughts. With our human limitations we can neither comprehend the extent of our efforts nor enlarge their powers. Not so with God. He can do the abundant, even with our feeble efforts. An hour of fervent prayer may bring a flood tide of revival; a cup of cold water start a stream of never-ending blessing; a single copy of God's Word begin a chain of redeemed souls. Amelia Price Ayres has beautifully put the thought to rhyme as regards the gift of money for one Bible presented to a heathen heart.

PAMEII

You sent the money across the sea
That bought a Bible for young Sing Lee;
And young Sing Lee, when he'd read therein,
Proceeded to turn his back on sin.
Then he rested neither night nor day
Till his brother walked in the narrow way.
And his brother worked till he had won
Away from the gods his wife and son.
The woman told of her new-found joy,
And Christ was preached by the happy boy.

Some of the folks who heard him speak
Decided the one true God to seek.
It wasn't long till half the town
Had left its idols of wood and stone.
And the work's not ended yet, my friend.
You started something that ne'er shall end,
When you sent the money across the sea,
That bought a Bible for young Sing Lee.

AMELIA PRICE AYRES

What the law could not do, in that it was weak through the flesh, God sending His own Son in the likeness of sinful flesh, and for sin, condemned sin in the flesh: that the righteousness of the law might be fulfilled in us, who walk not after the flesh but after the Spirit. *Romans 8:3, 4.*

GOD has nailed the likeness of my self-life to the cross. The cross is the symbol of degradation and curse. Cursed is everyone that hangs on the cross. If, then, God has treated the likeness of my sinful self, when borne by the sinless Christ, as worthy of His curse, how terrible in God's sight it must be for myself to hug it and embrace it and live in it!

Oh, wondrous cross! But that is not all.

Christ and I are one. In Him I hung there. I came to an end of myself in Christ, and kneeling at His cross I took the position of union with Him in His death, and I consigned my self-life to the cross.

F. B. MEYER

I am crucified with Jesus
And He lives and dwells with me,
I have ceased from all my struggling,
'Tis no longer I, but He.

All my will is yielded to Him,
And His Spirit reigns within;
And His precious blood each moment
Keeps me cleansed and free from sin.

All my weaknesses I bring Him,
And He bears them all away,
All my fears and griefs I tell Him,
And my cares from day to day.

All my strength I draw from Jesus,
By His breath I live and move,
E'en His very mind He gives us,
And His faith, and life, and love.

For my words, I take His wisdom
For my work, His Spirit's power,
For my ways His ceaseless presence
Guards and guides me every hour.

Of my heart He is a portion,
Of my joy the boundless Spring,
Saviour, Sanctifier, Helper,
Glorious Lord and Coming King.

A. B. SIMPSON

The Lord hath prepared a sacrifice. *Zephaniah 1:7.*

DO YOU remember how Jonah was down inside the fish, riding around in that submarine? He came to the end of himself. He said, "When my soul fainted within me I remembered the Lord: and my prayer came in unto Thee, into Thine holy temple" (Jonah 2:7). By faith Jonah was remembering the brazen altar in that temple. He knew that if he was to be restored, he must come by the blood-sprinkled way. Now Christ, our Passover, is slain for us, and "if we confess our sins He is faithful and just to forgive us our sins and to cleanse us from all unrighteousness" (I John 1:9). Since Christ has been slain for us, we have a new and living way which He has consecrated for us through His flesh. The way back to fellowship with God is by the blood-sprinkled way of the sacrifice on the altar. It is by the way of confession, prayer, and supplication.

CHARLES E. FULLER

On life's raging ocean sailing,
Jesus' name I sought to bear;
But my doubts and fears prevailing,
Filled my soul with anxious care.
Falling always, always crying,
"Help me! save me! grace allow";
Came the answer sweet replying,
"Jesus saves thee, saves thee now."

Weary of myself deceiving,
Then His truth broke like a flood;
I go onward, just believing,
Trusting in my Saviour's blood.
Now the waters wild are sleeping,
Jesus speaks, the tempest stills;
And a holy peace comes creeping
Like the sunlight down the hills.

Christ alone the victory giveth,
Oh! how sweet, by faith to cry,—
"Surely my Redeemer liveth,
He hath conquered, and not I."
Strike my harp with loud thanksgiving,
Bind the laurel round my brow;
I was dead, but now am living,
Jesus saves me, saves me now.

R. KELSO CARTER

For if there be first a willing mind, it is accepted
according to what a man hath, and not according
to what he hath not.   *2 Corinthians 8 :12.*

GOD's effort through the ages has been to bring man to submis-
sive obedience. He will not coerce man. Man's will, that
sacred citadel of his being, will never be forced by his Creator. Man must voluntarily yield his will to the will of God, if God is to
exercise lordship over him. It is in our power to refuse or accept the
will of God. Tennyson wrote:

> *"Our wills are ours, we know not how;*
> *Our wills are ours, to make them thine."*

A Philadelphia bank once used an illustrated advertisement which
read like this: "Divided key—one part useless without the other.
Thus two persons have joint control of securities." The picture shows
the two separate parts of this clever invention: a key with two parts,
each part by itself, and then the two brought together and fitted one
upon the other so that, united, they form what looks like the usual flat
key of a safety deposit box. Either of the two persons controlling the
securities in such a box may take his part of the key and try to open
the box, but without result. But when the two persons go together,
and unite their two parts of the key, the box opens instantly. May we
say that the will of God and the will of a child of God are the two
parts of the divided key which can unlock priceless securities? As we
yield our will wholly to His, these two parts of the otherwise divided
key are brought together, and then treasures indeed are released.
Shall we not make sure then that, so far as we are concerned, despite
what sense, reason and infidelity may suggest, the portion of the key
which God has placed in our care—our wills—shall always be in His
hands to unite with His will for His use at any time and at all times?
"Wherefore . . . present yourselves unto God . . . and your members as instruments of righteousness unto God."

> *"God knows the way, He holds the key,*
> *He guides us with unerring hand;*
> *Sometime with tearless eyes we'll see;*
> *Yes, there, up there, we'll understand."*
>   HOWARD W. FERRIN

Ye know the grace of our Lord Jesus Christ, that, though He was rich, yet for our sakes He became poor, that ye through His poverty might be rich.

2 Corinthians 8:9.

WE MIGHT well consider what He was lent during His earthly pilgrimage. For strange to say He came into the world with resources so slender that continually He had (and I use the word advisedly) to be beholden to people, mostly poor people around Him, for the common necessities of life. This was by His Father's and His own deliberate choice, for we are specially told: "Ye know the grace of our Lord Jesus Christ that though He was rich (beyond compare), yet for our sakes He became poor." Had we been having a son born into the world to die on a cross, we might have planned to have him born in a king's palace, that he might have all he desired on the way to death. But this was not the plan of God. So Christ went through life a poor Man. There were evidently no savings from those years of toil in Nazareth. He became deliberately poor. He remained deliberately poor, so poor that one day they borrowed from a fish the tribute money for Himself and Peter! Here are lines which express His extreme poverty on His shining way to the cross:

"They borrowed a bed to lay His head,
When Christ the Lord came down;
He borrowed the ass on the mountain pass,
That He might ride to town;
But the crown that He wore, and the cross that He bore,
Were His own, the cross was His own.

"He borrowed the bread, when the crowd He fed,
On the grassy mountain-side,
He borrowed the dish of broken fish,
With which He satisfied.
He borrowed a room on the way to the tomb,
The Passover Feast to eat.
They borrowed a cave, for Him a grave,
They borrowed a winding-sheet.
But the crown that He wore, and the cross that He bore,
Were His own, the cross was His own."

These I think are moving words. They bring to our minds something of the cost of His poverty on His journey to the cross. They seem true. Yet when you come to think of it, they are just the truth reversed. The poet has taken poetic license indeed! For the bed and the ass, the bread and the fish, the room and the cave were really

His own. He had created them. It was men who had borrowed them! But the very things the poet says were His own, were not His at all, but ours! We had deserved the cross, and should have died on it. But in grace, He died on it in our stead, that we might go free.

Northcote Deck

MARCH 2

Delight thyself also in the Lord. . . . *Psalm 37:4*.

ow beautiful the phrase! The literal significance is this, "Seek for delicacies in the Lord." Yes, and if we only set about with ardent purpose to discover the delicacies of the Lord's table, we should have no time and no inclination to fret. But this is just what the majority of us do not do. We take the crumbs from the Master's table, and we have no taste of the excellent delicacies. Now the delicacies of anything are not found in the elementary stages; we have to move forward to the advanced. The delicacies of music are not found in the first half-dozen lessons; it is only in the later stages that we come to the exquisite. And so it is in art, and so it is in literature, and so it is with the "things of the Lord." "Eye hath not seen, nor ear heard, neither have entered into the heart of man, the things which God hath prepared for them that love Him." Let us be ambitious for the excellent! God has not yet given to us of His best. He always keeps the best wine until the last. We shall never reach God's superlative! The "unsearchable riches of Christ" will reveal themselves more and more to us throughout the glorious seasons of the eternal day. When we sit at the table of the Lord, tasting of His delicacies, fretfulness will be unable to breathe.

J. H. Jowett

MARCH 3

Christ also hath once suffered for sins, the just for the unjust, that He might bring us to God.
1 Peter 3:18.

hen George Fox, the founder of the Friends, or the Quakers, was lying in a filthy dungeon at Lancaster, a friend went to Oliver Cromwell and offered himself, body for body, to lie in the prison in his stead, if Cromwell would accept the substitution and let Fox go free. Cromwell was so struck with the offer that he said to the great men of his Council, "Which of you would do as much for me if I were in the same condition?"

Christ is the Friend who died for you. He took your place on the cross. Just as truly as that robber Barabbas, for whom the people asked, lived and did not die, because it was he that was released and Christ who was crucified, so you can live and inherit eternal life because Christ died for you. That was the wonderful friendship, that the marvelous love of which He spoke when He said, "Greater love hath no man than this that a man lay down his life for his friends."

> *"Which of all our friends, to save us,*
> *Could or would have shed their blood?*
> *But our Jesus died to have us*
> *Reconciled in Him to God,*
> *This was boundless love indeed;*
> *Jesus is a Friend in need."*
>
> CLARENCE EDWARD MACARTNEY

MARCH 4

There is that scattereth, and yet increaseth . . . the liberal soul shall be made fat: and he that watereth shall be watered also himself. *Proverbs 11:24, 25.*

PERHAPS the loving sacrifice of those who give to the support of the Old Fashioned Revival Hour accounts in a large measure for the success of the message in reaching the hearts of the spiritually needy. The following letter is an example of the sort of giving which makes the soul of the giver "fat."

"*Dear Brother Fuller*: I am a minister in a small church here in Kansas but I have a big Gospel. I have no salary but there is a box for offerings at the door. This morning there was $6.25 in it for my needs. I went to my apartment and turned on my midget radio while eating a good dinner, most of which had been donated. We listened to the Pilgrim Hour. When you prayed and told of the need, I was impressed by the Spirit to take out $5 of the money I received this morning and send it. Somehow I feel that if this country had established a 10% Club for Christ we would not be asked for it for war.

"The last few weeks I have been carpentering to help out. May the Lord bless you."

Have you given for the support of the gospel message until it involves real sacrifice? Common honesty with God requires you to

57

give at least ten percent of your income. Although we are not under law we certainly cannot wish to give less under grace than those who lived under law were required to give. Real joy and blessing commences when we go beyond and give more than the minimum standard. Be a spendthrift for God!

MARCH 5

As Thou hast sent Me into the world, even so have
I also sent them into the world. *John 17:18.*

HE WANTS to use your lips; but, even more, He wants to use your life. Much as He may use your lips, He will use your personality, your presence, your life ten times more, when you are wholly unconscious of it. He loves men so much. He longs to save them. But He needs us—you and me—as channels through which His power shall flow to touch and mightily influence those whom we touch. How often has He turned away disappointed because the channel had broken connections, or could not be used?

"He was not willing that any should perish;
Jesus, enthroned in the glory above,
Saw our poor fallen world, pitied our sorrows,
Poured out His life for us, wonderful love.

"Perishing, perishing, thronging our pathway,
Hearts break with burdens too heavy to bear;
Jesus would save, but there's no one to tell them,
No one to save them from sin and despair."

Someone says: "You are putting an awful responsibility upon us. Would you have us go out and begin speaking to everyone we meet?" No, that is not what I am saying just now. Though there is a truth there. But this: Surrender yourself to Jesus as your Master, for Him to take possession. Turn the channel over to Him, that He may tighten the connections, upward and outward, and clean it out, and then use as He may choose. He has a passion for winning men, and He has marvelous tact in doing it. Let Him have His way in you. Keep quiet and close to Him, and obey Him, gladly, cheerily, constantly, and He will assume all responsibility for the results.

S. D. GORDON

58

Lovest thou Me?   *John 21:16.*

You can be very religious and not be in love with Christ. You can be very orthodox and not be in love with Christ. You can be very nice and sweet and lovely, and not be in love with Christ. You see, religion is an assent to certain teachings, but Christianity is being in love with the Lord Jesus Christ. Christians have a Man they love and adore and worship and follow; other religious people have a system of things that they are expected to believe and do.

WALTER L. WILSON

More love to Thee, O Christ,
More love to Thee!
Hear Thou the prayer I make
On bended knee;
This is my earnest plea,—
More love, O Christ, to Thee,
More love to Thee!

Once earthly joy I craved,
Sought peace and rest;
Now Thee alone I seek,—
Give what is best;
This all my prayer shall be,—
More love, O Christ, to Thee.
More love to Thee!

Let sorrow do its work,
Send grief and pain;
Sweet are Thy messengers,
Sweet their refrain,
When they can sing with me,
More love, O Christ, to Thee,
More love to Thee!

Then shall my latest breath
Whisper Thy praise,
This be the parting cry
My heart shall raise;
This still its prayer shall be,—
More love, O Christ, to Thee,
More love to Thee!

MRS. E. P. PRENTISS

But whosoever drinketh of the water that I shall give him shall never thirst; but the water that I shall give him shall be in him a well of water springing up into everlasting life.   *John 4:14.*

WHEN you eat or drink anything it becomes part of you. If you drink from this Fountain of Life and eat the Word, that Word becomes part of you and you possess it. Those who drink of the water that this world has to offer thirst again, but the water of life gives eternal satisfaction. The fountain of life is available to everyone. "Whosoever" includes every son of Adam. This fountain is like no other, for it may be carried about constantly. It is "living water" in the very heart of the believer. In other words, when you invite Christ to come into your heart you have the source of supply for your every need.

At what fountain are you drinking? Are you following "clouds without water"? Are you trying to find water in "broken cisterns"? Are you following some form of religion that gives you not bread but a stone? God help you to find the Living Water.

CHARLES E. FULLER

There flows from Calvary a stream
For every sinner's pain,
And he that drinketh, Jesus said,
Shall never thirst again.

Earth's foundations fair but mock our souls,
Like desert phantoms lure,
And they that drink the fainter grow,
The keener thirst endure.

This stream from Calvary still flows,
To bless and cleanse and heal,
And he that drinketh, Jesus said,
New life and rest shall feel.

Oh, blessed stream of pure delight!
Oh, balm for every pain!
To thee I haste, for Jesus said,
I'll never thirst again.

MAY AGNEW STEPHENS

The bond, with its requirements, which was in force against us and was hostile to us, He cancelled, and cleared it out of the way, nailing it to His cross. And the hostile princes and rulers He stripped off from Himself, and boldly displayed them as His conquests, when by the cross He triumphed over them. *Colossians 2:14, 15 (Weymouth).*

CHRIST's conquests of the human heart are the marvels of the centuries, unsurpassed and unsurpassable. Listen to the testimony of the great Napoleon. Conversing one day at Saint Helena, as his custom was, about the great men of antiquity, and comparing himself with them, he suddenly turned to one of his suite with the inquiry, "Who was Jesus Christ?" The officer evaded the interrogation by saying that he had not yet taken time to consider. "Well, then," said Napoleon, "I will tell you." He began by comparing Christ with himself, and with the heroes of the past, and he showed how Jesus far surpassed them all. Said he: "I think I know somewhat of human nature, and I tell you all these were men, not one is like unto Him. Jesus Christ was more than man. Alexander, Caesar, Charlemagne, and myself founded great empires, but upon what did the creations of our genius depend? Upon force. Jesus alone founded His empire upon love, and to this very day there are millions who would gladly die for Him. . . . Men wonder at the conquests of Alexander; but here is a Conqueror who draws men to Himself for their highest good; who unites to Himself and incorporates into His kingdom, not a nation, but the whole human race."

Men may devise what theories they like concerning the doctrine of the atonement, but they cannot get away from the incontestable fact that the magnetism of Jesus centers in His cross. His ethical doctrine has a charm peculiarly its own. His sinless life in the midst of a sinful world is the miracle of all the ages. But it is the uplifted Saviour, the gospel of the Crucified, that makes the irresistible appeal. Some men endeavor to get rid of this factor, to explain it away, and relegate it to an inconspicuous place in their theology. They lay the emphasis upon the Sermon on the Mount, and declare the teaching therein contained to be sufficient to reform the world. Christ did not think so. To Him the cross was the center of the whole circumference, His death the key to every revelation.

R. MOFFAT GAUTREY

Master, if you had been here, . . . my brother
would not have died. And even now I know that
whatever you ask from God, He will give you.
John 11:21, 22 (Weymouth).

CHRISTIAN reader, here lies the true secret of the whole matter.
Let nothing shake your confidence in the unalterable love of
your Lord. Come what may—let the furnace be ever so hot; let
the waters be ever so deep; let the shadows be ever so dark; let the
path be ever so rough; let the pressure be ever so great—still hold
fast your confidence in the perfect love and sympathy of the One who
has proved His love by going down into the dust of death—down
under the dark and heavy billows and waves of the wrath of God,
in order to save your soul from everlasting burnings. Be not afraid
to trust Him fully—to commit yourself, without a shadow of reserve
or misgiving, to Him. Do not measure His love by your circumstances.
If you do, you must, of necessity, reach a false conclusion. Judge not
according to the outward appearance. Never reason from your surroundings. Get to the heart of Christ, and reason out from that
blessed center. Never interpret His love by your circumstances; but
always interpret your circumstances by His love. Let the beams of
His everlasting favor shine upon your darkest surroundings, and
then you will be able to answer every infidel thought, no matter
whence it comes.

> *"Judge not the Lord by feeble sense,*
> *But trust Him for His grace:*
> *Behind a frowning providence*
> *He hides a smiling face."*

C. H. M.

Sorrow not . . . as others which have no hope.
1 Thessalonians 4:13.

A YOUNG couple before marriage were professed Christians, but
afterwards drifted from God. Their little daughter, who was
their idol, suddenly died at the age of four. The mother's heart
grew bitter, and her health became so gravely impaired by the trouble
that fear of her reason failing caused her to be sent into the coun-

62

try for rest and change. One morning when walking in the fields, she became interested in watching a shepherd with his flock. He wanted to get the sheep from one field to another. A stream flowed between the two fields, and the shepherd could not get the sheep to cross the stream. They ran about in all directions. Presently, picking up a tiny lamb, the shepherd carried it across the stream and placed it in the other field. The mother sheep no longer hesitated, but bounded over to the other side, to be quickly followed by the whole flock.

"I had learned my lesson," said the sorrowing mother, "and alone in that field, with the blue sky above me, I knelt on the grass and cried, 'O Jesus, I thank Thee for this sight. I see now why you have taken my darling over the stream, so that I might follow.' And there and then I came back to the Saviour, who freely pardoned me. I returned home rejoicing in salvation."

AUTHOR UNKNOWN

> Should waters sweep down, of affliction or loss,—
>   The more as thy heart would beat true,—
> "Led safely" by Him thou need'st not fear to cross,
>   All safely He will bring thee through.
>
> Should darkness o'ertake thee and fill thee with dread,
>   In Him thou art still quite secure;
> If He leads thee on, thou art still "safely led,"
>   And faith is for "dreading" the cure.
>
> "Led safely" by Him, in the way He deems best,
>   Through sunshine, or sorrow and pain,—
> "Led safely" by Him, with thy heart quite at rest,
>   "Led safely"—be this thy refrain.

J. DANSON SMITH

MARCH 11

O send out thy light and thy truth: let them lead me. *Psalm 43:3.*

THERE are three ways in which God reveals His will to us— through the Scriptures, through providential circumstances, and by means of the direct voice of His Holy Spirit, making impressions upon our hearts and upon our judgments. The Scriptures come first. If you are in doubt upon any subject, you must first of all consult the Bible about it, and see if there is any law there to direct you. Until you have found and obeyed God's will as it is there revealed, you must not ask nor expect a separate direct personal revelation. Where our Father has written out for us a plain direction about anything, He will not, of course, make an especial revelation to us about that thing. And if we fail to search out and obey the Scripture rule, where there is one, and look instead for an inward voice, we shall open ourselves to the deceptions of Satan, and shall almost inevitably get into error. No man, for instance, needs, or could expect any direct revelation to tell him not to steal, because God has already in the Scriptures plainly declared His will about it. There are not many important affairs in life for which a clear direction may not be found in God's Book.

H. M. SHUMAN

MARCH 12

This is a faithful saying, and worthy of all acceptation, that Christ Jesus came into the world to save sinners. *1 Timothy 1:15.*

WHAT source of indescribable assurance to know that in this world of deceit and shattered promises we have one unquestioned, rock-grounded truth! What uplifting confidence to realize that even though human prophecies miscarry and human promises are rudely broken, even though husbands and wives prove unfaithful, friends unreliable, sons and daughters ungrateful,—this love of Christ will never be altered! Your own experiences may have embittered you or made you suspicious. The last years have taught us how promises signed by great corporations, treaties sealed by powerful nations, are disavowed. Yet if you have lost trust in men, find new faith in God! Put a question mark behind any human utterances if you must, but write "Amen" behind the faithful sayings of God! Doubt anything if you will, when men speak, but when God offers you grace in Christ, then with all your heart and soul and mind accept this as the truth of all truth that it is.

WALTER A. MAIER

I will believe, though all around my way
Dark shadows fall, and wintry winds be chill;
I know that after night shall come the day—
My Father cares, and naught can work me ill.

I will believe, though all my days be spent
In ceaseless toil from morn until the night;
My Father knows, and I can rest content—
His trusting child is precious in His sight.

I will believe—though faith be sorely tried,
God's promises forever shall endure;

All needful things will surely be supplied—
I will not doubt, but rest in Him secure.

I will believe—when life's last task is done,
I know that I shall see the Christ I love;
And fellowship so sweet on earth begun
Shall evermore endure with Him above.

BESSIE PATTEN GILMORE

MARCH
13

I . . . am persuaded that He is able to keep. . . .
2 Timothy 1:12.

GIVE yourself wholly up to Jesus, and He will keep you. Will you dare to say that He can hold the oceans in the hollow of His hand, and sustain the arch of heaven, and fill the sun with light for millenniums, but that He can not keep you from being overcome by sin, or filled with the impetuous rush of unholy passion? Can He not deliver His saints from the sword, His children from the power of the dog? Is all power given Him in heaven and on earth, and must He stand paralyzed before the devils that possess you, unable to cast them out? To ask such questions is to answer them.

F. B. MEYER

When in storms of life the sky is clouded,
When the hidden sun I fail to see;
When in mystery my path is shrouded,
I can trust the Man who died for me!

When the pilgrim-way is sad and dreary;
When from earth-born care I would be free—
When my soul is all perplexed and weary—
I can trust the Man who died for me.

Sins of word and deed, sins of omission,
Sins of thought oft throng the memory.
When the teardrops fall in deep contrition,
I can trust the Man who died for me.

World and flesh still strive against the spirit,
And the foe oft claims the victory,
But in faith I claim my Saviour's merit.
I can trust the Man who died for me.

Once He left His glorious Home in Heaven.
Once He shed His blood on Calvary's tree.
Saved by grace, redeemed, restored, forgiven—
I can trust the Man who died for me.

Love Divine, in love's complete surrender
All I am and have I yield to Thee.
All my heart's love unto Thee I tender.
I can trust Thee! Thou hast died for me!

ANNA HOPPE

MARCH
14

For God sent not His Son into the world to condemn the world; but that the world through Him
might be saved.   *John 3:17.*

WHEN Adam was created in God's image, God breathed into
him His own life and Adam became a living soul. Before the
entrance of sin Adam was perfect in relationship and fellowship with his Creator. Then sin entered and as a result spiritual death
took place. Adam became spiritually alienated or cut off from the
life which was in God. That part of him capable of communion and
fellowship with God was severed from the Life-Giver. Though Adam
still existed in his natural life yet he was dead in trespasses and sins.

Everyone that is born into the world since Adam's fall is shapen
in iniquity. He may walk and talk but he is without God-conscious-
ness. He walks in disobedience according to the course of this age,
according to the spirit that now worketh in the children of disobedience.

Now we are brought face to face with a great truth. In Christ
and in Christ alone there is eternal life. This cuts across the path of
all false, worldly, and bloodless systems of religion. And we are told
how to obtain this life. It is in that familiar passage of Scripture,
John 3:16. Your sins may be as high as the highest building, your
hands may be stained with blood, you may be of all men most
miserable, but God's Word says, "Whosoever believeth in Him shall
not perish, but have everlasting life."

CHARLES E. FULLER

God loved the world of sinners lost
And ruined by the fall;
Salvation full, at highest cost,
He offers free to all.

E'en now by faith I claim Him mine,
The risen Son of God;
Redemption by His death I find,
And cleansing through the blood.

Love brings the glorious fulness in,
And to His saints makes known
The blessed rest from inbred sin,
Through faith in Christ alone.

MRS. STOCKTON

MARCH 15

Enlarge the place of thy tent, and let them stretch forth the curtains of thine habitations: spare not, lengthen thy cords, and strengthen thy stakes.

Isaiah 54:2.

"CHILD of mine," speaks the still, small Voice, "I would have filled you with My own fullness, taken possession of you, used you to My praise, but you would not. It was not your littleness, your limited capacity that hindered Me, but that you did not turn your littleness over to Me as a channel through which My fullness could have reached other lives. That was all I asked of you, but you limited Me. You wanted to be a reservoir, where the water is stagnant and soon dries up. I wanted to make you a spring, overflowing constantly to others. You wanted to be blessed. I wanted to bless others through you. I wanted you to become a living prayer, releasing my power; you made prayer a duty. I would have made you My mouthpiece, speaking forth My searching, convicting, saving, enlightening, comforting words, but you limited Me. You dabbled in the philosophies of mortals, you cringed before the opinions of men, you bowed to the popular, and I could not use you. I would have made you a whirlwind to uproot and shake and sweep clean, and you preferred to be a nice little breeze that made people happy.

"My child, it is not too late. Much of your life has been wasted, but will you give Me what remains? 'Little is much, when God is in it.' Will you turn your ear from what men are saying and tune your heart to My message? You once said that you wanted My best at any price. Did you mean it, or was it only a well-sounding phrase of a public prayer? If you meant it, I will accept your challenge, for My power is limited for lack of people who want My best. Do you dare to be scorned, and misunderstood, and marked as a fanatic? Do you dare to risk your salary and your prestige among men? Do you dare to trust Me for the impossible? Then, O child of My infinite love, 'fear ye not, stand still, and see the salvation of the Lord.'"

ANNA J. LINDGREN

MARCH 16

If . . . we receive comfort, it is for your comfort.
2 Corinthians 1:6 (Weymouth).

IT IS an amazing thing to watch the new color which our sorrow assumes when we go out to minister to others. The rawness goes out of our own wound while we are dressing the wounds of our neighbor. Our own pang is lessened when we seek to take the pang out of another's soul. "I felt as though my heart would break, so I just got up and went out to help a poor body who I knew was in need." Yes, and while she went to bring comfort to her needy sister the heart's-ease came into her own soul. This is the beautiful, gracious way of God. We can go out with a broken heart to minister to other broken hearts, and a cooling balm is applied to our own feverish pain and fears.

J. H. JOWETT

I have heard my Saviour calling,
To the harvest rich and fair;
Where the workmen now are busy,
I must take my station there.
Though I may not with the reapers
Gather large and heavy sheaves,
I, like Ruth, may catch stray handfuls
Which some careless gleaner leaves.

Or, perhaps there may be standing,
Hid among the weeds of sin,
Golden grain to grace the garner,
Which the lab'rers have not seen.
These are mine to speak of Jesus,
Mine to point the way above,
Mine to carry with thanksgiving,
To the Saviour's arms of love.

Yes, I'm ready for His service,
In my gracious Master's name
I'll devote my every talent
That He may His lost reclaim.
These my hands and feet shall labor;
This my heart His all shall be,
While my lips exclaim with rapture
"Here am I, O Lord, send me."

KENNETH MACKENZIE

For we are . . . created in Christ Jesus UNTO GOOD WORKS which God hath BEFORE OR- DAINED that we should WALK IN THEM.

Ephesians 2:10.

GOD hath an ordained plan of good works in Christ Jesus, and as each member of the body of Christ yields himself or herself to Him absolutely to do His ordained works, He will give to, and reveal to, that individual member his or her particular works, so that they may walk in them. This is a plain promise of guidance, not only into a practical life-work for each one yielded to Him, but the life-work which God has ordained for each one of His children "from before the foundation of the world." Is this incredible to you, beloved? Nay, anything else is incredible! For that God should have a purpose for every drop of dew glittering in the morning sunlight; for every blade of grass that upsprings from the earth; for every flower that blooms on hill or heath; and yet not have a plan for the lives of the men and women for whom these were created, is indeed in the last degree incredible!

And do you reply that there are myriads of lives of His children apparently afloat upon the stream of a purposeless existence? Alas, yes. But it is because God can not reveal His will to an unrenounced self-will; can not make clear His plans to a life full of self-plans. Such unyielded self-plans and self-will become the fleshly cataract that veils the spiritual vision to God's plan and God's will. But when you yield your life wholly to Him, God will take away that veil and sooner or later show you your life-work. This is true, it matters not how dark the way is now, how hedged in by adverse circumstances, how trying or complicated your present position. You may have to wait; you must needs be patient; but God will assuredly extricate you from all entanglements, and work out His blessed will through you, if you will but trust, wait, and obey as He guides.

JAMES H. McCONKEY

There was a certain creditor which had two debt-
ors: the one owed five hundred pence, and the
other fifty. And when they had nothing to pay, he
frankly forgave them both. Tell me therefore,
which of them will love him most? Simon answered and said, I suppose that he, to whom he
forgave most. And He said unto him, Thou hast
rightly judged.   *Luke 7:41–43.*

THE remarkable ministry of the Old Fashioned Revival Hour in
the prisons is a story that would require volumes to tell. These
men who have been caught in Satan's net as well as the
clutches of the law are susceptible to the Gospel. They know they
are sinners. They know they need a Saviour. They listen eagerly to the
songs and the heart-warming message. Many a lonely prison cell has
become an altar. Here is the letter of one prisoner who found freedom
in Christ Jesus.

"*Dear Mr. Fuller*: Just now I am listening to you from my
cell. I thank my God for being able to listen to the gospel hymns.
One cannot fully appreciate their power and comfort, nor the
great love and mercy of Christ, until he has been brought from
the depths of despair and shame. I humbly praise God that He
is no respecter of persons.

"We have Bible classes here where instruction in the Word
makes us wise unto salvation. Also, through the Salvation Army
Prison Corps (all inmates), we hold open air services every Sunday and on holidays. Satan is very reluctant to release his slaves
but we know God's Word will not return unto Him void. Many
men are seeing the light and turning to God. Pray, with us, that
God will save many in this wicked and sinful place. The need
is great."

Money and time invested in reaching such men for Christ are
certainly very well spent. Perhaps you cannot visit a prison today but
you can help to send the message through the radio and you can pray.

For the fruit of the light is in all goodness.

Ephesians 5:9 (R. V.)

T HE works of darkness are all degrading and destructive. Light generates light which is fruitful and edifying. What, then, are the distinguishing characteristics of those who are light in the Lord? Paul mentions three.

"All goodness"—beneficence in action in all things and toward all persons. There should be no action in the Christian's life that could possibly react harmfully upon another. We constantly hear one who indulges in some questionable form of amusement say, "But I can do that and it won't harm me." Is one's personal harm the only thing to be considered? Goodness forbids the Christian from doing anything that would be detrimental to another. He will guard his influence over others with studious care, and will gladly give up even a lawful thing if there is in it the slightest possibility of leading another away from Christ and into sin. Goodness is a most practical virtue, and exercises itself even in the realm of eating and drinking and in all commonplaces of daily conduct. It puts an absolute ban upon every form of selfishness, and compels the Christian not to seek his own but the other's good.

RUTH PAXSON

I do not ask for mighty words
To leave the crowd impressed,
But grant my life may ring so true
My neighbor shall be blessed.

I do not ask for influence
To sway the multitude;
Give me a "word in season" for
The soul in solitude.

I do not ask to win the great—
God grant they may be saved!—
Give me the broken sinner, Lord,
By Satan long enslaved.

Though words of wisdom and of power
Rise easily to some,
Give me a simple message, Lord,
That bids the sinner come.

A group of boys and girls may be
My God-appointed task;
Help me to lead each one to Thee—
What greater could I ask?

I ask no place of prominence
Where all the world can see,
But in some needy corner, Lord,
There let me work for Thee.

No task too great, no task too small,
Sufficient is Thy grace;
The darkened heart, my mission field,
My light, the Saviour's face.

BARBARA CORNET RYBERG

MARCH
20

He that believeth on the Son hath everlasting life.
John 3:36.

THERE is only one thing in all the world that every human being can do and that is to believe. God found one thing which could be done by every human being from infancy to maturity. The rich can believe and so can the poor. The sick and weak can trust, and so can the strong and well. The blind can believe and so can those who see. The uneducated can believe and the educated can do no more. God asks for faith, a true faith, a living faith, a faith that believes His Word. He does not ask for money, for many have none. He does not ask for service for salvation, because the sick, the weak, and the aged cannot serve. He does not ask merit for salvation, for no one has sufficient merit to be entitled to such a large payment as the Gift of Heaven. If God should put redemption, forgiveness, and salvation on any other basis than that of simple faith, then the entire human race would be shut out. But having put the gift of eternal life on the basis of receiving by believing, the whole human race is included and invited to accept it. Our God is a good God. He has made terms that are available to all and out of the reach of none.

WALTER L. WILSON

Sins of years are washed away,
Blackest stains become as snow;
Darkest night is changed to day,
When you to the fountain go.

Doubt and fears are borne along,
On the current's ceaseless flow;
Sorrow changes into song,
When you to the fountain go.

I'm believing and receiving,
*   While I to the fountain go;*
And my heart its waves are cleansing,
*   Whiter than the driven snow.*

H. H. BOOTH

MARCH 21

And this is His commandment, That we should believe on the name of His Son Jesus Christ, and
love one another, as He gave us commandment.
And he that keepeth His commandments dwelleth
in Him, and He in him.   *1 John 3:23, 24.*

IF YOU are really a member of the body of Christ and you have
confessed Him as your personal Saviour, there will be certain
marks or characteristics in your life. One will be obedience to
His Word. Another will be love for the brethren. And another will
be a forsaking of worldliness. Perhaps this will cut across the path of
some young people but God says in 1 John 2:15–17, "Love not the
world (system) neither the things that are in the world. If any man
love the world (system), the love of the Father is not in him." Those
are not my words. If you love the things of the world, the bright
lights of the palaces of sensual pleasure, the love of the Father is not
in you. Some day, all these things of the world system will come
under the fire of God and will pass away. But he that doeth the will
of God abideth forever.

CHARLES E. FULLER

Oh! the bitter shame and sorrow,
*   That a time could ever be,*
When I let the Saviour's pity
Plead in vain, and proudly answered,
*   "All of self, and none of Thee."*

Yet He found me: I beheld Him
*   Bleeding on the accursed tree,*
Heard Him pray, "Forgive them, Father!"
And my wistful heart said faintly:
*   "Some of self, and some of Thee."*

Day by day, His tender mercy
*   Healing, helping, full and free,*
Sweet and strong, and oh! so patient!
Brought me lower, while I whispered:
*   "Less of self, and more of Thee."*

Higher than the highest heavens,
Deeper than the deepest sea,
Lord, Thy love at last hath conquered!
Grant me now my soul's desire:
"None of self, and all of Thee."

THEODORE MONOD

MARCH
22

Whatsoever ye shall ask the Father in My name,
He will give it you. *John 16:23.*

TO PRAY in the name of Jesus is, in all likelihood, the deepest mystery in prayer. It is therefore exceedingly difficult for the Spirit of prayer to explain this to us. Furthermore, it is easier for us to forget this than anything else which the Spirit teaches us.

The name of Jesus is the greatest mystery in heaven and on earth. In heaven, this mystery is known; on earth, it is unknown to most people. No one can fathom it fully.

Behold, a sinner stands in the heavenly light which the Spirit of God has shed upon him. The longer he stands there, the more he sees of his own sins, his past life, his unclean thoughts, his impenitent heart, his aversion to God and his desire toward sin.

He knows that he must turn to God and that no one else can help him. But the closer he comes to God, the worse things seem. He feels that God cannot have anything to do with anyone who is as impure and dishonest in every way as he is.

To him the Spirit of prayer says, "Come in the name of Jesus. That name gives unholy men access to a holy God." The sinner protests and enumerates all the reasons why God cannot receive him. But, sooner or later, light dawns upon his soul. He begins to see what the name of Jesus means and enters into the presence of God with all his sin and with all the impurity and impenitence of his heart.

Then the Spirit says, "Now pray for whatsoever you will. In the name of Jesus you have permission, not only to stand in the presence of God, but also to pray for everything you need."

The sinner raises a number of objections again, "I cannot pray. I do not have enough faith. Nor do I have enough love and earnestness. My heart is not spiritual, and I am not sufficiently zealous."

The Spirit listens calmly to all his objections and says, "Everything you say is true. And there would be no hope for you if you were to pray in your own name. But listen again. You are to pray in the name of Jesus. It is for Jesus' sake that you are to receive what you ask for."

O. HALLESBY

Dost thou believe on the Son of God? *John 9:35.*

THE Lord Jesus invites us to believe in His own person. He is fairer than the sons of men. He is wonderful in His personality. He is worthy of the adoring worship of angels. He is of more value than any other person in the universe. If you will gaze upon Him in His triumphant death, you will say with the centurion, "Truly this was the Son of God." If you gaze upon Him in His glorious resurrection, you will say with Thomas, "My Lord and my God." If you gaze upon Him in the majesty of His ascension, as He sits upon the throne of His glory, you will like John fall at His feet in utter amazement. You are called upon to believe on His own blessed person. Believe on what He is and who He is. Believe in His attributes and purposes and plans. Believe in His ability and His sufficiency. Trust yourself fully to Him.

WALTER L. WILSON

I've found a joy in sorrow,
A secret balm for pain,
A beautiful tomorrow
Of sunshine after rain;
I've found a branch of healing
Near every bitter spring,
A whispered promise stealing
O'er every broken string.

I've found a glad hosanna
For every woe and wail,
A handful of sweet manna
When grapes of Eschol fail;
I've found a Rock of Ages
When desert wells were dry;
And, after weary stages,
I've found an Elim nigh—

An Elim with its coolness,
Its fountains, and its shade;
A blessing in its fullness
When buds of promise fade;
O'er tears of soft contrition
I've seen a rainbow light;
A glory and fruition
So near!—yet out of sight.

AUTHOR UNKNOWN

Wait on the Lord, and keep His way, and He shall
exalt thee.   *Psalm 37:34.*

ALL it what you will, there is a waiting before God that we
hurried modern mortals do not know, that sends a man back to
his task with the hand of God upon him in such a fashion that
waters part before him which are not moved at our command. It is
not that God puts a premium upon fastings and night-long prayers
and tears and austerities of the flesh. But He does reward a burning
desire for His very best that leaves no stone unturned and follows
Elijah to Jordan while others merely watch him go by. Our Lord
Himself certainly lived perfectly in the will of God, yet He found it
necessary to spend nights in prayer. And shall we poor failing mortals
casually snatch from heaven the power that others gained only by
fervent and importunate intercession? It is true that our Father giveth
liberally and upbraideth not; but He keeps His choicest blessings for
those who really mean business and will not stop at the Gilgal of a
mild average experience.

It is interesting to note that when Elijah seemed to be trying to
get rid of Elisha, his faithful follower said, "As the Lord liveth and
as thy soul liveth, I will not leave thee." Later in Elisha's ministry,
when the Shunammite woman comes to him in behalf of her son, he
tries to dispose of the matter by sending Gehazi with his staff, but
the woman says exactly what he said to Elijah: "As the Lord liveth
and as thy soul liveth, I will not leave thee." It is the man who holds
on for God's blessing to whom people will come for a blessing. If you
would have needy souls drawn to you for help, you must first have
clung to One who is greater.

VANCE HAVNER

Being justified freely by His grace through the redemption that is in Christ Jesus. . . .
                                    Romans 3:24.

RACE is one of the most wonderful words in the Bible. It means
the unmerited favor of God. Sometimes it is used in business
and banking circles in a way which is a good illustration of
what the word means in a spiritual sense. You go to the bank and
borrow a sum of money on your note. The day for payment approaches

and you discover that you aren't going to be able to meet it on time. You become alarmed and finally go with confusion of face and fear to the man in charge of loans. You tell him frankly that you are unable to pay the note on time but that if you may have three days additional you can meet it. He smiles sympathetically and relieves your distress by saying that the bank will allow you three days' "grace," that is, they will extend the time to permit you to arrange the payment. You do not deserve this extra time. It is only by the "favor" of the bank that you are helped.

Now the situation of the whole human race is this: Through Adam's sin, all men were condemned to eternal separation from God. That seems hard, doesn't it? It *IS* hard but it is justice and God is absolutely just. But God was also "plenteous in mercy," loving us with a love that is beyond our comprehension. Therefore He planned a way of escape for all. He came to earth in the person of Jesus, kept the law perfectly (a thing which not even one human being had ever done) and then bore in His own body the sentence of death that had been passed on the human race. So by His faithfulness He delivered all men from death. This, then, is the grace of God, about which Paul loved to preach and write. Just as all of us were condemned to death through one man's disobedience, so all who receive Christ as Saviour are set free by the obedience of One Man.

J. Elwin Wright

Amazing grace! how sweet the sound,
That saved a wretch like me!
I once was lost, but now am found;
Was blind, but now I see.

'Twas grace that taught my heart to fear,
And grace my fears relieved;
How precious did that grace appear,
The hour I first believed.

C. M. D.

MARCH 26

I am black, but comely.   *Song of Solomon 1:5.*

THERE is a sweet fable of the common brier that grew by the ditch. One day there came along the gardener with his spade. As he dug about its roots and lifted it from its lowly place, the brier said, "Why is he doing this? Does he not know I am only a worthless brier?" The gardener planted the brier in the bed beside the lordly roses. Again it said, "What a mistake, planting a poor

77

thing like me among the roses?" Then with his keen knife the gardener amputated a big part of the brier, made a slit in the wound, into which he set the stem of a royal rose, binding the wound; "budded it" the rosarians say. When the season turned again, and June days crowned the rose beds with beauty, rich, fragrant roses bloomed on the brier from the ditch. Passing, the gardener smiled, stooped and said to the brier, "Your beauty, old brier, is not due to that which came out of you, but to that which I have put into you." The marvel of God's grace in His people's lives is due, not to what they were by nature—wild briers, but to that which He puts into them, even "Christ in you, the hope of glory."

THE WATCHMAN-EXAMINER

Take me, Lord, as Thou hast found me,
Guilty, vile and far from Thee,
Satan's fetters fastened round me,
Take me, Lord, and make me free.

Make me, Lord, what Thou would'st have me,
Make me like Thyself to be,
Make me pure and make me holy,
Consecrated unto Thee.

MARY MOORE

MARCH 27

And He shall be as the light of the morning, when the sun riseth, even a morning without clouds; as the tender grass springing out of the earth by clear shining after rain. *2 Samuel 23:4.*

THE sway of Christ as King, according to David's description, is like "clear shining after rain," whereby the tender grass is made to spring out of the earth. So have we often seen it. After a heavy shower of rain, or after a continued rainy season, when the sun shines, there is a delightful clearness and freshness in the air that we seldom perceive at other times. Perhaps the brightest weather is just when the rain has ceased, when the wind has driven away the clouds, and the sun peers forth from his chambers to gladden the earth with smiles.

And thus is it with the Christian's exercised heart. Sorrow does not last forever. After the pelting rain of adversity cometh ever and anon the clear shining. Tried believer, consider this. After all thy afflictions there remaineth a rest for the people of God. There is a clear shining coming to thy soul when all this rain is past. When thy time of rebuke is over and gone, it shall be to thee as the earth when the tempest has sobbed itself to sleep, when the clouds have rent themselves to rags, and when the sun peereth forth once more as a bridegroom in his glorious array. To this end, sorrow cooperates with the bliss that follows it, like rain and sunshine, to bring forth the tender blade. The tribulation and the consolation work together for our good.

C. H. SPURGEON

> The world's fierce winds are blowing
> Temptations sharp and keen;
> I feel a peace in knowing,
> My Saviour stands between;
> He stands to shield me from danger
> When earthly friends are gone;
> He promised never to leave me,
> Never to leave me alone.

AUTHOR UNKNOWN

MARCH 28

We have sinned.   *Daniel 9:5.*

DANIEL made his personal confession to God. I wish to say that this is the greatest key to unlock the storehouse of blessing. In the secret place of God's presence, lay everything before Him and ask the Holy Spirit to put His finger upon the thing that is breaking fellowship and communion. Perhaps you have had an unruly temper. Perhaps you have rolled some sweet morsel of gossip under your tongue. Perhaps you have stirred up strife among your brethren by harsh, biting, bitter words.

If every one who names the name of Christ would follow Daniel's example and confess his sins and short-comings, there would be a revival which would startle the nation. "If my people, which are called by My name, shall humble themselves, and pray, and seek My face, and turn from their wicked ways; THEN WILL I HEAR" (2 Chronicles 7:14).

CHARLES E. FULLER

> There is a time, we know not when, a point, we know not where,
> That marks the destiny of men, for glory or despair.
> There is a line, by us unseen, that crosses every path,
> That marks the boundary between God's patience and His wrath.
>
> To pass that limit is to die, to die as if by stealth;
> It does not dim the beaming eye, or pale the glow of health.
> The conscience may be still at ease, the spirit light and gay;
> That which is pleasing still may please, and care be thrust away.

But on the forehead God has set indelibly a mark,
Unseen by man, for man as yet is blind and in the dark.
And yet the doomed man's path below, like Eden, may have bloomed;
He did not, does not, will not know or feel that he is doomed.

He thinks and feels that all is well, and every fear is calmed;
He lives, he dies, he wakes in hell, not only doomed but damned!
O where is this mysterious bourne by which our path is crossed,
Beyond which God Himself hath sworn that he who goes is lost?

How far may we go on in sin? How long will God forbear?
Where does hope end, and where begin the confines of despair?
An answer from the skies is sent: Ye that from God depart,
While it is called TODAY, repent, and harden not your heart.

J. A. ALEXANDER

MARCH 29

Abide in Me, and I in you. As the branch cannot bear fruit of itself, except it abide in the vine; no more can ye, except ye abide in Me. *John 15:4.*

Only a smile, yes, only a smile,
That a woman o'erburdened with grief
Expected from you; 'twould have given relief,
For her heart ached sore the while.
But, weary and cheerless, she went away,
Because, as it happened that very day,
You were out of touch with your Lord.

Only a word, yes, only a word,
That the Spirit's small voice whispered, "Speak";
But the worker passed onward, unblessed and weak,
Whom you were meant to have stirred
To courage, devotion and love anew,
Because, when the message came to you,
You were out of touch with your Lord.

Only a note, yes, only a note,
To a friend in a distant land;
The Spirit said, "Write," but then you had planned
Some different work, and you thought
It mattered little. You did not know
'Twould have saved a soul from sin and woe—
You were out of touch with your Lord.

Only a song, yes, only a song,
That the Spirit said, "Sing tonight;

Thy voice is thy Master's by purchased right."
But you thought, "Mid this motley throng,
I care not to sing of the City of God";
And the heart that your words might have reached
grew cold—
You were out of touch with your Lord.

Only a day, yes, only a day,
But oh! can you guess, my friend,
Where the influence reaches and where it will end
Of the hours that you fretted away?
The Master's command is, "Abide in Me";
And fruitless and vain will your service be
If out of touch with your Lord.

AUTHOR UNKNOWN

MARCH 30

And one shall say unto Him, What are these wounds in Thine hands? Then He shall answer, Those with which I was wounded in the house of My friends.   *Zechariah 13:6.*

THOSE symbols of shame are Christ's chief marks of honor now. He wears them as a warrior wears his scars. They tell of the battle in which He fought and vanquished sin. There was never a warrior in all earth's history who travailed and triumphed as He did. It was a stern fight, but not a sterile one. So many so-called victories are indistinguishable from defeat. But in His triumph all the ages share. That glorified body of the world's Redeemer is the only body in the universe which was wounded for sin. Other bodies have been wounded by sin. Yours has, and mine. Oh, how scabbed and botched we are, disfigured and polluted by its stain! Ah, what scars we carry in our conscience, and how carefully we conceal our shame. But His were vicarious wounds, endured for the sake of others, and they mark Him out from every other member of the race. Was not His name called Jesus, that He should save His people from their sins? That is the function upon which all His fame is built, and apart from it His name is a misnomer. By His suffering came salvation, by His wounds our healing, by His death our glorious deliverance. All His dignity, in heaven and on earth, is based on that. In the midst of the throne there standeth a Lamb, as though it had been slain. And gazing on that wondrous spectacle, the saints cry "Alleluia," and all the angels say "Amen."

R. MOFFAT GAUTREY

When I survey the wondrous cross
  On which the Prince of glory died,
My richest gain I count but loss,
  And pour contempt on all my pride.

Forbid it, Lord! that I should boast,
  Save in the death of Christ, my God;
All the vain things that charm me most,
  I sacrifice them to His blood.

See! from His head, His hands, His feet,
  Sorrow and love flow mingled down;
Did e'er such love and sorrow meet?
  Or thorns compose so rich a crown?

ISAAC WATTS

MARCH 31

When He seeth the blood upon the lintel, and on the two side posts, the Lord will pass over the door, and will not suffer the destroyer to come in unto your houses to smite you.   *Exodus 12:23.*

THIS story is the perfect type of salvation through the shed blood of the Lamb of God.

God told the children of Israel to take a spotless lamb, let the lamb be slain and the blood applied to the lintel and door posts of the house. The blood was to be applied with hyssop, a little clinging vine within reach of everyone. Obedience to God's command was an evidence of the faith of that family, for it meant that they believed that God would see the blood and pass over them. If the shed blood had not been applied the destroying angel would have done his work.

Now, listen! Nineteen hundred years ago Christ died on Calvary and when the Roman soldiers pierced His side blood and water came out. That blood avails for your sin and provides your salvation. What good has that blood done you, friend of mine? Have you reached out with appropriating faith and applied that shed blood to your unregenerate heart?

You can talk about Christ, read about Christ, praise Christ as a wonderful teacher and believe that He was a great and good man but until you personally apply the blood you will not know His regenerating power. Remember, He is saying, "When I see the blood, I will pass over you."

CHARLES E. FULLER

'Twas I that shed the sacred blood,
I nailed Him to the tree,
I crucified the Christ of God,
I joined the mockery.

Yet not the less that blood avails,
To cleanse away my sin,
And not the less that cross prevails
To give me peace within.

HORATIUS BONAR

The Lord is . . . not willing that any should perish,
but that all should come to repentance.

2 Peter 3:9.

THE voice of radio reaches into the strangest places! Here sits a man with a bottle of rum before him and—But let's get the story in his own words:

"'Friend of mine, sitting there by your radio . . . you are listening to an old fashioned preacher.'

"Pastor Fuller, do you know who you were talking to? The greatest sinner you ever hoped to reach, sitting with a bottle of rum on the one hand and the devil on the other—dead in sin. Sir, your program will save me from death. Please tell your radio audience how your message pierced my fogged brain as never before. I want all your listeners to know how Christ can send your voice to one who could be reached by none other, when all hope had failed.

"Please excuse mistakes due to my condition from drinking. Christ must be at your side to give you the power to reach me—who has hated righteousness."

Pray that the gospel message may catch the ear of many more, this week, as they listen. Think of the many broken homes that may be restored if you are faithful in praying and giving.

I WISH THEE PEACE!

—the peace of sins all taken,
All washed away through Christ's atoning blood;
The peace that rests, untroubled and unshaken,
Since God's redeeming grace is understood.

J. DANSON SMITH

There is at Jerusalem by the sheep market a pool
. . . called . . . Bethesda, having five porches. In
these lay a great multitude of impotent folk, of
blind, halt, withered, waiting for the moving of the
water. *John 5:2, 3.*

"IN THESE lay a multitude of them that were sick, blind, halt,
withered."

Where? In the place of healing. But they were not healed.

And into the place of healing steps the Healer, and out of the
multitude only one (so far as the record goes) was healed.

Where is the place of healing today? Where the Healer is—in the
Church.

And as it was said about the pool of Bethesda, so can it be said
about the Church today, "There lay a multitude of them that were
sick, halt, blind, withered."

"Wilt thou be made whole?"

"But I am not sick."

That is your great tragedy—that you do not know it.

How about the "inner chamber," the place of secret fellowship
with God? The place of intercession? How often do you enter it, and
with what emotions, what results? Are you strengthened there, daily,
"with might in the inner man," fortified against the influences of the
world, the flesh, and the devil? And are lives touched and energized
everywhere, because of your prayer life?

Feebleness of prayer is the mark of disease. Impotence to walk
is in the Christian, as in the natural life a terrible proof of some
evil in the system that needs a physician.

There is a disease affecting orange trees that is called root-disease.
At first nothing wrong can be detected by an ordinary observer, for
the tree still bears, but an expert can detect signs of the deadly
malady.

The Church of Christ and the spiritual life of thousands of its
members suffer from root-disease; the neglect of secret intercourse
with God.

"Wilt thou be made whole?"

ANNA J. LINDGREN

God's free gift is eternal life in Christ Jesus our
Lord.   Romans 6:23 (Weymouth).

THIS gift is one which does not change with the changing seasons. He is given and may be taken in the summer or in the
winter, in the spring or in the autumn. It is not so with other
gifts. We do not give overcoats in June, nor melons in December.
The gifts of earth are suited to the seasons and to the circumstances.
Different gifts are given according to the need which is manifested
at the time. Not so with Christ! There is always the need for Him, in
summer or in winter, in the sunshine or in the shadow, by day or by
night. Christ is given and Christ may be taken at any time. There is
never any season of the year or hour of the day when He is not
needed, nor when He is withheld.

This lovely gift does not change with the times. If you observe
old photographs, you are amused at the strange hats that were worn
in former days, the peculiar sleeves and the unusual cut of the coat.
We say that those styles are out of date, and are not in fashion. Christ
Jesus is never out of date. He is always in fashion. The Christian
graces which He bestows, and the salvation which He gives, are just
as attractive and desirable today as in the years past. He adorns those
who trust Him. He beautifies those who receive Him. He dignifies and
makes honorable those who make Him Lord of the life. No form of
education, nor of man-made religion has ever been found which will
do for the soul and for the life what Jesus Christ will do.

WALTER L. WILSON

> *Nearer to Him that hath loved me,*
> *Nearer to Him who hath died;*
> *Nearer through crosses and trials,*
> *Nearer the crucified.*
>
> *Nearer, nearer to Him,*
> *Nearer to Jesus, my Saviour,*
> *Nearer the crucified.*

R. B. LOCKWOOD

Except ye repent, ye shall all likewise perish.
Luke 13:3.

IN ORDER that a great revival may sweep over the land today there must be a cleaning up. Judgment must begin at the House of God. Away with your card players and dancers that come in to make merchandise of the House of God. Listen to me. My Bible says, "Come out from among them and be ye separate . . . and touch not the unclean thing."

You are listening to an old-fashioned preacher. God is a jealous God, and He will have no other god before Him. When we cast out the idols in our hearts and worship Him alone, God will answer our prayers. There are not only idols of silver and gold but of pride, covetousness, pleasure and lust.

Do you remember how God told Israel, when the first Passover was observed, to put away the leaven out of their houses? Leaven is always a type of sin. If you want God's blessing there must be a time of searching your own heart and letting God search you to find all the leaven and put it away. Is there some hidden leaven in a vessel in your house today? Don't expect your heart to be revived until you put it away.

CHARLES E. FULLER

If I gain riches, friends and power,
And neglect my soul to free
From scarlet, crimson sins,
What doth it profit me?
If I should spend my time,
Time given by God alone,
At selfish, trivial tasks,
And neglect to feed my soul,
What doth it profit me?

FLORENCE A. SMITH

Call upon Me in the day of trouble: I will deliver thee, and thou shalt glorify Me. *Psalm 50:15.*

WE MAKE a most serious mistake when, in any time of need or pressure, we turn to the creature for help or sympathy. We are sure to be disappointed. Creature-streams are dry. Creature-props give way. Our God will make us prove the vanity and folly of all creature-confidences, human hopes, and earthly expectations. And on the other hand, He will prove to us, in the most touching and forcible manner, the truth and blessedness of His own word, "They shall not be ashamed that wait for Me."

No, never! He, blessed be His name, never fails a trusting heart. He cannot deny Himself. He delights to take occasion from our wants, our woes and weaknesses, to express and illustrate His tender care and lovingkindness, in a thousand ways. But He will teach us the utter barrenness of all human resources. "Thus saith the Lord; Cursed be the man that trusteth in man, and maketh flesh his arm, and whose heart departeth from the Lord. For he shall be like the heath in the desert, and shall not see when good cometh; but shall inhabit the parched places in the wilderness, in a salt land and not inhabited."

Thus it must ever be. Disappointment, barrenness and desolation are the sure and certain results of trusting in man. But, on the other hand—and mark the contrast, reader—"Blessed is the man that trusteth in the Lord, and whose hope the Lord is: for he shall be as a tree planted by the waters, and that spreadeth out her roots by the river, and shall not see when heat cometh, but her leaf shall be green; and shall not be careful in the year of drought, neither shall cease from yielding fruit."

C. H. M.

APRIL 6

In whom we have redemption through His blood, the forgiveness of sins, according to the riches of His grace.   *Ephesians 1:7.*

THE Apostle uses an expression some eleven times in this epistle which suggests the measure of God's ability "to do." The expression is "according to." We will not mention the entire number, but call your attention to only a few. In the first chapter of Ephesians he writes: "According to the good pleasure of His will" (vs. 5); "according to the riches of His grace" (vs. 7); "according to His good pleasure" (vs. 9); "according to the purpose of Him who worketh all things after the counsel of His will" (vs. 11); and in the third chapter, "according to the riches of His glory (vs. 16); and "according to the power that worketh in us" (vs. 20).

A beloved friend of mine rejoiced my heart by pointing out the significance of this expression. He said there was a vast difference between God giving us "out of" His riches, and His giving us "according to" His riches. Then he illustrated it after this manner. If Henry Ford gave me something out of his riches, he might give me ten dollars or one hundred dollars or even one thousand dollars, or he might give me only ten cents. On the other hand, if Henry Ford gave me according to his riches, who can estimate the largeness of the gift he might bestow upon me? God measures His gifts to us not by our puny scale of measurement but "according to" the riches which He possesses in Himself, and in which He has abounded toward us through Jesus Christ our Lord. Surely, if He does something through Christ, it will not be a scanty doing—it will be "exceeding abundantly."

HOWARD W. FERRIN

> *The Rose-Garden Gate half open stands,*
> *   And Roses are peeping out*
> *As if to invite—"Come, fill your hands*
> *   With beauty! Don't go without!*
> *We're blossoming here*
> *Just to give you cheer;*
> *   Come, gather us, do not doubt!"*
>
> *As I came and filled my heart and hands*
> *   With their fragrant loveliness,*
> *I thought of One who pleading stands,*
> *   Longing to give and bless;*
> *"Come! Gather! Take! All you will," He pleads,*
> *"There is more than enough for all your needs."*

MARGARET ELIZABETH MYERS

APRIL 7

In that day there shall be a fountain opened to the house of David and to the inhabitants of Jerusalem for sin and for uncleanness. *Zechariah 13:1.*

IF EVER we are with joy to draw water out of the wells of salvation, it is to Calvary we must come. If ever we are to find ease for the festering wounds inflicted upon our life by sin's envenomed fang, we must apply the balm distilled from the wounds of Christ. How those wounds of His heal our broken hearts and cleanse our stricken consciences from all their guilty stain, no theology man invented has ever adequately explained. Every theory of atonement is an attempt to explore a mystery so profound that mortal mind is baffled. But facts are finer than theories and more impressive than theologies. The healed man is still the unanswerable argument which routs the logic of the scribes. Right down the centuries the church has witnessed the miracles of personal redemption. Shattered lives have been recreated by the mystic touch of the Nazarene. Souls defiled by hideous transgression have been made clean every whit by His indwelling. Cannibals have been converted, and devil priests subdued by His matchless grace. The vilest sinners the world has known have learned in the school of the Crucified the very genius of sainthood.

> *"I ask them whence their victory came;*
> *They, with united breath,*
> *Ascribe their conquest to the Lamb,*
> *Their triumph to His death."*

What happened in the dread transaction of Calvary we shall never be able to state exhaustively in terms of human speech. But this, at least, we know assuredly, there was opened that day in the house of David a fountain for sin and for all uncleanness.

R. MOFFAT GAUTREY

APRIL 8

For He is our peace, who hath made both one, and hath broken down the middle wall of partition between us; having abolished in His flesh, the enmity, even the law of commandments contained in ordinances; for to make in Himself of twain one new man, so making peace; and that He might reconcile both unto God in one body by the cross, having slain the enmity thereby.

Ephesians 2:14–16.

THE Lord Jesus accomplished on the cross the thing which God had promised, that the seed of the woman should bruise the serpent's head. "To this end was the Son of God manifested, that He might destroy the works of the devil" (1 John 3:8). God tells us that the devil has been robbed of his power over us and that Jesus destroyed the work which he has done. This was accomplished on the cross, so that we can glory in the cross of Christ, for it actually brings our freedom. Today it stands between us and our foe. It is a standard which God has raised up for us, through which we may have victory over our foe, the devil. It is the emblem of his defeat. On the cross of Christ the world, the flesh, and the devil, each in his own way, were dealt with forever.

Christ on the cross removed the barriers which separated me from God—my guilt, my sin, the law; and He dealt with my enemies— the world, the flesh, the devil. These six things were dealt with, so that we need no longer be in bondage through fear and that we may come boldly to the throne of grace. Have we all given a hearty assent to these things which Christ did for us? Or have we, as we read the Word, drifted by them, taking things for granted? Let us lay hold of that for which God has laid hold of us. Let us gird up the loins of our minds and consent to that which He did. Let us enter into all that which being united to Christ as the Head means. Let us rejoice in all that was accomplished for us on Calvary.

L. L. LEGTERS

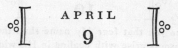

APRIL
9

Whom God hath raised up, having loosed the pains of death: because it was not possible that He should be holden of it. *Acts 2:24.*

THE Lord Jesus Christ was wonderful in His resurrection. When His body was laid in the grave, Pilate gave orders at the request of the Pharisees to seal the sepulchre. "Make it as sure as ye can" (Matt. 27:65). And they did! Nature made it as sure as she could, for a large stone was before the sepulchre, but "up from the grave He arose," the angel of the Lord rolled the stone away and sat upon it. The Roman government made it as sure as it could and placed its seal upon the grave; but "up from the grave He arose" to break the seal of Rome as later He broke the back of Rome and as even later He will smash the last Roman world empire. Unbelief made it as sure as it could for Pharisaism tried to discredit His resurrection but "up from the grave He arose" and whenever unbelief thinks it has buried the truth, the "corpse" always comes to life in the midst of the funeral to outlive all the pallbearers. Death made it as sure as it could but "up from the grave He arose" and now He carries the keys of death and hell. The world, the flesh, and the devil conspired to keep Him in the grave but "up from the grave He arose" that "death might be swallowed up in victory."

VANCE HAVNER

> Rise, glorious Conqueror, rise;
> Into thy native skies,—
>   Assume Thy right;
> And where in many a fold
> The clouds are backward rolled—
> Pass through those gates of gold,
>   And reign in light!
>
> Victor o'er death and hell!
> Cherubic legions swell
>   Thy radiant train;

Praises all heaven inspire.
Each angel sweeps his lyre,
And waves his wings of fire,—
Thou Lamb once slain!

M. BRIDGES

APRIL
10

But unto you that fear My name shall the Sun of righteousness arise with healing in His wings.

Malachi 4:2.

EVERY man knows that the sun is the true light, feels it to be such, and without hesitation affirms it to be supreme. There is no debate as to whether the sun or the moon is the light of the world. Imagine a dark night, and an observer who has never seen the sun: a star suddenly shows itself, and the observer hails it with delight; presently the moon shines with all her gentle strength, and the observer says: "This is the fulfillment of the promise; can ought be lovelier, can the sky possibly be brighter?" In due course the sun comes up; every cloud is filled with light; every mountain is crowned with a strange glory; every leaf in the forest is silvered; the sea becomes as burnished glass, and secrecy is chased from the face of the earth: under such a vision, the observer knows that this is the true light—the sovereign, all-dominating flame. It is so in the revelation of Jesus Christ. When the eyes of men are opened to see Him in all His grace and wisdom and sympathy—in all the sufficiency of His sacrifice and the comfort of His Spirit—the heart is satisfied, and every rival light is lost in the infinite splendor of God the Son.

JOSEPH PARKER

Sun of my soul! Thou Saviour dear,
It is not night if Thou be near;
O may no earth-born cloud arise
To hide Thee from Thy servant's eyes.

Be near to bless us when we wake,
Ere through the world our way we take;
Till in the ocean of Thy love,
We lose ourselves in heav'n above.

JOHN KEBLE

Revive Thy work in the midst of the years.
Habakkuk 3:2.

W E N E E D to stand in these stormy times of the world's history and say, "I believe God." I believe with all my heart that God will bring a revival, even exceedingly above that which we ask or think, when we really meet the conditions. God forbid that any child of His should say that there cannot be another, great, sweeping revival before Jesus comes. God forbid that we should fold our hands and sit quietly by when souls are rushing headlong to everlasting separation from Him. God forbid that we should fail to meet His conditions for revival. There will be a sweeping revival when and if we meet the conditions.

The only revival which will amount to anything must be prayed down, not just promoted. We read in 1 Samuel of such a revival. Five conditions brought this about. First, there was a sense of deep need. Secondly, a destruction of idols. Thirdly, prayer. Fourthly, confession of weakness and sin. Fifthly, faith in the cleansing power of the blood of the Lamb. The same conditions will bring about a revival today.

The closing chapters of the book of Judges and the opening chapters of 1 Samuel depict one of the darkest periods of Israel's history. The same apostasy and sin are in our land today, but the same God still lives and will deliver when we come to Him in true repentance and confession.

CHARLES E. FULLER

Lord, speak to me, that I may speak
In living echoes of Thy tone;
As Thou hast sought, so let me seek
Thy erring children lost and lone.

O lead me, Lord, that I may lead
The wandering and the wavering feet;
O feed me, Lord, that I may feed
The hungering ones with manna sweet.

O strengthen me, that while I stand
Firm on the Rock, and strong in Thee,
I may stretch out a loving hand
To wrestlers with the troubled sea.

O teach me, Lord, that I may teach
The precious things Thou dost impart;
And wing my words, that they may reach
The hidden depths of many a heart.

FRANCES RIDLEY HAVERGAL

He . . . took a towel. . . .   *John 13:4.*

IS THERE a church that is not bruised, wounded, and bleeding because of pride and self-seeking among its own? Is there a Christian of maturer years who does not carry about in his bosom sensitive scars that ever break open, because a fellow-Christian—a loved one—inflicted the wound? And the forgiveness asked and granted never went deep enough to pour in the oil that heals and erases the memory of the hurt.

And here we go, supersensitive to the slightest touch of real or fancied hurt, wrapped about with our dignified rights and our "righteous indignation" and our wounded pride. And the stain remains, and the wound never heals, and the work of God is arrested, because no one is great enough to be small enough to get down on his bare knees on the floor and with the towel of humility wipe the feet and heart of the offender.

The pride of flesh—our heritage from beneath—cries out: "Not I! What would people think? I am the one sinned against! I must uphold my position!" Who is the one sinned against? The One who "rose from the throne, laid aside the garment of light which He had worn as His vesture, took up the poor towel of humanity, and wrapped it about His glorious Person; poured His own blood into the basin of the Cross, and set Himself to wash away the foul stains of human depravity and guilt."

"He took a towel."

Shall we?

ANNA J. LINDGREN

The tree is known by his fruit.   *Matthew 12:33.*

DO YOU remember Paul's list of the traits of character that mark a Christian life—love, joy, peace, long-suffering, gentleness, goodness, meekness, faithfulness, self-control? Suppose for a moment you think through a list of the opposites of those nine characteristics—bitterness, envy, hate, low-spiritedness, sulkiness, chafing, fretting, worrying, short-suffering, quick temper, hot-temper, high-spiritedness, unsteadiness, unreliability, lack of control of yourself. May I ask, have you any personal acquaintance with some of these qualities? Is there still some need in your life for the other desirable traits? Well, remember that it is only as the Holy Spirit has control that this fruit of His is found. For notice that it is not we that bear this fruit, but He in us. We furnish the soil. He must have free sway in its cultivation if He is to get this harvest. And notice, too, that it does not say "the fruits of the Spirit," as though you might have one or more, and I have some others. But it is "fruit"—that is, it is all one fruit and all of it is meant to be growing up in each one of us. And let the fact be put down as settled once for all that only as we tarry and receive the Master's promise of power can we live the lives He longs to have us live down here among men for Him.

S. D. GORDON

There's a prayer my heart is pleading,
More than all desires above.
Not to understand all mysteries,
Not alone to feel His love,
Not to make all men take notice
Of the talents I can show;
But to know whom I've believed,
My dear Lord Himself, to know.

My great longing is for power,
Only His, that I may know
That whate'er my lips may utter,
His own precious Word may go
Deep into the heart I'm touching,
With His resurrection power.
How my heart is praying, longing,
For His fulness, hour by hour!

McQUAT

APRIL 14

For it is God which worketh in you both to will and to work, for His good pleasure.

Philippians 2:13 (Weymouth).

THIS statement occurs between two injunctions. The first has reference to personal salvation, and the second declares the duty of man in relation to the world. The first reads, "Work out your own salvation with fear and trembling"; and the second, "Do all things without murmurings and disputings; that ye may be blameless and harmless, children of God without blemish, in the midst of a crooked and perverse generation, among whom ye are seen as lights in the world."

The declaration referred to brings both the positive and relative statements within the realm of practical possibility, "For it is God

95

which worketh in you." This divine inworking makes the human out-working easy, simple, and delightful. For every demand made upon us as Christian men and women, there is sufficient, overwhelming supply in the communication of divine energy.

G. Campbell Morgan

> O blessed life! the heart at rest
>   When all without tumultuous seems,
>   That trusts a higher will, and deems
> That higher will, not mine, the best.
>
> O blessed life! the mind that sees
>   Whatever change the years may bring;
>   A mercy still in everything,
> And shining through all mysteries.
>
> O blessed life! the soul that soars,
>   When sense of mortal sight is dim,
>   Beyond the sense—beyond to Him
> Whose love unlocks the heavenly doors.
>
> O blessed life! heart, mind and soul
>   From self-born aims and wishes free
>   In all—at one with Deity
> And loyal to the Lord's control.
>
> O life! how blessed, how divine!
>   High life, the earnest of a higher!
>   Saviour, fulfil my deep desire,
> And let this blessed life be mine.

W. Tidd Matson

APRIL 15

Whither shall I go from Thy Spirit? Or whither shall I flee from Thy presence? . . . If I take the wings of the morning, and dwell in the uttermost parts . . . even there shall Thy hand lead me.

Psalm 139:7–10.

THIS scripture was made true to one who was followed by the prayers of a faithful mother in Sweden and by the message of radio over the trackless forests of northern Canada.

"*Dear Mr. Fuller*: I used to work where it was thickly pop-ulated but never took time to listen to God's Word. I didn't care for it. When I moved up here in the woods to work last year I built a shanty and have been living all alone. I bought a radio to hear the news. I really heard some news, too! I started to listen to your program last fall. It was the same sort of preaching I had heard at home as a kid. I knew I was a sinner, lost forever. Sunday after Sunday I listened. Then came a day when I couldn't stand it any longer so I cried to God for mercy. He forgave my sins and I am cleansed in the blood of His Son, Jesus Christ. Some people tell me I can't *know* until after I am dead but, thank God, I *know* now. I know it in my heart and I know it from God's Word.

"I have a mother in Sweden who has been praying for me all these years. I know now that God took me away from my friends down South and moved me up here where I could hear His Word through Mr. Fuller and be saved."

This man probably would never have been won to Christ in church but radio found him in his isolated wilderness cabin—and he found God because faithful Christians made the Old Fashioned Revival Hour possible. Is it worth while? Pray today for those in lonesome occupations—in the mines, on the sheep ranches, in the lumber camps, and on the lonely desert.

APRIL 16

Ye must be born again.   *John 3:7.*

THAT rebirth changes everything. It changes you, the impulses of your heart, the words of your lips, the conduct of your life. The new birth transforms fear to courage, doubt to conviction, afflictions to blessings, death to life! Instead of surrendering to despair, twice-born men and women can find happiness even in the chaos of adversity. Bishop Ken, suffering in his last days from painful disease, his sleep gone, yet blessed by the quiet of a reborn soul, could sing his immortal "Praise God, from whom all Blessings flow." Ray Palmer, a young teacher, alone and discouraged in New York City, harassed by religious doubts, brought his sorrow to Christ, and in his reborn trust exulted, "My faith looks up to Thee, Thou Lamb of Calvary." Anne Steele experienced one of the hardest afflictions that can come to a woman: her lover was drowned only a few hours before their wedding-day. Yet because she was reborn in Christ, she could look to Jesus and say:

"Give me a calm and thankful heart,
From every murmur free;

97

The blessings of Thy grace impart
And make me live to Thee."

I promise you that, no matter how many failures may have embittered you, no matter how much misery and heartache may have marked your life, no matter how often you have been swayed by sin, you, too, can begin life anew in Christ and find blessing in that rebirth.

WALTER A. MAIER

APRIL 17

But we all, with unveiled face reflecting as in a mirror the glory of the Lord, are transformed into the same image from glory to glory, even as from the Lord the Spirit. *2 Corinthians 3:18 (R. V.).*

ONE day Christ will come again to take every Christian into His immediate presence. In that eternal tomorrow there will be perfect likeness of every Christian to his Lord, for he will be glorified both in spirit and in body.

1 John 3:2: "Beloved, now are we the sons of God; and it doth not yet appear what we shall be; but we know that, when He shall appear, we shall be like Him; for we shall see Him as He is."

Oh! is it any wonder that Scripture describes such a calling as high (Phil. 3:14); holy (2 Tim. 1:9); and heavenly (Heb. 3:1)? What does the hope of such a calling inspire in you? Is it glorious enough to inspire hatred of all that is of the world, the flesh and the devil? Is it attractive enough to wean you from the world with all its soul-destroying pleasures and pursuits? Is it real enough to make you loathe self that would dethrone Christ as your Lord? Is it precious enough to make you seek those things which are above, where Christ sitteth on the right hand of God? Is it strong enough to create within you the passionate desire to have Christ all in all to you?

RUTH PAXSON

Through the love of God our Saviour,
All will be well;
Free and changeless is His favor,
All, all is well.
Precious is the blood that healed us,
Perfect is the grace that sealed us,
Strong the hand stretched forth to shield us,
All must be well.

Though we pass through tribulation,
All will be well;

98

Ours is such a full salvation,
All, all is well.
Happy still in God confiding;
Fruitful, if in Christ abiding;
Holy, through the Spirit's guiding:
All must be well.

MARY BOWLEY

APRIL 18

God . . . hath . . . spoken.   *Hebrews 1:1, 2.*

HERE in the very beginning of this marvelous epistle we are brought face to face with God. A man's word can carry weight only as his wisdom and his veracity give him standing in the community. But in this epistle One has spoken whose Word is eternal, never changing and always authoritative.

How foolish to follow the wisdom of man, even though his words are intellectual, when he speaks contrary to God's holy Word! How foolish to build one's trust for eternity upon the sandy foundation of the empty words of unsaved men, when God has spoken. He spoke of old through the prophets but now He has spoken unto us by His Son. There is no other approach to God but through Him; no other name, no other way, no other foundation, no other hope. For this reason we ought to give the more earnest heed to His words, which are a marvelous revelation. "Faith cometh by hearing and hearing by the Word of God."

CHARLES E. FULLER

Have faith in God! for He who reigns on high
Hath borne thy grief and hears the suppliant's sigh,
Still to His arms, thine only refuge, fly.
    Have faith in God!

Fear not to call on Him, O soul distressed!
Thy sorrow's whisper woos thee to His breast;
He who is oftenest there is oftenest blest.
    Have faith in God!

Lean not on Egypt's reeds; slake not thy thirst
At earthly cisterns. Seek the kingdom first.
Though man and Satan fight thee with their worst,
    Have faith in God!

Go tell Him all! The sigh thy bosom heaves
Is heard in heaven. Strength and grace He gives
Who gave Himself for thee. Our Jesus lives;
    Have faith in God.

AUTHOR UNKNOWN

99

And they took Jesus, and led Him away. And He
bearing His cross went forth into a place called
the place of a skull, which is called in the Hebrew,
Golgotha: where they crucified Him.

John 19:16–18.

You and I have grown accustomed to the vision of the Crucified.
We have seen the spectacle of Calvary so often that we can pass
it by as though it were a common sight. Our hearts have grown
callous, because accustomed, to His anguish. We are no longed awed
by the unutterable sorrow of the Lamb. If angels have hearts to
break, they must have broken their very hearts when they saw what
man had done to God's Well-Beloved. If angels have tears to shed,
they must have wept tears of blood as they marked the base indigni-
ties which man had heaped upon the wondrous Saviour of the world.
It was a sight at which heaven shuddered, and from which the angels
veiled their faces with their wings, unable to behold the tragic evi-
dences of our tremendous shame.

The Heir of the vineyard came but once to claim His heritage,
and by wicked husbandmen was cast out and slain. That is the
world's greatest tragedy. Once in the midst of the ages God deigned
to be the Guest of earth, and all the hospitality we offered Him was
a manger bed and a borrowed sepulcher. He stooped from a throne
of glory, and we nailed Him to a tree.

Yet those wounds, which were once the objects of derision, have
become the objects of adoration. It is the broken heart of Christ that
has healed the broken heart of the world. It is the nail-pierced hands
of Christ that have cleansed our leprosy, opened our blind eyes and
quickened our dead soul into newness of life.

R. MOFFAT GAUTREY

Above the sweetest songs of earth,
Through all the strife of gain and loss,
Above the sounds of grief and mirth,
I hear the story of the cross.

That story is a tale of love,
That wipes away the sinner's tears,
It makes him heir of heav'n above,
And gives him joy through endless years.

Oh, none but Jesus bore such scorn,
No stricken lamb so meek as He;
No other brow so bruised by thorn,
No other heart so bled for me.

No other feet the wine-press trod,
No other hand so freely gave,
No Saviour like the Son of God!
No love like His to reach and save!

Oh, blessed cross of sacrifice,
Where Jesus died for me, for me!
The cross of my Redeemer, Christ,
Who makes the guilty captive free!

That shining cross shall ever stand
For all of love that man can know;
Yet none may fully understand
The love that God alone can show.

CARRIE E. BRECK

APRIL 20

He hath raised us up together, and made us sit together in heavenly places in Christ Jesus.

Ephesians 2:6.

ALL those who are born of the Spirit and are united to the Lord Jesus Christ are seated with Him in the heavenlies. To many of us the thought of being seated with Him in the heavenlies seems like an absurdity. We are so conscious of the material things of this world and of our weakness and frailty that we either regard this truth as a mere doctrine with no practical bearing upon life or refuse even to think of it. Many Christians think that they have been sitting in the heavenlies when they have attended a revival meeting or a conference where there has been great manifest blessing. There is a glorious reality in all that God has revealed. He has never spoken one idle word. It may be true that we have never apprehended what God means, but that does not change the glorious reality of a life in the heavenlies.

We must remember that each one of us who is in Christ Jesus is "a new creation," that we are "sons of God," that we are "of the household of God," that we are the "beloved of God, called saints." Though we have not yet received our new bodies, we are united with Him who is now seated at the right hand of God. It would be easy to grasp this great truth if we now had our resurrection bodies, but our present condition—a new creation in human bodies, liable to sickness, pain, and physical death—makes this truth hard to be understood. God has clearly and repeatedly stated in the letter to the Ephesians that we are now seated in the heavenlies, and in the Epistle to the Hebrews He reveals what life in the heavenlies is. Because we are seated in the heavenlies, it is now possible to live heavenly lives in earthly bodies—miracle lives.

L. L. LEGTERS

APRIL
21

That I may know Him, and the power of His resurrection. *Philippians 3:10.*

I WANT you to feel that power today. I would have you feel the surge of eternal life throbbing in your bosom, filling you with glory and the hope of immortality. Are you cast down? Are you defeated? Do the evil influences about you, in the home, in the office or factory, drag you into the filth of fleshly practices? Hear me, my friend; the remedy lies in the mighty life of the risen Son of God who rose from the dead that first Easter morning. It is said that after many years of ministry Dr. Dale, the great scholar of Birmingham, read the Bible with a new light, and one day while in his study, leaped to his feet and shouted, "Jesus is alive! Jesus is alive!" and went forth to preach with new power.

I pray God that this truth of a risen Redeemer will grip your soul afresh, and with a shout of victory you, too, will begin to rejoice in a new life lived in the power of His resurrection.

Come, live a God-like life! His life is full of His power. Take it! It is yours. The whole sea of divine grace is before you! Plunge in! We have all seen boys in swimming. One of them goes to the edge of the water and dips his toes in, only to start back and cry, "Oh, it's cold." Another wades in slowly, shivering more violently each moment. But see! another runs to the springboard and takes a header! He rises all in a glow. His blood is circulating and he cries in exquisite glee, "Come on in; it's great!" That is the boy who truly enjoys the swim.

HOWARD W. FERRIN

APRIL
22

Thou art my hiding place; Thou shalt preserve me from trouble; Thou shalt compass me about with songs of deliverance. *Psalm 32:7.*

How blessed the thought that God Himself becomes our bomb-proof shelter. Our lives are hidden with Christ in God. Nothing can touch us to do us harm until all the defensive power of His omnipotence is exhausted. Is there any possible excuse for you to carry around that load of worry under these circumstances?

When great cities prepare to withstand a siege it is usual for their armies to provide a multiple ring of defenses. Even so every Christian is provided with numerous encirclements, each one of them invincible before the fiery assaults of Satan. It is interesting and significant that one of these lines of defense is "songs of deliverance" with which, according to our verse, God encompasses us.

The power of trustful rejoicing in times of testing is greatly underestimated. God wants you to have a singing heart. Let it be one of your lines of defense.

J. ELWIN WRIGHT

> *If a wren can cling*
> *To a spray a-swing*
> *In a mad May wind, and sing, and sing,*
> *As if she'd burst for joy;*
> *Why cannot I,*
> *Contented lie,*
> *In His quiet arms, beneath His sky,*
> *Unmoved by earth's annoy?*

AUTHOR UNKNOWN

APRIL 23

Eye hath not seen, nor ear heard, neither have entered into the heart of man, the things which God hath prepared for them that love Him. But God hath revealed them unto us by His Spirit.
1 Corinthians 2:9, 10.

BEFORE you have the power of the Holy Ghost you will be curious about many questions; but when the Holy Ghost shall come you shall know all things clearly with the heart. I often think that woman's nature enables me to understand how we know in the power of the Holy Ghost. A man is said to reason his way, a woman by the quick glance of her intuition sees what she cannot reason, and she jumps to a conclusion to which her husband reasons his way ten minutes later. So it is with the heart when it is illumined by the Holy Spirit. The pure heart of the believer leaps to conclusions which eye hath not seen, nor ear heard, nor the reason of man conceived. The faculty of knowledge is altered: we no longer seek it by the intellect, but by the heart. The busy intellectual disputant becomes the deep intuitioner.

F. B. MEYER

> *"Is anyone there?" the soul cries out,*
> *Closed in by thickening fogs of doubt.*
> *There is, I know, for He answered me.*

103

Is anyone there when the glad heart sings
And all but bursts with the joy life brings?
There is, I know, for He sang with me.

Is anyone there at the turn of the road,
Waiting to guide and help with the load?
There is, I know, for He guided me.

Is anyone there by the hard sick-bed
To heal with a hand on the fevered head?
There is, I know, for His touch healed me.

Is anyone there when the soul takes flight,
To say, "Beloved, come in to the light"?
There is, I know, for He promised me.

EDITH DUNN BOLAR

APRIL 24

With Thee is the fountain of life. *Psalm 36:9.*

EVEN if we had the assurance that there is a life beyond the grave and that death is not the final chapter, we should still be confronted by the searching inquiry: "What shall I do to inherit eternal life? How can I be saved for this new existence, purified for the blessings of the next life?" For when people think of death, they think of sin; they think of judgment; all the follies and pretenses of life fade, and the glib excuses vanish. When life lingers in its last moment, men take no time to catalog their virtues and add up their accomplishments; but as the irrepressible monitor of conscience draws before their eyes in rapid panorama the sins of their existence,—in these moments, before a soul launches into eternity, men need the promise of a ransom that can pay the wages of sin, the pledge of an "Advocate with the Father"; they need what culture and learning can never give: the surety of the divine, redeeming Presence.

Then it is, when reason falters and self-reliance fails, that Christ comes with the assurance that through His suffering, His death, His resurrection, all our sins are cancelled, our guilt removed, our indebtedness to God entirely paid, our sin-stained souls washed completely white by His blood, and, all praise to His Saviour love! our death transformed to life. It is the glory of our Christian faith, not only that it teaches men that they come from God, but it also shows them that through faith in Christ and His atonement—and through that faith alone—they will return to God. Because this is the answer to humanity's paramount need and its deepest fear, and the promise of its highest joy and happiness, Christ has heaped the promises of this blessed eternity. Listen to Him as He pledges: "I am the Resurrection and the Life." "I say unto you, He that heareth My Word and believeth on Him that sent Me hath everlasting life." "Verily, verily, I say unto you, He that believeth on Me hath everlasting life." "My sheep hear My voice, . . . and I give unto them eternal life." "Because I live, ye shall live also." Take Him at His word! Trust Him! Believe Him! Live with Him!

WALTER A. MAIER

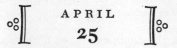

APRIL
25

Now before the feast of the passover, when Jesus knew that His hour was come that He should depart out of this world unto the Father, having loved His own which were in the world, He loved them unto the end. *John 13:1.*

T H O S E two little words, "His own," should be underlined in your Bible. All through these wonderful chapters, from the thirteenth to the end of the seventeenth, we see Christ alone with "His own." These were they who had received Him. He had come unto "His own" in the sense of natural relationship and they had not received Him, but "as many as received Him, to them gave He power to become the sons of God, even to them that believe on His name." Thus they entered into a spiritual relationship with Him and became "His own."

Now in these chapters we find Christ leading His disciples into a deeper understanding of their new place before the Father and their new position in the world. "His own" were being enlightened. Back in the Old Testament God said to Abraham, one day, "Shall I hide from Abraham that thing which I do?" No, He revealed His secrets to Abraham and He will reveal His secrets to every born-again child of God who is walking with Him and living a life separated from the world.

It was to this little group whom He loved unto the end that He could say, in the fourteenth chapter, "Let not your heart be troubled," and in the fifteenth, "I am the true vine and My Father is the Husbandman." And again, "Ye are the branches."

CHARLES E. FULLER

Though I forget Him, and wander away,
Still He doth love me wherever I stray;
Back to His dear, loving arms would I flee,
When I remember that Jesus loves me.

Oh, if there's only one song I can sing,
When in His beauty I see the Great King,
This shall my song in eternity be:
"Oh, what a wonder that Jesus loves me!"

P. P. BLISS

APRIL 26

**And the Spirit of the Lord came mightily upon him,
. . . he had nothing in his hand.** *Judges 14:6.*

As a boy, I got the impression from illustrated Bible stories that Samson was a massive giant about three times the size of an average man. As a matter of fact, the Word states nothing to indicate that. Indeed, that was exactly the thing that puzzled Samson's enemies: there was nothing about him to give the impression of tremendous strength. He was just an ordinary man separated unto the Lord. Ordinary men separated unto the Lord have always been a riddle to this world, and men are bewildered trying to account for the secret of their power. The Spirit of the Lord comes mightily upon men who go down to Timnath unimpressive in self and with nothing in their hands.

I am sure that if I were walking to the next town today and knew that somewhere on the way there was the possibility that a lion would roar upon me, I would not set out with nothing in my hand. I would carry the biggest gun available, and even then I would likely change my mind and not go at all! But Samson started out empty-handed. If there was to be power to cope with lions it must come from somewhere else and it did. And the application is this: In the Christian experience the power of the Lord comes mightily upon those who carry nothing in their hands.

VANCE HAVNER

APRIL 27

Yet amid all these things we are more than conquerors through Him who has loved us.
Romans 8:37 (Weymouth).

Man's extremity is God's opportunity." This is a very familiar saying. It often passes among us; and, no doubt, we fully believe it; but yet, when we find ourselves brought to our extremity, we are often very little prepared to count on God's opportunity. It is one thing to utter or hearken to a truth, and another thing to realize the power of that truth. It is one thing, when sailing over a calm sea, to speak of God's ability to keep us in the storm, and it is another thing altogether to prove that ability when the storm is actually raging around us. And yet God is ever the same. In the storm and in the calm, in sickness and in health, in pressure and in ease, in poverty and in abundance, "the same yesterday, and today, and forever"—the same grand reality for faith to lean upon, cling to and draw upon, at all times and under all circumstances.

C. H. M.

> *More than conquerors, when tribulation*
> *Tries the soul continually;*
> *In the furnace heat of sore affliction,*
> *Christ doth give the victory.*
>
> *More than conquerors, when dangers threaten*
> *Thee; look up, take heart, and sing;*
> *Sheltered, safe with Christ, no ill can harm thee*
> *In the shadow of His wing.*
>
> *More than conquerors, through Christ who loves us,*
> *Our defense—His righteousness;*
> *Neither height nor depth, nor any creature*
> *From His love can sever us.*

BESSIE PATTEN GILMORE

APRIL 28

Can the Ethiopian change his skin, or the leopard his spots? then may ye also do good, that are accustomed to do evil. *Jeremiah 13:23.* But we . . . are changed into the same image from glory to glory, even as by the Spirit of the Lord. *2 Corinthians 3:18.*

How hard and difficult it is to try to live a Christian life when one is not a Christian! How laborious it is to try to be good when the life of the good God and His good Spirit are not within us! What a grind it is to try to lay aside the habits of the week in order to be a good Christian on Sunday! God's plan is not this plan; God's way is not this way.

God has designed an entirely different arrangement, whereby He gives to the soul who trusts Jesus Christ a new life, His own life. It is called in one place, "The Divine Nature." There are two ways of keeping a pig out of a mud puddle. Man's way is to surround the mud puddle with ten or more coils of barbed wire, fencing it in with the wires spaced closely together, so that the pig cannot get through them to the mud. God's way is to change the pig into a sheep, so that the new nature which it receives will create a desire to stay out of the mud and to rejoice in the clover patch instead. God is not in the business of training, moulding, and improving man's normal nature. He is occupied in giving to men a new nature, which is His own life implanted in the heart of the believer. The gift of this new life is assured to the believer in the verse which we are contemplating. The gift of this life is a miracle. In no other way can enemies be brought together.

WALTER L. WILSON

> He died for me that I might die
> To Satan, self, and sin;
> O death so deep! O life so high!
> Help me to enter in.
>
> He lives for me that I may live
> As spotless e'en as He;
> Saviour, to me Thy nature give,
> And live Thy life in me.

A. B. SIMPSON

APRIL 29

He first findeth his own brother Simon, and saith unto him, We have found the Messias . . . and he brought him to Jesus.   *John 1:41, 42.*

OUR scripture is the story of one who found Jesus and couldn't rest until he led his brother to Him. And that's a bit like our letter from a lady in California who was led to Jesus by an elderly person who had found Him in the broadcast of the Old Fashioned Revival Hour.

"*Dear Mr. Fuller*: Until a few months ago I was wandering through life aimlessly. I had all sorts of bad luck, depression, family troubles, sickness and despair. Where was I to turn? I had the good fortune to come in contact with a lady of elderly years, who through listening to your radio program and reading your book passed on the idea to me.

"Life started for me again. I now have a new partner, God, and a new light has been cast on all my problems.

"I am writing to thank you for your wonderful inspiration. I witnessed your broadcast last Sunday and was more than amazed at the sincerity and realness of your service."

If the Old Fashioned Revival Hour has been a blessing to you why not urge your friends to listen? You can become a missionary by so doing. Pray today for those who are like the lady in this letter "wandering aimlessly."

APRIL 30

I delight to do Thy will, O my God. *Psalm 40:8.*

EVERY prohibition of God, and every command He lays upon men, have their reason in His good-will toward men. Nothing is denied to the subjects of His kingdom capriciously, or merely for the satisfaction of some motive outside these subjects. Love prohibits that which, if permitted, would blight the life and mar the pleasure. It is also true that every commandment calling to paths of duty is the outbreathing of love. There are moments when such pathways are rough and thorny and tortuous; but love never sends men along them save when, in the way, something is to be gained which will more than compensate for the suffering, and which can only be gained through the suffering.

> "Every joy or trial
> Falleth from above,
> Traced upon our dial
> By the Sun of love."

Man's capacity for pleasure finds its full satisfaction when his life is surrendered to the will of God. There is first the immediate delight of obedience. The response to love is in itself the essence of delight. This is illustrated from all that we know of love in the human relation, but its highest realization is to be found in this realm of submission to the government of God. Infinite meaning lies within the words of Christ, "I delight to do Thy will, O my God."

G. CAMPBELL MORGAN

For I delight in the law of God after the inward man: but I see another law in my members, warring against the law of my mind, and bringing me into captivity to the law of sin which is in my members. O wretched man that I am! who shall deliver me from the body of this death? I thank God through Jesus Christ our Lord. *Romans 7:22-25.*

EVERY man's heart is a battlefield. If self has possession, Jesus is lovingly striving to get possession. If possession has been yielded to Jesus, there is a constant besieging by the forces of self. And self is a skilled strategist. In every heart there is a cross, and a throne, and each is occupied. If Jesus is on the throne, ruling, self is on the cross, dying. But if self is being obeyed, and so is ruling, then it is on the throne. And self on the throne means that Jesus has been put on the cross.

S. D. GORDON

Live out Thy life within me,
O Jesus, King of kings!
Be Thou Thyself the answer
To all my questionings.
Live out Thy life within me,
In all things have Thy way!
I, the transparent medium
Thy glory to display.

The temple has been yielded,
And purified of sin;
Let Thy Shekinah glory
Now flash forth from within.
And all the earth keep silence,
The body henceforth be
Thy silent, docile servant,
Moved only as by Thee.

Its members every moment
Held subject to Thy call;
Ready to have Thee use them,
Or not be used at all.
Held without restless longing,
Or strain or stress or fret,
Or chaffings at Thy dealings,
Or thoughts of vain regret.

But restful, calm and pliant,
From bend and bias free,

Permitting Thee to settle
  When Thou hast need of me.
Live out Thy life within me,
  O Jesus, King of kings!
Be Thou the glorious answer
  To all my questionings.
                    FRANCES RIDLEY HAVERGAL

MAY 2

That the trial of your faith, being much more precious than of gold that perisheth, though it be tried with fire, might be found unto praise and honour and glory at the appearing of Jesus Christ.
                                        1 Peter 1:7.

A FEW days ago I was resting quietly under one of the giant Sequoias up in the High Sierras. As I looked up through the enormous limbs to the top of the tree I noticed that the wind was swaying its branches. I said to myself, "They tell me this tree is four thousand years old. If the wind and storms had not come at various times to strengthen it, how could it have stood when the tempest in all its fury beat against it?"

And how are you, friend, going to stand unless God tests your faith? Job had to discover that truth. God allowed disaster to overtake him and he was brought to the ash heap. In the end of his testing, Job testified, "I have heard of Thee by the hearing of the ear: but now mine eye seeth Thee, wherefore I abhor myself, and repent in dust and ashes." The whole book of Job deals with the process of the consecration of a saint.

                                        CHARLES E. FULLER

Make me a captive, Lord,
And then I shall be free;
Force me to render up my sword,
And I shall conqueror be.
I sink in life's alarms
When by myself I stand;
Imprison me within Thine arms,
And strong shall be my hand.

My heart is weak and poor
Until it master find:
It has no spring of action sure—
It varies with the wind.
It cannot freely move
Till Thou has wrought its chain;

Enslave it with Thy matchless love,
And deathless it shall reign.

GEORGE MATHESON

MAY 3

When they had lifted up their eyes, they saw no man, save Jesus only. *Matthew 17:8.*

ONCE you look to Jesus and see Him who walked humbly as a man among men, transfigured, in His divine glory, as the Son of God in the radiance of His dazzling splendor; once you read of His death in Moses and the prophets with their predictions of the atoning, ransoming, justifying, substituting love by which, as Isaiah of old foretold eleven times in eight verses, He was to be "wounded for our transgressions" and to be "bruised for our iniquities"; once, like the same three disciples who witnessed His glory only to see Him later in the agony of the Garden, you behold Jesus with the sweat of anguish dropping from His pallid countenance, as He prepares to suffer in His own body the punishment and the consequences of my sins, your sins, all sins; once you approach Calvary and its central cross and see Jesus, not glorified, but "despised and rejected of men, a man of sorrows and acquainted with grief," and with all your heart you acclaim Him your Saviour, His precious blood the cleansing of your sin, His death your life, His grace your assurance of heaven,—then the forces of fear have been completely routed because your sins are forgiven. As you clasp that cross with faith-filled eyes, let the world pass into the murky shadows of insignificance; beholding "Jesus only," the Saviour's calming, comforting, quickening "Fear not" becomes your guarantee of sustaining grace.

WALTER A. MAIER

MAY 4

Thou knowest my downsitting and mine uprising, thou understandest my thought afar off.
Psalm 139:2.

CAN we think that when Jesus looked up at Zacchaeus and bade him come and offer hospitality, it was the first time He had seen him? Nay, I think He had often passed him in the streets, He had seen the shadow over his face. There was unrest and trouble in his eye. He looked like a man who was often awake at night. For Zac-

112

chaeus often went home with a full purse and a very empty and impoverished heart. He was often "under the fig-tree," in gloom and despondency, casting fitful glances at the better life. And so when the Master called to him, there was something in the very tone which revealed that he was understood.

We are not told what they talked about on their way to the publican's house, but I think I can hear the Master saying to His newly-found disciple, "When thou wast under the fig-tree I saw thee." I say this is the way of the Master. He sees us in the faint beginning and gropings of the spiritual life. "When he was yet a long way off his father saw him!" That is characteristic of the divine eyes. He sees us in the long distance! The first faint impulses are recognized; the first turning is known. When we are under the fig-tree He sees us!

J. H. JOWETT

> In tenderness He sought me,
> Weary and sick with sin,
> And on His shoulders brought me,
> Back to His fold again.
> While angels in His presence sang
> Until the courts of heaven rang.
>
> He washed the bleeding sin-wounds,
> And poured in oil and wine;
> He whispered to assure me,
> "I've found thee, thou art Mine";
> I never heard a sweeter voice,
> It made my aching heart rejoice!
>
> Oh, the love that sought me!
> Oh, the blood that bought me,
> Oh, the grace that brought me to the fold,
> Wondrous grace that brought me to the fold!

W. SPENCER WALTON

MAY 5

Henceforth there is laid up for me a crown of righteousness, which the Lord, the righteous judge, shall give me at that day: and not to me only, but unto all them also that love His appearing.

2 Timothy 4:8.

THE New Testament Christians were not only ready, they were expectant, hilariously anticipating the Lord's return. And we are bidden not only to prepare but to look for our Lord. "Looking for and hasting unto the coming of the day of the Lord"; "Looking for that blessed hope, and the glorious appearing of the great God and our Saviour Jesus Christ"; "Look up, and lift up your heads; for your redemption draweth nigh." It is one thing to be ready for someone to come; it is another thing eagerly to expect and await the coming of someone. In my pastoral calling, I am sure that many of my church members were ready for my visits who were not thrilled with anticipation.

If you grew up at home with a sister, I am sure you recall how that when an ordinary friend called, she was ready but not particularly excited about it; but when the one of her heart's desire was expected, you could tell the difference hours ahead of time. The program of beautification began at least by noon and by the middle of the afternoon the hands on the clock seemed to have stuck, so slowly moved the hours.

One wonders about these believers who say they are ready but who act as though it did not matter whether the Lord came or not. It is evident from the Scriptures that joyful expectancy is an evidence of readiness.

VANCE HAVNER

MAY
6

For this is the will of God, even your sanctification.
1 Thessalonians 4:3.

THE one and only law of life that sets a man free from all the forces that blight and destroy is the will of God. Show me a man who lives for one day wholly, utterly, in word and thought and deed in the will of God, and I will show you a man who is antedating heaven, and who for that day reaches the plane of life which is at once broadest, freest, and gladdest.

The Word of God is given to man not that he may have a correct theory, but that he may have the truth. Truth is a sanctifying force, and a man holds the truth only when he is held by the truth. When truth possesses a man, all its glory and beauty are manifested through his life and character. The truth the Bible reveals is the will of God for man. Sanctification by truth is the bringing of man into the will of God.

"The means of grace" are means to an end, that end being the realization of the will of God. Every one of them tends to that issue.

"The hope of glory" is the hope that ultimately the will of God will be done upon the earth as in heaven, or that the spirit of man, passing into the heavenly state, shall realize all the full blessedness of that will.

G. CAMPBELL MORGAN

114

I can do all things through Christ which strengtheneth me. *Philippians 4:13.*

"B UT I do not feel strong," says Joshua, "and I am not at all courageous. The men who withstood Moses to the face and rewarded his patience with apostasy, will dispute my authority also; and what credentials can I carry that none shall dare to controvert?"

And the Unseen breaks in almost abruptly, and closes the conversation with this: "Have not I commanded thee? Be strong and of a good courage; be not afraid, neither be thou dismayed: for the Lord thy God is with thee, whithersoever thou goest."

At that point the dialogue ceases, the disputation ends. Every doubt has been dissolved, the spirit of fear cast out. The man who had trembled upon his knees rises already a victor. He has conquered himself. Nay! shall I not rather say that God has conquered him? Yes! that is the better way of putting it, God has conquered him; and the man who has been subdued by the Holy Spirit will be subdued by none beside.

R. MOFFAT GAUTREY

Stand up, my soul, shake off thy fears,
And gird the gospel armor on;
March to the gates of endless joy,
Where thy great Captain Saviour's gone.

What though thine inward lust rebel;
'Tis but a struggling gasp for life;
The weapons of victorious grace
Shall slay thy sins, and end the strife.

Then let my soul march boldly on,
Press forward to the heavenly gate;
There peace and joy eternal reign,
And glittering robes for conquerors wait.

ISAAC WATTS

The Spirit itself maketh intercession for us with
groanings which cannot be uttered. *Romans 8:26.*

𝕴 N T E R C E S S O R Y prayer is without doubt not only the highest
form of Christian service, but also the hardest kind of work. To the
person who is not an intercessor such a statement seems absurd.
Prayer to most people is looked upon as an easy occupation. Difficulties are unknown. But that is because they know nothing at all of the
ministry of intercession. Their prayers, for the most part, are centered
upon themselves, their loved ones and their own personal interest,
with an occasional petition for the perishing heathen. They spend,
perchance, five to fifteen minutes in the morning and the same again
at night. To set aside a special hour during the day, or to wait before
God for half a night never enters their mind. Their prayer life is
spasmodic. It is considered a side issue and is readily neglected if
other things demand attention. Such persons are in no way affecting
the kingdom of Satan. Hence, prayer, so-called, is easy.

But the Christian who enters upon the ministry of intercession will
pass through a very different experience. Satan will do everything in
his power to hinder and obstruct. There will be a conscious realization
of his presence and opposition. Interruptions innumerable will come.
The telephone will ring, visitors will call, and a hundred other things
that never would have bothered otherwise will have to be taken into
account. We are living in the twentieth century. Never have we known
such bustle and rush and hurry. The whole world is forging ahead at
a terrific pace. Hours of quietness and retirement are becoming more
and more difficult to observe. Thus the work of intercession becomes
hard.

Full well Satan knows that prayerless work will be powerless and
fruitless. Hence if he can only keep us busy so that we do not have
time to pray he will have accomplished his purpose.

> *"Away with work that hinders prayer,*
> *'Twere best to lay it down;*
> *For prayerless work, however good,*
> *Will fail to win the crown."*
>
> OSWALD J. SMITH

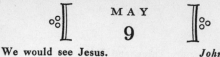

We would see Jesus. *John 12:21.*

𝔍 WISH that every one of you would underline those words, "We would see Jesus." They were spoken by a group of Greeks who had come up to Jerusalem to worship at the time of the Passover. We may learn something about their motive when we consider the word "desire." They desired of Philip, saying, "Sir, we would see Jesus." The leaders of Israel sought to slay Him. But these men humbly desired to see Him.

It was more than idle curiosity that prompted them to seek Him. If it had been only a physical glimpse of Him that they desired they could easily have obtained that as He passed in and out of the temple. They did not ask to witness one of His mighty miracles. What they wanted was a personal, intimate acquaintance with Christ. The Psalmist expressed it centuries before when he said, "As the hart panteth after the water brooks, so panteth my soul after Thee, O God."

These Greeks were tired of their culture and philosophy. Their religion produced no heart satisfaction. They wanted reality.

There is a deep lesson in all this for all of us, beloved friends of mine, members of the body of Christ. Let us not be so much occupied with what Christ can do for us in the way of physical or spiritual blessings. Let us be occupied with Christ Himself. When the Lord took His disciples to the mount of transfiguration, they saw Moses and Elijah as well, for a time, but there came a moment when they again lifted their eyes and saw no man save Jesus only. And that is your need today.

CHARLES E. FULLER

We would see Jesus—the strong Rock foundation
Whereon our feet are set by sovereign grace;
Not life nor death, with all their agitation,
Can thence remove us if we see His face.

ANNA B. WARNER

And all Mine are Thine, and Thine are Mine.

John 17:10.

OF OLD the mighty men of Israel were willing to swim the rivers at their flood, to come to David, their uncrowned but God-appointed king. And when they met him, they cried, "Thine are we, David, and on thy side, thou son of Jesse." They were his because God had given them to him, but they could not rest content till they were his also by their glad choice. Why then should we not say the same to Jesus Christ? "Lord Jesus, I am Thine by right. Forgive me that I have lived so long as if I were my own. And now I gladly recognize that Thou hast a rightful claim on all I have and am. I want to live as Thine henceforth; and I do solemnly at this hour give myself to Thee. Thine in life and death. Thine absolutely and for ever."

F. B. MEYER

No time for trifling in this life of mine;
Not this the path the blessed Master trod,
But strenuous toil; each hour and power employed
  Always and all for God.

Time swiftly flies; eternity is near,
And soon my dust may lie beneath the sod.
How dare I waste my life or cease to be
  Always and all for God.

I catch the meaning of this solemn age;
With life's vast issues all my soul is awed.
Life was not given for trifling; it must be
  Always and all for God.

I see the heathen perishing around
While heaven asks, "Where is thy brother's blood?"
How dare I meet my Lord if I am not
  Always and all for God.

Full soon will come to us the harvest time,
The reaping of the seed that here we strawed;
Oh, then we'll not regret we spent earth's spring
  Always and all for God.

A. B. SIMPSON

Do not be anxious, therefore, about tomorrow, for
tomorrow will bring its own anxieties.
Matthew 6:34 (Weymouth).

"IN NOTHING be anxious." Nothing is made up of no-thing. It is
impossible to put anything into no-thing. Nothing is a circle with
everything excluded. Your child's sickness; your boy's wayward-
ness; your neighbor's meanness—all are excluded. They are but tests
of your willingness to obey God rather than the promptings of human
nature.

There is a reason. Worry is incompatible with a life of prayer. It
prevents us from praying and God from working. Do not worry,
"but—(adopt the prayer method instead)—in everything by prayer
and supplication. . ." Now we understand God's ways with us. Everything is excluded from care that it might be included in prayer. He,
our Father, wants the opportunity of caring for the things that
concern us.

NORMAN B. HARRISON

The love of God has hung a veil
Around tomorrow,
That we may not its beauty see
Nor trouble borrow.

But, oh, 'tis sweeter far, to trust
His unseen hand,
And know that all the path of life,
His wisdom planned.

I know not if tomorrow's way
Be steep or rough;
But when His hand is guiding me,
That is enough.

And so, although the veil has hid
Tomorrow's way,
I walk with perfect faith and trust,
Through each today.

AUTHOR UNKNOWN

Thou hast ascended on high, Thou hast led captivity captive: Thou hast received gifts for men.
. . . Blessed be the Lord, who daily loadeth us
with benefits.   *Psalm 68:18, 19.*

MOST of the gifts of earth deteriorate with time and with use.
The gold ring, placed so tenderly on the maiden's finger at the
marriage altar, becomes thin and worn with the years. The
wedding dress must be soon laid away, for its materials are so thin
and frail that a little use soon destroys its usefulness. The automobile,
made of steel and wood, becomes damaged by the hazards of the
road, wears out with the long mileage, and must be replaced. Houses
become uninhabitable by reason of the storm, the wind, and the
weather. Cities become buried in the sand because of the destroying
winds from the desert. Ships strike hidden reefs and rocks, and floun-
der in the depths of the sea. Strong bodies fade and fall. Fine woods
are eaten by the worms, and the best of books become powder by reason of air and dampness. Only Christ remains! The Scripture has said,
"They shall fail, but Thou remainest."

WALTER L. WILSON

Joy of my soul, thou Saviour dear,
It is so sweet when Thou art near;
In Thy blest love all fear I hide,
Most gracious Lord, in me abide.

Keep Thou the vigil of my heart,
Lest from my soul Thy grace depart;
Oh! may Thy love fill every need,
For of Thy bounty I would feed.

Oh! may no earthly shadow fall,
Around my heart, Lord, keep it all;
Be Thou the light of heavenly fire;
Thy Spirit, Lord, I so desire.

JOSEPH SWAIN

Keep that which is committed to thy trust, avoiding profane and vain babblings, and oppositions of science falsely so called: which some professing have erred concerning the faith.

1 Timothy 6:20, 21.

THERE is no greater tragedy in the nation than the crime of educators who deliberately wreck the faith of young people. This letter from Iowa should stir your heart to a realization of the plight of scores of thousands of our young people in high schools and colleges.

"*Dear Rev. and Mrs. Fuller*: I am now listening to your program. I realize that I need a real spiritual experience. I believe all you say and think your efforts are wonderful.

"I am a senior in the — University. My major is sociology. My professors do not accept the principles of the old fashioned religion. They believe that man is supreme and that by developing one's own potentialities one becomes religious. I am in mental confusion for I cannot accept this. I know there must be the possibility of an inner confidence and peace which are in contrast to my present state.

"I ask to be remembered in your prayers that I may find God in a real way and not be influenced by the ideas of my professors or the authors of some of my text books. I have thought about going to one of my professors who seems to be a Christian but I am afraid he will suggest my seeing a psychiatrist and that will not help. I have read many good books but I need God. It's awful not to be able to find the way. Pray that God will help me to believe."

Pray for the young people in our colleges. Urge them to attend churches where the Gospel is preached. Encourage them to listen to the Old Fashioned Revival Hour. It may save them from infidelity.

Think it not strange concerning the fiery trial which
is to try you, as though some strange thing happened unto you: but rejoice, inasmuch as ye are
partakers of Christ's sufferings; that, when His
glory shall be revealed, ye may be glad also with
exceeding joy. *1 Peter 4:12, 13.*

INTO the life of every child of God there must come pain, sorrow,
sickness, and suffering; loss and disappointment; misunderstanding, loneliness, and weariness. No one can escape these things, it
is impossible to side-step them, for hereunto were we called. The
question is not how to avoid these things, but how to have victory
in them. For victory in these personal circumstances of life that press
in upon us, there is but one way, "Looking unto Jesus the author and
perfector of our faith, who for the joy that was set before Him endured
the cross, despising the shame, and hath sat down at the right hand
of the throne of God" (Heb. 12:2 R. V.).

There is but one way—keeping our eyes on the "Prince Leader,"
who also suffered. There is glorious overcoming power while our
eyes are fixed on Him and not on circumstances. He suffered, the
just for the unjust. He had done no wrong, yet He suffered. It may not
be for chastening in your life that you suffer or are in pain or are
grieved; God may be using this in the life of another.

Can we trust the all-wise God, who bought us with His own blood,
to send into our lives just those things which He can use, the things
He sees are best for us, and the things He can use in the lives of
others?

L. L. LEGTERS

Think it not strange,—partaker of Christ's sufferings;
Tested and tried,—thou art exalted sure:
Not to consume are these "strange" things permitted,
But to enrich, if we will but endure.

Think it not strange! Rejoice, rejoice the rather!
Forward thy gaze—until shall Glory be;
Then, oh, the joy, the wonder, and the rapture,
When thou shalt find His glory shared with thee.

J. DANSON SMITH

Blessed be the God and Father of our Lord Jesus Christ, who hath blessed us. . . . *Ephesians 1:3.*

FOR His beloved Son's sake the God and Father of our Lord Jesus Christ blessed us. We shall miss one of the deepest truths in Ephesians if we fail to see that everything the Father does for the Church and for the Christian, He does primarily for the glory of His own grace and for the sake of His dear Son who voluntarily laid down His human body on the Cross in a moment of time that He might possess His mystical Body in the heavenlies now and in all the ages to come.

Years ago a very dear friend of mine died, the only child of her parents. I had gone in and out of the home as another daughter. Among her papers was an envelope addressed to her parents, to be opened in case of her death. It contained just one request, that they would regard me as a daughter and do for me as they would have for her.

Is this not the request which the Son made of His Father for all the other sons who had believed on Him? Did He not express His desire to share with them all that was His, even to His oneness with the Father and their home in glory?

John 17:21, "That . . . as Thou, Father, art in me, and I in Thee, that they also may be one in Us."

John 17:24, "Father, I will that they also, whom Thou hast given Me, be with Me where I am; that they may behold My glory."

RUTH PAXSON

Thou hast given Him power over all flesh.
John 17:2.

BETHANY was the home of Martha, Mary, and their brother Lazarus. The Lord often lodged there for He had no home—no place to lay His head. Martha was a perfect housekeeper, but Mary loved to sit at Jesus' feet drinking in His wonderful words.

Now Lazarus was taken sick. It was literally a sinking sickness. Therefore the sisters sent for Jesus. This was a blessed thing for them to do. They sought the Lord and unburdened their hearts. My friend, trouble will do one of two things for you. It will either make you bitter and hard-hearted or it will drive you closer to the Lord.

What did they do? They left their burden in His hands. The thirty-seventh Psalm says, "Commit thy way unto the Lord, trust also in Him and He shall bring it to pass."

When Jesus got the news, He did not go at once to the house of His friends. He said, "This sickness is not unto death but for the glory of God." God's answer to our prayers is often delayed for God's glory. Oh, that we might learn this lesson!

Before Jesus arrived Lazarus was dead. Not only dead, but corruption had set in. He had been dead four days. There is no greater miracle than this one. The sick may get well but only Christ can raise the dead. All are dead in trespasses and sins. But Jesus loved Lazarus and God loves every sinner. "While we were yet sinners, Christ died for the ungodly."

Jesus cried, "Lazarus, come forth." And Lazarus came forth. Had Jesus not mentioned him by name all Sheol might have been emptied. When Jesus gets hold of a man, whether he be dead spiritually or physically, He has power to loose him from the bondage of corruption. And He will impart to him His resurrection life.

CHARLES E. FULLER

MAY 17

For ye are the temple of the living God; as God hath said, I will dwell in them, and walk in them.
2 Corinthians 6:16.

THE Spirit of God in working among men seeks embodiment in men, through whom He acts. The amazing truth is that not only is He willing to enter into and fill you with His very presence, but He seeks for, He wants, yes, He needs your personality as a channel or medium, that living in you He may be able to do His work among the men you touch even though you may not be conscious of much that He is doing through you. Is not that startling? He wants to live in your body, and speak through your lips, and look out of your eyes, and use your hands, really, actually. Have you turned your personality over to Him as completely as that?

S. D. GORDON

In His heart my Saviour hides me,
And He holds me in His hand;
At His feet I sit and listen,
And I go at His command.

In His heart no ill can reach me;
In His hand no fear I know:

At His feet I love to linger,
At His call I love to go.

At Thy feet new lessons learning,
Teach and mold me day by day;
List'ning for Thy least commandment,
Let me joyfully obey.

While within Thy heart abiding,
Let my heart be filled with Thine;
While Thy hand protects and guides me,
Fill my hands with tasks divine.

A. B. SIMPSON

MAY 18

And the same day, when the even was come, He (Jesus) saith unto them, Let us pass over unto the other side. And when they had sent away the multitude, they took Him even as He was in the ship. And there were also with Him other little ships. And there arose a great storm of wind, and the waves beat into the ship, so that it was now full. And He was in the hinder part of the ship, asleep on a pillow. *Mark 4:35–38.*

HERE, then, we have an interesting and instructive scene. The poor disciples are brought to their extremity. They are at their wits' end. A violent storm—the ship full of water—the Master asleep. This was a trying moment indeed, and assuredly we, if we look at ourselves, need not marvel at the fear and agitation of the disciples. It is not likely that we should have done better had we been there. Still, we cannot but see wherein they failed. The narrative has been penned for our learning, and we are bound to study it, and seek to learn the lesson which it reads out to us.

There is nothing more absurd and irrational than unbelief when we come to look at it calmly. In the scene before us this absurdity is very apparent; for what could be more absurd than to suppose that the vessel could possibly sink with the Son of God on board? And yet this was what they feared. It may be said they did not just think of the Son of God at that moment. True, they thought of the storm, the waves, the filling vessel, and, judging after the manner of men, it seemed a hopeless case. Thus it is the unbelieving heart ever reasons. It looks only at the circumstances, and leaves God out. Faith, on the contrary, looks only at God, and leaves circumstances out.

C. H. M.

125

MAY
19

Having made known unto us the mystery of His will. *Ephesians 1:9.*

ALL prayer lies within the two petitions of the pattern prayer the Master taught His disciples: "Thy kingdom come; Thy will be done." There is no prayer beyond that. It may be divided into sentences and syllables, and made to fit the necessity of the hour; but when prayer moves the heart of God, it is because it is confined within that compass.

Allow your imagination to carry you back to the past ages. Amid the silences of that immeasurable eternity you are conscious of perfect peace, perfect happiness, perfect love. The explanation is to be found in the fact that the will of God was perfectly done. None can declare the genesis of evil, but its nature is clearly known—it is rebellion against the will of God. The mystery of how that first came to be, is absolutely inscrutable, but the fact is established beyond question.

We are but infinitesimal portions of the universe of God, but the being of the smallest particle of created things is conditioned in His will, and its success or failure depends upon its realization of, or failure to realize, that will. The supreme subject in every life, then, is that His will should be discovered and obeyed.

G. CAMPBELL MORGAN

MAY
20

There remaineth therefore a rest to the people of God. *Hebrews 4:9.*

IT IS indeed a pity that so many of God's people have failed to cross over Jordan into the land of plenty which God has provided for them. To many, Canaan is simply a type of heaven, a country which may not be entered except by way of death. But God wants us to move out of the wilderness into His promised land right here and now. He has provided a place of rest for weary hearts which requires no years of waiting to attain, only the courage and faith to appropriate immediately.

God can give to you rest *in* the struggle before the time comes for you to rest *from* the struggle. In other words, He can so encompass your heart that in the midst of every conflict with the unseen forces of evil there will be no interruption of your inward calm of spirit. You may possess a hilltop in the Land of Beulah, surrounded by an invincible garrison of heavenly hosts through which no enemy can break. From this vantage point you may watch His victory in your behalf with assurance which is incapable of unrest.

J. ELWIN WRIGHT

> There is a rest that deeper grows
>   In midst of pain and strife;
> A mighty conscious willed repose
>   In depth of deepest life.
> To have and hold the precious prize
>   No need of jealous fear;
> But windows open to the skies,
>   And skill to read the stars.
>
> Who dwelleth in that secret place,
>   Where tumult enters not,
> Is never cold with terror base,
>   Never with anger hot.
> For if an evil past should dare
>   His very heart invest,
> God's in his deeper heart, and there
>   He enters into rest.
>
> When mighty sea winds madly blow,
>   And tear the scattered waves;
> Peaceful as summer woods below
>   Lie darkling ocean caves.
> The wind of words may toss my heart,
>   But what is that to me!
> 'Tis but a surface storm—Thou art
>   My deep, still, resting sea.

GEORGE MACDONALD

MAY 21

That . . . He might shew the exceeding riches of His grace in His kindness toward us through Christ Jesus. *Ephesians 2:7.*

JESUS comes to a sinner, awakens him from his sleep in sin, converts him, forgives him his sins and makes him His child. Then He takes the weak hand of the sinner and places it in His own strong, nail-pierced hand and says: "Come now, I am going with you all the way and will bring you safe home to heaven. If you ever get into trouble or difficulty, just tell Me about it. I will give you, without reproach, everything you need, and more besides, day by day, as long as you live."

My friend, do you not also think that that is what Jesus really meant when He gave us prayer?

And that is the way we should make use of it. That is the way He desires to answer our prayer, graciously and abundantly. Prayer should be the means by which I, at all times, receive all that I need, and, for this reason, be my daily refuge, my daily consolation, my daily joy, my source of rich and inexhaustible joy in life.

From this it is very apparent also that a child of God can grieve Jesus in no worse way than to neglect prayer. For by so doing he severs the connection between himself and the Saviour, and his inner life is doomed to be withered and crippled, as is the case with most of us. Many neglect prayer to such an extent that their spiritual life gradually dies out.

I seem to hear some of the bitter sorrow which proceeds from the heart of God when He is compelled to say to us, "Ye have not, because ye ask not" (James 4:2).

He has all that we need, and there is nothing that He would rather do than impart to us His gifts. But we do not ask. We do not have time, we say. Or we forget to pray. The result is that we go about at home and in the assembly of believers like spiritual cripples or dwarfs, spiritually starved and emaciated, with scarcely enough strength to stand on our own feet, not to speak of fighting against sin and serving the Lord.

O. HALLESBY

MAY 22

Awake, awake; put on thy strength, O Zion; . . .
Shake thyself from the dust; arise.

Isaiah 52:1, 2.

WE LIVE in an hour when the foundations of civilization are crumbling, the night of apostasy is deepening, lawlessness runs wild to its awful climax, the powers of anti-Christ increase and abound, and wars and rumors of wars belt the globe. Yet the Church of God, with the only hope and cure for mankind's sin and misery, rests, for the most part, at ease in Zion, and we who claim that Name above every name make mud pies and daisy chains and twiddle our thumbs while a world sweeps over the brink of disaster. We preach a Gospel that is God's dynamite and we live firecracker lives. We sing of showers of blessing and the old-time power and faith, the victory and higher ground, and then we leave it all in the hymn books and go home.

We read that when our Lord held a service the congregation went home amazed and glorifying God and filled with fear and saying, "We have seen strange things today" (Luke 5:26). How many, do you think, go from our meetings today in such a frame of mind? The early church lived in such power that men durst not join themselves unto them; they stood in awe of pentecostal fire. . . . "Where is the Lord God of Elijah?"

I am afraid that too many of us are like these theological students who saw Elijah and Elisha go by. They believed theoretically that Elijah was to be taken, but so weak was their actual faith that they wanted later to send out a scouting party to look for him lest the Spirit of God had cast him upon a mountain or into a valley! Here was knowledge without faith, the same sort that talks and sings today about the great realities of the Gospel but never actually believes them. We study Sunday-school lessons about Elijah, but who seeks his mantle? We read and sing about Pentecost, but who is willing to live as those Christians lived?

VANCE HAVNER

MAY 23

His right hand, and His holy arm, hath gotten Him the victory. *Psalm 98:1.*

I WANT you to see in Jesus the Conquering One. How I love to read in Colossians about His victory over all the forces of evil when "He blotted out the handwriting of ordinances that was against us, which was contrary to us, and took it out of the way, nailing it to His cross; and having spoiled principalities and powers He made a shew of them openly, triumphing over them in it." He conquered them all for us. We have no need to live in fear.

Knowing Jesus as the Conqueror gives us peace of heart. He said, "These things have I spoken unto you that ye might have peace. In the world ye shall have tribulation but be of good cheer, I have overcome the world."

How did He win the victory? The second chapter of Philippians tells us. This Christ, the Eternal Son of God, left the glory above. He who was rich for our sakes became poor that we through His poverty might become rich. He humbled Himself, even to die on the cross. "Wherefore God hath highly exalted Him and given Him a name that is above every name." He has all power. Paul caught the vision of what this means to us when he said, "We are more than conquerors through Him that loved us and gave Himself for us."

In another place Paul said, "I can do all things." But don't stop reading there. How? "Through Christ which strengtheneth me." I love to draw near to Paul and just breathe in some of that holy boldness that he had in Christ.

CHARLES E. FULLER

> *Soldiers of Christ, arise,*
> *And put your armor on,*
> *Strong in the strength which God supplies*
> *Through His Eternal Son;*
> *Strong in the Lord of hosts,*
> *And in His mighty power,*
> *Who in the strength of Jesus trusts*
> *Is more than conqueror.*

AUTHOR UNKNOWN

MAY 24

Then spake Jesus again unto them, saying, I am the light of the world: he that followeth Me shall not walk in darkness, but shall have the light of life. *John 8:12.*

ONE moment of voluntary darkness over a continent—a world—in tribute to the genius that brought to the world the blessings of derived light and power, brings home with tremendous force the meaning of light. Should that moment of darkness be forced and complete, stark tragedy would be the result, but what if the very Source and Mainspring of light were suddenly shut off! The pulse of life would cease. Chaos would ensue.

Thy claim is unique. Had anyone else declared, "I am the light of the world," the world would have buried him in derision and scorn, but Thy claim still stands unchallenged. Thou art "higher than the highest thought can reach."

Thou art "the sun of righteousness." In Thy light I see light. In Thee I see God—His love, His holiness, His power, His plan. And in Thee I see self—stumbling and groping in the abysmal darkness of sin, crying after "light." And I see that following Thee is the only deliverance from the midnight of the soul.

ANNA J. LINDGREN

> *Light of the world, we hail Thee,*
> *Flushing the eastern skies;*
> *Never shall darkness veil Thee*
> *Again from human eyes;*
> *Too long, alas, withholden,*
> *Now spread from shore to shore;*
> *Thy light, so glad and golden,*
> *Shall set on earth no more.*

Light of the world, Thy beauty
Steals into every heart,
And glorifies with duty
Life's poorest, humblest part;
Thou robest in Thy splendor
The simple ways of men,
And helpest them to render
Light back to Thee again.

Light of the world, illumine
This darkened earth of Thine,
Till everything that's human
Be filled with what's divine;
Till every tongue and nation,
From sin's dominion free,
Rise in the new creation
Which springs from love and Thee.

JOHN S. B. MONSELL

MAY
25

**Casting all your care upon Him; for He careth
for you.** *1 Peter 5:7.*

IN WHATEVER measure you fail to live without anxious care you
are living beneath your privilege in Christ. Your anxiety is a
proof of your doubt of either God's ability or His willingness to
care for you adequately. Fretting over your trial delays the day when
God can remove it. He knows all about it and designed it only for
your enrichment and the perfecting of His work in you.

J. ELWIN WRIGHT

There is a faith unmixed with doubt,
    A love all free from fear;
A walk with Jesus, where is felt
    His presence always near.
There is a rest that God bestows,
    Transcending pardon's peace,
A lowly, sweet simplicity,
    Where inward conflicts cease.

There is a service God-inspired,
    A zeal that tireless grows,
Where self is crucified with Christ,
    And joy unceasing flows.
There is a being "right with God,"
    That yields to His command
Unswerving, true fidelity,
    A loyalty that stands.

There is a meekness free from pride,
That feels no anger rise
At slights, or hate, or ridicule,
But counts the cross a prize.
There is a patience that endures
Without a fret or care,
But joyful sings, "His will be done,
My Lord's sweet grace I share."

There is a purity of heart,
A cleanness of desire,
Wrought by the Holy Comforter
With sanctifying fire.
There is a glory that awaits
Each blood-washed soul on high,
When Christ returns to take His bride
With Him beyond the sky.

AUTHOR UNKNOWN

MAY 26

The fruit of the Spirit is love, joy, peace, longsuffering, gentleness, goodness, faith. *Galatians 5:22.*

THE word "gentleness" is translated "kindness" in the Revised Version, and this is to be preferred. If longsuffering is love's passivity, kindness is love's activity. We may help others by kindly thoughts, or words, or deeds. It is a Christian exercise in which we need never be idle. God is rich in goodness or kind acts (Rom. 2:4). His supreme act of kindness was the gift of His well-beloved Son to be the Saviour of mankind (Eph. 2:7; Titus 3:4). By means of this kindness God would constrain men to repent, and return to Himself (Rom. 2:4).

The natural man has nothing of such kindness, because it is expressive of the grace of the new life in Christ (Rom. 3:12). The Christian, as a child of God, is to show to others the gracious kindness that God has shown to him (2 Cor. 6:6; Col. 3:12). If we rendered kindness only to those who deserved it, we should not be kept very active. If God had extended His kindness only to those who deserved it, which of us should have known it? Should not this thought make our dealings with others more kindly. True kindness is never artificial or patronizing. In rendering a kindness, love gives itself.

NEIL McLACHLAN

The day was long, the burden I had borne
Seemed heavier than I could longer bear,

132

And then it lifted—but I did not know
Someone had knelt in prayer.

Had taken me to God that very hour,
And asked the easing of the load; and He,
In infinite compassion, had stooped down
And taken it from me.

We cannot tell how often as we pray,
For some bewildered one, hurt and distressed,
The answer comes; but many times those hearts
Find sudden peace and rest.

Someone had prayed, and Faith, a reaching hand,
Took hold of God, and brought Him down that day!
So many, many hearts have need of prayer—
Oh, let us pray.

GRACE NOLL CROWELL

MAY 27

And they that be wise shall shine as the brightness
of the firmament; and they that turn many to righteousness as the stars for ever and ever. *Daniel 12:3.*

H E R E ' s a rather typical instance of a young girl who, at eighteen,
had become sceptical. The gospel message, however, quickly
melted her heart and she is now a happy Christian—all because
someone invited her to listen to the Old Fashioned Revival Hour.

"*Dear Mr. Fuller:* I'm just a young girl who hasn't even got
any real parents so I have to work real hard for everything I get.
I've had many unpleasant experiences the past year and whenever anyone talked to me about God and how He sent His Son to
save sinners I laughed at them because I thought it was too easy
a way to get out of trouble—just to pray and believe. I wouldn't
think of going to church because, when I was younger, I was
taught (by a heretical set) that the church was the place where
the devil did the most harm and that all ministers who have been
taught in schools are ravening wolves in sheep's clothing.

"I was raised by my grandparents, who didn't teach me right
from wrong. I was brought up as a heathen. After I came to Min-
neapolis the woman I am working for put on your program. For
the first time in my life I listened with her and I believe the
Holy Ghost came into my heart. I realized how much I had sinned
and how powerless I was without Christ, my Saviour. I've been

to church and I am going every Sunday now. What wonderful peace I have through Christ. I am only eighteen years old."

Pray for the thousands of young people cast adrift without praying relatives or friends. Many of them can be reached by a friendly word of testimony and an invitation to a gospel service. Is your life counting for Christ? Will you have some sheaves of precious grain to lay at His feet when you appear in His presence?

᥍ MAY ᥍
28

Blessed is everyone who does not take offence at my claims.   *Matthew 11:6 (Weymouth).*

𝕴N THE providence of God, Herod was allowed to shut up John in prison, and later to behead him. But John had kept the faith! For, languishing in prison, when he had proclaimed a Messiah who was to set the captive free, he still sent his last quavering question: "Art Thou He that should come?" Thereby he showed his perplexity at the strange lack of action of the One who was to "bind up the broken-hearted," yet seemed to have no concern for his breaking heart. Yet his triumphant conviction that Messiah must and would come shone forth in the rest of his message: "Art Thou He that should come, or look we for another?" "For if Thou art not He, we shall go on looking for Him; we can never abandon the hope, the search, for God's Anointed."

Here was faith perplexed yet persistent, which betokened the greatness of John. Here was a man so great that the Lord was able to leave His servant in prison, without an explanation but just a promise, "Blessed is he whosoever shall not be offended in Me." It is surely only His choicest saints with whom He can deal like that, and still He finds it good for us and pleasing to Himself, to ask sometimes for faith which does not ask for explanations. "Lord, increase our faith!"

NORTHCOTE DECK

What can these anxious cares avail,
    The never-ceasing moans and sighs?
What can it help us to bewail
    Each painful moment as it flies?
Our cross and trials do but press
The heavier for our bitterness.

Only thy restless heart keep still,
And wait in cheerful hope, content

To take whate'er His gracious will,
His all-discerning love, hath sent.
Nor doubt our inmost wants are known
To Him who chose us for His own.

GEORGE NEUMARCK

MAY 29

I pray, that your love may abound. *Philippians 1:9*.

WHEN I arrived home one evening, there was a pile of mail on my desk. I went into the kitchen and kissed my sweetheart, put down the satchel, and started opening the letters. Soon I heard a step, and the wife came into the office. Putting her face next to mine, she said, "Lover, when are you going to think more of me than you do of the mail?" I looked up into her face, and said, "Right now." I helped her put the food on the table, and after the meal was over, said to the children, "You children can clean up the table; your mother and I are going to have a good visit." We went into the front room, sat down on the davenport, and had a grand time of fellowship together. I had been paying the bills, buying her clothes, giving her money, and had been a real husband to her, I thought; but that wasn't what she wanted. It wasn't my money, but myself that she was interested in.

There is such a thing as being satisfied with the affairs of God, and missing His lovely Person. We are so busy doing church work that we are missing Him. This service is very lovely—I wish we had much more—but that isn't what He is talking about. "If any man thirst. . . ." "If you want Me, come and drink." Just drink in the Spirit of God. Drink in the Lord Jesus. Co and take all you can get of Him. He wants us to be good customers of His. Get everything He has for you. We want You, Lord Jesus, and we want all we can get of You.

WALTER L. WILSON

Oh! fill me, Jesus! Saviour! with thy love!
My woes but drive me to the fount above:
Thither may I in childlike faith draw nigh,
And never to another fountain fly
But unto Thee!

MARY SHEKELNOT

135

The Lord . . . hath had compassion on thee.

Mark 5:19.

𝕴 W A N T you to see Jesus as the Compassionate One. Listen! "When He (that is, Christ) saw the multitude He was moved with compassion on them because they fainted and were scattered abroad as sheep having no shepherd." And again it is recorded that He said to His disciples, "I have compassion on the multitude because they continue with Me now three days and have nothing to eat and I will not send them away fasting lest they faint by the way."

Then there is the incident of the leper, (what a loathsome disease leprosy is) who came to Him and knelt down beseeching Him, saying, "If Thou wilt, Thou canst make me clean." It is recorded that Jesus, "moved with compassion," put forth His hand and touched him. Think of it! The sinless Son of God touching this foul leper.

And He said to the leper, "I will, be thou clean."

Indeed we have in Jesus a compassionate deliverer, not "an high priest which cannot be touched with the feeling of our infirmities." No matter what your burden may be or what perplexity you are facing, you can go to your High Priest, the one Mediator between God and man, the man Christ Jesus, and obtain mercy and find grace to help in time of need.

CHARLES E. FULLER

No mortal can with Him compare
Among the sons of men;
Fairer is He than all the fair
That fill the heavenly train.

He saw me plunged in deep distress,
He flew to my relief;
For me He bore the shameful cross,
And carried all my grief.

SAMUEL STENNETT

For the Lord loveth judgment, and forsaketh not
His saints.   *Psalm 37:28.*

ALL the biographers of Michael Faraday agree that he was the
most transparently honest soul that the realm of science has ever
known. He moved for fifty years amidst the speculations of
science, whilst, in his soul, the certainties that cannot be shaken were
singing their deathless song. . . . In life, as in death, he rested his soul
upon certainties. And if you ask what the certainties were, his biographers will tell you they were three: First, he trusted implicitly in
his Father's love. Secondly, he trusted implicitly in the redeeming work
of his Saviour. Thirdly, he trusted implicitly in the written Word.
. . . In him the simplicities were always stronger than the sublimities;
the child outlived the sage. As he lay dying, they tried to interview the
professor, but it was the little child in him that answered. "What are
your speculations?" they inquired.

"Speculations? I have none! I am resting on certainties. I know
whom I have believed, and am persuaded that He is able to keep that
which I have committed unto Him against that day." And, reveling like
a little child in those cloudless simplicities, his great soul passed away.
. . . Happy the heads that, in the soul's last straits, find themselves
pillowed serenely there!

F. W. BOREHAM

I have chosen you . . . that ye should go and bring
forth fruit. *John 15:16.*

If we do the little duties of life faithfully, punctually, thoughtfully, reverently—not for the praise of man, but for the "Well done" of Christ—not for the payment we may receive, but because God has given us a little piece of work to do in His great world—not because we must, but because we choose—not as the slaves of circumstances, but as Christ's freed ones—then far down beneath the surge of common life the foundations of a character are laid, more beautiful and enduring than coral, which shall presently rear itself before the eyes of men and angels, and become an emerald islet, green with perennial beauty, and vocal with the songs of Paradise.

We ought, therefore, to be very careful how we fulfil the common tasks of daily life. We are making the character in which we have to spend eternity. We are either building into ourselves wood, hay, and stubble which will have to be burnt out at great cost; or the gold, silver, and precious stones, that shall be things of beauty and joy forever.

F. B. MEYER

Since Thou hast chosen us, O God,
Thy message to convey
To all the weary, sinsick world,
That some may find the way,
Give us Thy heart that will not quail,
Thy faith that cannot fail,
Thy arm of power for darkest hour
When evil hosts assail.

Since Thou hast chosen us, O Lord,
Fruitful we, too, would be;
We would not come with empty hand
At close of day to Thee.
Oh, give us fruit that shall remain,
Nor let us toil in vain.
Use us to bring the lost ones in
Till Thou shalt come again!

CORA MAE TURNBULL

I go to prepare a place for you. And if I go and prepare a place for you, I will come again, and receive
you unto Myself, that where I am, there ye may be
also.   *John 14:2, 3.*

IN THAT passage from St. John's Gospel is this very impressive
sentence, "If it were not so, I would have told you." There Christ
invites us to rest all our faith in the life to come in Him and in His
words. "If it were not so, I would have told you." If what were not so?
Why, that there is no life after death. Christ stakes His honor, His
reputation, on His testimony to the life to come. By every consideration of truth and honor, if there is no future life, He was bound to
have told His disciples. But He never told them that. Neither by word
nor by inference, nor by His life did He ever in the least degree intimate that this life is the end of all. On the contrary, by the purity
of His life, by the tone of His preaching, by His constant appeal to
life to come, and by His own definite affirmation of the life after death,
Christ told His disciples that this life is not the end and that there is
a greater and a nobler life which is to come.

CLARENCE EDWARD MACARTNEY

*We are waiting for the dawn
    Of that everlasting day,
When the night of earth shall end
    And the shadows flee away.
Morn of morns and day of days!
    How we wait and watch and pray
Till the dawn of heaven shall break,
    And the shadows flee away.*

*Then our tears shall cease to flow,
    Loved ones meet to part no more;
Sin and pain and death shall cease
    And our sorrows all be o'er;
Every mystery shall be solved,
    Every night be turned to day,
Every wrong shall be made right
    When the shadows flee away.*

A. B. SIMPSON

Remember the words of the Lord Jesus, how He
said, It is more blessed to give than to receive.
Acts 20:35.

E GET the words, not from any of the Gospels, but from St. Paul. They were given him by some of the disciples of the Lord, and they are thoroughly in keeping with the mind of the Master, who gave Himself for us.

Giving is a lovely virtue. Abraham crowned his life by saying, "Of all Thou hast given me have I given a tenth unto Thee." Every son of Abraham brought his tithe to his priest: that was his least. Many more gifts followed throughout the year. Let not the Jew put to shame the Christian. A tenth is our least: much more than that should be our most. The Jew's minimum should not be the Christian's maximum.

But circumstances must rule: and the poor widow's two mites, being all she had, may far exceed in love the millions of a millionaire. The words of Christ remain true to all, "It is more blessed to give than to receive." So many wish only to get. Their whole life is spent in drawing all the fish into their own net, and securing all the grist for their own mill.

But Love likes to give. Its highest pleasure is found in parting with its possessions. It gives its money to help the needy; it shares its wealth with the wayfarers who have fallen by the wayside. It gives its kind words in sympathy with the sufferers. It gives its prayers in intercession for all. It forgets not the foreign nations any more than the home people.

Was there ever a finer epitaph than that placed on General Gordon's memorial stone which you see as you enter St. Paul's Cathedral: "He gave his strength to the weak, his sympathy to the suffering, his substance to the poor, and his heart to God." It is so compact of all the good virtues, and so true of the hero of Khartoum that all Britain mourned the loss of one who was the model of faith, of courage, and of conscientiousness. His diary, discovered after his death at Khartoum, is one of the most wonderful records to be found of modern heroism, of humility and unselfish beneficence.

W. S. BRUCE

If My people, which are called by My name, shall
humble themselves, and pray, and seek My face,
and turn from their wicked ways; then will I hear
from heaven, and will forgive their sin, and will
heal their land.   *2 Chronicles 7:14.*

BY THE term "revival" we usually mean that Spirit-given condition in which an entire group, larger or smaller, participates and shares mutual blessing, rather than the spiritual state of an individual Christian as distinct from his fellows, be that individual experience ever so blessed. It is in this sense of a revived Christian community that we are now writing. For a picture of such revival, witness the early Church. We read in Acts (4:33) that "great grace was upon them all," and that their condition was further characterized by great power, great fear or reverence, great persecution, and great joy. In speaking of these Christians the Holy Spirit used this word "great" five times. Revival is an unusual and superlative work of God, the results of which are to abide in the life even when God may have withdrawn certain manifestations of revival.

Never is one so conscious of the sovereign grace of God as when he is walking in the holy atmosphere of revival. Never is he so keenly aware of the fact that he is deserving of nothing. Accordingly the Christian will not expect to be able to produce revival, not even by his fervent prayer, and certainly not by trying to imitate certain outward manifestations through which previous seasons of revival blessing have come. In the truest sense, revival prayer must be, in the words of Habakkuk (3:2): "O Lord, revive thy work."

The heart of the New Covenant is that God worketh in us for our sanctification and our service. It is His work in us that we long to have revived. When we honestly, really, want His work in our lives, nothing else, nothing more, nothing less, then we can pray for revival. This means dealing with anything in our lives that hinders His working, dealing with it definitely in the presence of God by confession and full surrender. Revival will come when we want not so much a revival, as we without any reserve want the Lord Jesus to be magnified in our bodies every moment we live and with every breath we take.

G. ALLEN FLEECE

JUNE
5

After these things I heard as it were a great voice
of a great multitude in heaven, saying, Hallelujah.
. . . And a second time they say, Hallelujah. . . .
And the four and twenty elders and the four living
creatures fell down and worshipped God that sitteth on the throne, saying, Amen; Hallelujah . . .
And I heard as it were the voice of a great multitude, and as the voice of many waters, and as the
voice of mighty thunders, saying, Hallelujah.
Revelation 19:1-6 (R. V.).

HERE first the song, and then the submission, and yet again the
song. It is that vision of the perfect consummation that inspires
the song.

At last all opposing forces are overcome, and the kingdom of the
heavens is realized through all the vast realms over which it is God's
right to reign.

At last the prayer taught by Christ is answered, the Name is
hallowed, the kingdom come, the will is done, and the unending
Hallelujah follows the unlimited Amen.

Then begins the absolutely perfect service of which all the imper-
fect service of these probationary days is the hardly articulate prophecy. Then life moves unchecked, unhindered, toward highest forms of
expression and most glorious inter-relation, because it is absolutely
homed in the will of God.

G. CAMPBELL MORGAN

Bear me on Thy rapid wing,
Everlasting Spirit!
Where bright choirs of angels sing,
And Thy saints inherit;
Waiting round the eternal throne,
Joys immortal are their own:
This the cry of every one—
"Glory to the Incarnate Son!"

Four and twenty elders rise
From their princely station,
Shout His glorious victories—
Sing His great salvation,
Cast their crowns before the throne,
Cry, in reverential tone,
"Holy, Holy, Holy One,
Glory be to God alone!"

Hark! the thrilling symphonies
Seem within to seize us;
Add we to their holy lays—
Jesus, Jesus, Jesus!
Sweetest note in angels' song,
Sweetest sound on mortal tongue,
Sweetest anthem ever known,
Jesus, Jesus reigns alone.

AUTHOR UNKNOWN

JUNE
6

He that is washed needeth not save to wash his
feet, but is clean every whit.   *John 13:10.*

I WANT you to get clearly the fact of relationship and fellowship. It is possible to be in relationship with God because you have accepted Jesus Christ as your personal Saviour and have been born again, and yet be out of fellowship with Him because your feet have become contaminated with the dust of your daily journey. You need a daily cleansing of your feet.

All the disciples except Judas Iscariot had definitely and experimentally received Christ as their Saviour. Christ called them His own. But He had a great spiritual lesson to teach them, in this thirteenth chapter of John. It was their need of a daily cleansing of their feet. And so He laid aside His garments, took a towel, and began to wash the disciples' feet.

Our feet have to do with our walk. "Blessed is the man that walketh not in the counsel of the ungodly." "For we walk by faith, not by sight." "This I say, then, walk in the Spirit and ye shall not fulfil the lusts of the flesh."

In our walk as pilgrims our feet become defiled daily and we need a daily cleansing.

When Jesus came to Peter with the basin, Peter said, "Thou shalt never wash my feet."

But Jesus said to Peter, "If I wash thee not, thou hast no part with Me."

Fellow believer, if Christ does not wash you continually, there is no fellowship. You will be saved so as by fire but you will lose the joy of fellowship with Him.

When Peter heard the Lord say that it was necessary for him to have his feet washed, he said impetuously, "Lord, not my feet only, but also my hands and my head."

But Jesus replied, "He that is washed needeth only to wash his feet."

143

There is a washing at conversion that the believer has in Christ that never needs to be repeated. "For by one offering He hath perfected forever them that are sanctified" (Hebrews 10:14). But there is also a daily washing for the believer if he would live in fellowship. It is "the washing of water by the Word" (Ephesians 5:26).

CHARLES E. FULLER

JUNE 7

Now . . . manifest to His saints: . . . the riches of the glory of this mystery. . . . Christ in you, the hope of glory. *Colossians 1:26, 27.*

THIS God-established union is a hidden life, "For ye died, and your life is hid with Christ in God" (Col. 3:3), but it is wondrously real. Here is a box marked "God," within it another marked "Christ," and as you open it you see another box marked "you"; your life in Christ and Christ in God. This union we have with Christ in God assures perfect safety and is burglar proof. Before you can be reached, Christ must be put out of the way, and before He can be reached, God must be set aside. "Your life is hid with Christ in God." Here is rest and peace and quietness and victory over the devil. Let us thank God for the truth of it, whether or not it has been made a reality in our lives.

The Lord Jesus Himself laid emphasis on this same fact, but He made it even more intimate. He said, "In that day ye shall know that I am in My Father, and ye in Me, and I in you" (John 14:20). Could it be more intimate or more personal, "I am in My Father, . . . ye in Me, . . . I in you"? This world never has and never can see with human eyes or human understanding how we are united to the Son of God. As we cannot explain the mystery of the Trinity so no one can explain the mystery of our union with the beloved Son of God. I cannot explain it but I can believe it and give a hearty assent to it. One day when we appear with Him in glory it will be fully manifested; in the meantime let us rejoice and be glad and rest in His word—"in Christ Jesus."

L. L. LEGTERS

This is my wonderful story,
Christ to my heart has come;
Jesus, the King of Glory,
Finds in my heart a home.

I am so glad I received Him,
Jesus my heart's dear King;

I who so often have grieved Him,
All to His feet would bring.

Now in His bosom confiding,
This my glad song shall be;
I am in Jesus abiding,
Jesus abides in me.

A. B. SIMPSON

JUNE 8

Arise, go up to Bethel, and dwell there; and make there an altar unto God, that appeared unto thee when thou fleddest from the face of Esau thy brother. *Genesis 35:1.*

E HAVE here a most exquisite feature in the divine method of dealing with souls. There is not one word said about Shechem, its pollutions and its confusions. There is not a word of reproof for having settled down there. Such is not God's way. He employs a far more excellent mode. Had we been dealing with Jacob we should have come down upon him with a heavy hand, and read him a severe lecture about his folly in settling at Shechem, and about his personal and domestic habits and condition. But oh, how well it is that God's thoughts are not as our thoughts, nor His ways like ours! Instead of saying to Jacob, "Why have you settled down in Shechem?" He simply said, "Arise, go up to Bethel"; and the very sound of the word sent a flood of light into Jacob's soul by which he was enabled to judge himself and his surroundings. "Then Jacob said unto his household, and to all that were with him, Put away the strange gods that are among you, and be clean, and change your garments: and let us arise, and go up to Bethel; and I will make there an altar unto God, who answered me in the day of my distress, and was with me in the way which I went."

C. H. M.

To every man there openeth
  A Way, and Ways, and a Way,
And the High Soul climbs the High Way,
  And the Low Soul gropes the Low;
And in between, on the misty flats,
  The rest drift to and fro.
But to every man there openeth
  A High Way, and a Low,
And every man decideth
  The Way his soul shall go.

JOHN OXENHAM

145

I will be with thee: I will not fail thee, nor forsake thee. Be strong and of a good courage.

Joshua 1:5, 6.

THERE are some natures so shallow that they have no depths to sound; and they go through life, apparently, without discovering how superficial they really are. Their existence is all upon the surface, seen in a moment, withering in an hour. They have no center of faith, no hidden altar at which the soul, robed in the raiment of reverence, ministers as priest before the Lord. But the man of finer faculty, who has made his body a temple of the Holy Ghost, knows full well that he has this treasure in a very earthen vessel, and its capacity is often taxed to contain the glory and fulfill the word which has been revealed to him.

That was the case with Joshua as he stood that day before the Lord of hosts. He was not afraid of God. He was afraid of himself. There is a fear that is born of guilt, coming swiftly on the heels of conscious wrongdoing. There is a fear that is born of cowardice, and at a crisis it breeds a fatal paralysis of mind and will. But Joshua was afflicted with neither of these. He could meet the divine scrutiny with heart unveiled, because he carried within him a conscience void of offense. In the fateful hour of battle he had never faltered, nor turned his back to the foe. But as he looked that day across Jordan and thought of the coming days and of the part that he must play therein, he was conscious of a tremor he had never felt before. Hitherto the supreme responsibility had rested upon another. Henceforth, it was a burden which he himself must bear, and he felt unequal to the load. To him, God spoke in this hour, saying, "Be strong—I will not fail thee."

R. MOFFAT GAUTREY

As helpless as a child who clings
Fast to his father's arm,
And casts his weakness on the strength
That keeps him safe from harm;

So I, my Father, cling to Thee,
And thus I every hour
Would link my earthly feebleness
To Thine almighty power.

J. D. BURNS

JUNE 10

Cast thy bread upon the waters: for thou shalt find it after many days. *Ecclesiastes 11:1.*

SOMEONE has said, "I keep shovelling out and God keeps shovelling in. But there is always an increase because God's shovel is bigger than mine." We are sure this faithful pastor will find it even so.

"*Dear Brother Fuller*: I am a minister to a small congregation in a rural section (of Tennessee) and I, along with hundreds of other such ministers, need these messages of the Pilgrim Hour so much. They are as cool water to a thirsty soul. It is such a joy to sit around the King's table and enjoy His Word with you as you lead us into the deeper things of His riches. We have little opportunity such as the cities afford to attend Bible conferences.

"We are so prone to receive God's bounties without shouldering our part of the responsibility. Your announcement today aroused me to the fact that I was being blessed without responding in a way to continue to receive that blessing. It is true that my salary for my family is very small, only $12.50 a week. (I am not grumbling. Thank God, thus far He has graciously supplied every need.) Here is $5.60 to help keep the Pilgrim Hour going. Believe me, I shall be praying. 'Behold, I am the God of all flesh. Is there anything too hard for Me?' We shout back, with victorious voices, 'Oh, Lord God, Thou hast made heaven and earth with Thy mighty power and stretched-out arm. There is NOTHING too hard for Thee.' "

Pray for the thousands of faithful pastors, like this one, who are carrying on in places where few see or appreciate their labor of love for Christ. Perhaps there is one near you who needs the word of encouragement which you can give.

JUNE 11

. . . and to the church in thy house. *Philemon 2.*

WHEN the Saviour is enthroned in any home, regardless of size, location, and appearance; when He is worshipped in any family circle, irrespective of financial or social rating; when His Word is read and reverenced, His Name invoked in personal prayer, His glories sung in family hymns, that home becomes a blessed

147

sanctuary, a temple of the living Christ; that family, by His own promise, "Where two or three are gathered together in My name, there am I in the midst of them," becomes a church, a house of God.

WALTER A. MAIER

Friend of the home: as when in Galilee
The mothers brought their little ones to Thee,
So we, dear Lord, would now the children bring,
And seek for them the shelter of Thy wing.

Draw through the child the parents nearer Thee,
Endue their home with growing sanctity;
And gather all, by earthly homes made one,
In heav'n, O Christ, when earthly days are done.

HOWELL E. LEWIS

JUNE 12

Withhold not good . . . when it is in the power of thine hand to do it. *Proverbs 3 :27.*

My hands were filled with many things
That I did precious hold,
As any treasure of a king's—
Silver, or gems, or gold.
The Master came and touched my hands,
(The scars were in His own)
And at His feet my treasures sweet
Fell shattered, one by one.
"I must have empty hands," said He,
"Wherewith to work My works through thee."

My hands were stained with marks of toil,
Defiled with dust of earth;
And I my work did ofttimes soil
And render little worth.
The Master came and touched my hands,
(And crimson were His own)
But when, amazed, on mine I gazed,
Lo! every stain was gone.
"I must have cleansed hands," said He,
"Wherewith to work My works through thee."

My hands were growing feverish
And cumbered with much care!
Trembling with haste and eagerness,
Nor folded oft in prayer.
The Master came and touched my hands,
(With healing in His own)

And calm and still to do His will
They grew—the fever gone.
"I must have quiet hands," said He,
"Wherewith to work My works for Me."

My hands were strong in fancied strength,
But not in power divine,
And bold to take up tasks at length,
That were not His but mine.
The Master came and touched my hands,
(And might was in His own!)
But mine since then have powerless been,
Save His are laid thereon.
"And it is only thus," said He,
"That I can work My works through thee."

AUTHOR UNKNOWN

JUNE 13

Let not your heart be troubled: ye believe in God,
believe also in Me. *John 14:1.*

THESE words were spoken to the eleven disciples after the Last Supper. Judas had already departed, otherwise Jesus could not have said them.

In the natural, there were many things to trouble the hearts of the disciples. They were troubled over the warning that Christ had given to Peter that he would deny Him thrice. They were troubled because He had told them He was going away. And they were troubled because they could see that the Lord was deeply burdened.

How beautifully the Lord brings His disciples to a place of peace. This is a chapter on how to cure heart trouble. "Let not your heart be troubled." The cure is in two words, "Believe Me." Let us note the other places where it occurs in this chapter: "Believe Me that I am in the Father, and the Father in Me" (verse 11). "Believe Me for the very works' sake" (verse 11). "He that believeth on Me, the works that I do shall he do also" (verse 12). "I have told you before it come to pass that . . . ye might believe" (verse 29).

What does it mean to believe? It means simply to take God at His Word and trust Him.

You will remember how, after God brought Israel out of the bondage of Egypt and was taking His people through the wilderness journey, He began to tell them about the land flowing with milk and honey. A goodly land! But when they arrived at Kadesh-Barnea, on the border of the land, they said, "Let's go over and see if the land is good." They appointed twelve spies to find out if God had told them

149

the truth. That is unbelief. Because of that unbelief ten of the twelve came back with trembling knees, admitting that the land was good but with their eyes on the giants. Only two believed and were not troubled in their hearts.

Now here is the difference. All of them saw the giants. All of them saw the fruits of the land. But ten looked at the conditions while two had their eyes on God.

God can cure your heart trouble only if you take Him at His Word and disregard the difficulties.

CHARLES E. FULLER

JUNE

14

I have been crucified with Christ, and it is no longer I that live, but Christ lives in me; and the life which I now live in the body I live by faith in the Son of God who loved me and gave Himself up for me. *.Galatians 2:20 (Weymouth).*

BELOVED, are we so dissatisfied with self as to feel the supreme need of Christ alone? Do we realize that in ourselves we are dead men and women? The very fact that a man must be born again: do we realize this to be in itself the most tremendous indictment against, and proof of the utter worthlessness of our own natural self-life, that a holy God could ever array against us? Have we accepted the logical consequences of regeneration, in their bearing on holy living? Do we realize our need of living in God, as well as being born of God? Are we conscious of our need of abiding? Are we "following after," abiding? Surely its reward is rich, for He Himself hath said, "Abide in Me and I in YOU!"

JAMES H. MCCONKEY

Once it was the blessing, now it is the Lord;
Once it was the feeling, now it is His Word;
Once His gift I wanted, now the Giver own;
Once I sought for healing, now Himself alone.

Once 'twas painful trying, now 'tis perfect trust;
Once a half salvation, now the uttermost;
Once 'twas ceaseless holding, now He holds me fast;
Once 'twas constant drifting, now my anchor's cast.

Once 'twas busy planning, now 'tis trustful prayer;
Once 'twas anxious caring, now He has the care;
Once 'twas what I wanted, now what Jesus says;
Once 'twas constant asking, now 'tis ceaseless praise.

Once it was my working, His it hence shall be;
Once I tried to use Him, now He uses me;
Once the power I wanted, now the Mighty One;
Once for self I labored, now for Him alone.

Once I hoped in Jesus, now I know He's mine;
Once my lamps were dying, now they brightly shine;
Once for death I waited, now His coming hail;
And my hopes are anchored safe within the vail.

A. B. SIMPSON

JUNE 15

And it shall come to pass in the last days, saith God, I will pour out of My Spirit upon all flesh.

Acts 2:17.

GOD has declared that in the "last days" He would pour out of His Spirit. That promise was partially fulfilled on the day of Pentecost. But it remains for us to see the final and complete fulfilment. Let me again remind you that this is still the dispensation of the Holy Spirit. Have we, then, Scripture to warrant the hope of another great outpouring of the Spirit of God as we enter the "last hours" of the last days of this age? I believe we have. It is my deep, deep conviction that God is waiting to pour out His Spirit once again, and that wherever He can find a people who will meet His conditions, He will give flood-tides of mighty revival. And this, the outpouring of the Holy Spirit, is, I am convinced, the greatest need of the hour.

But is this outpouring for a select few? Is it only for spiritual leaders, and for men alone? By no means. Thank God, His Word is absolutely clear and conclusive. "I will pour out of My Spirit," He declares, "upon all flesh." Yes! Upon old flesh and young flesh, upon rich flesh and poor flesh, upon high and low flesh—"all flesh."

"And your sons and your daughters shall prophesy . . . and on My servants and on My handmaidens I will pour out in those days of My Spirit; and they shall prophesy." Not the men only but the women; not the old only but the young; not the high only but the low. Daughters will prophesy, and handmaidens as well.

All may claim a part. It is to be a great universal outpouring for all peoples everywhere. Any one may have it, any church may expect it. This is the solution of all problems. Not money, but the outpoured Spirit. Not how to get the attention of the people, but how to secure the operation of the Holy Ghost. Not better preaching, but Holy Ghost preaching. "I will pour out of My Spirit upon all flesh." This, my brethren, is the greatest need of the hour.

OSWALD J. SMITH

151

But thou, when thou prayest, enter into thy closet, and when thou hast shut thy door, pray to thy Father which is in secret; and thy Father which seeth in secret shall reward thee openly.

Matthew 6:6.

THINK of God, His greatness, His holiness, His unspeakable glory, and then on the inestimable privilege to which He invites His children, that each one of them, however sinful or feeble he may be, every hour of the day, may have access to Him, and hold converse with Him as long as he wishes. If he enters his Inner Chamber, then God is ready to meet him, to have fellowship with him, to give him the joy and strength which he needs with the living assurance in his heart that He is with him and will undertake for him in everything. In addition He promises that He will enrich him in his outward life and work with those things which he has asked for in secret. Ought we not to cry out with joy? What an honor! What a salvation! What an overflowing supply for every need!

One may be in the greatest distress, or may have fallen into the deepest sin, or may in the ordinary course of life desire temporal or spiritual blessing; he may desire to pray for himself or for those belonging to him, or for his congregation or church; he may even become an intercessor for the whole world—the promise for the Inner Chamber covers all: "Pray to thy Father which is in secret; He will reward thee openly."

We might well suppose that there would be no place on earth so attractive to the child of God as the Inner Chamber with the presence of God promised, where he may have unhindered intercourse with the Father. The happiness of a child on earth if he enjoys the love of his father; the happiness of a friend as he meets a beloved benefactor; the happiness of a subject who has free access to his king and may stay with him as long as he wishes; these are as nothing compared with this heavenly promise. In the Inner Chamber you can converse with your God as long and as intimately as you desire, you can rely on His presence and fellowship.

Oh, the wonderful love of God in the gift of an Inner Chamber sanctified by such a promise! Let us thank God every day of our lives for it as the gift of His wonderful love. In this sinful world He could devise nothing more suitable for our needs, as a fountain of unspeakable blessing.

ANDREW MURRAY

JUNE 17

She hath done what she could. *Mark 14:8.*

EVERYONE may not be called to be a Paul or a Deborah, but all can emulate the simple, loving and sacrificial service of Mary. Too many times, in our emphasis on her attitude of devotion and quiet waiting before Jesus to hear from His lips secrets which could not be shared with others, we forget that Mary, as well as Martha, served. The service of Martha was to His physical need, that of Mary was to His spirit. How much deeper was that need of the spirit than His need of food!

Should not this be a lesson to us in our ministry to "the least of these"? We have not adequately fulfilled our service to the needy when we have shared with them the material things of which God has made us stewards, unless they have been made to feel our deep concern for the wounds of their spirits. We may have little to give of money or worldly goods but the poorest of us can become channels through which the Holy Spirit may heal broken hearts. A word in season, a loving touch, a sympathetic tear or some simple act of understanding fellowship which you can render today may make a world of difference to someone.

J. ELWIN WRIGHT

Lord, let me do the little things
  Which may fall to my lot;
Those little inconspicuous ones
  By others oft forgot.

A staff for age to lean upon,
  Strong hands to help the weak;
A loving heart with open door
  To all who solace seek.

To hold my tongue when hot words rise,
  Speak kindly ones instead;
Nor harshly judge my fellow men
  In what they've done or said.

To share another's heavy load
  By word of courage given;
To help a fallen brother rise
  And bring him nearer heaven.

If, like the Master, I can give
  Myself for those I love,
Rich joy and peace shall come to me,
  Sweet rest in heaven above.

FRA MORTON SIMS

153

He who believes in me, from within him—as the
Scripture has said—rivers of living water shall
flow.   *John 7:38 (Weymouth).*

THE Dead Sea has water from the Jordan flowing into it continually, but nothing ever flows out of that sea, and therefore it is
dead. You can attend every Bible conference and every meeting, and be dead because nothing ever flows out. "He that believeth
on Me . . . out of him shall flow. . . ." If there is a spring within,
there will be a river flowing without. You can't hold it in. It will spring
up of itself. You will have to talk to be refreshed. "I will speak, that I
may be refreshed" (Job 32:20). "I believed, and therefore have I
spoken" (2 Cor. 4:13).

WALTER L. WILSON

Like the wondrous river of the prophet's vision,
So the Holy Spirit floweth full and free.
Larger, deeper, fuller, still the river groweth
Till it reach the fullness of the Crystal Sea.

First a little streamlet, lo! it softly trickled
From the sacred fountain of the holy heart.
Let us not despise the day of small beginnings,
From the feeblest droppings, mightiest rivers start.

Waters to the ankles, lo! the river deepens,
And we bathe our steppings in the heavenly flood.
Walking in the Spirit, stepping in His foot-prints,
Living in obedience, walking with our God.

Waters to the loins, we've reached the mighty river,
'Tis the promised baptism of the Holy Ghost.
Plunge into the torrent, let it bear us onward
Till our lives repeat the days of Pentecost.

A. B. SIMPSON

JUNE
19

For he that is dead is freed from sin. Now if we be dead with Christ, we believe that we shall also live with Him.   *Romans 6:7, 8.*

ONCE read a story which makes this truth clear. During the Civil War, when men were drawn by lot to join the army, a man named Wyatt was called to fight for the South. He was the main support of his family and, realizing this hardship, another young man named Pratt volunteered to go in his stead. He was accepted, and drafted, and bore the name and number of Wyatt. Eventually Pratt was killed in action, and having died as the substitute and in the name of the other man, the name of Wyatt was recorded. At a later date Wyatt was again called upon for service, but at the recruiting office he calmly stated he had already been killed in action. The entry was found, and Wyatt, although alive and well, was dead in the eyes of the authorities because he was identified with his substitute.

Even so the believer died with Christ, was buried with Christ, and was raised to newness of life in Him. As Christ died to sin, the believer died to sin. This is a fact. God has established it as such. Christ died on Calvary for you long before you lived and appropriated that fact for the forgiveness of your sins; even so you died with Christ on Calvary although up to the present time you have never appropriated His death to sin as your death to sin. So let each Christian know that his death with Christ on the cross is a fact. He will then be in a position to obey the injunction of Romans 6:11, which reads: "Likewise reckon ye also yourselves to be dead indeed unto sin, but alive unto God through Jesus Christ our Lord."

HOWARD W. FERRIN

JUNE
20

I am the Good Shepherd.   *John 10:14.*

WE HAVE a contrasting picture here. The Pharisees were the religious leaders of that day but they were false shepherds. Christ was the true Shepherd.

The Pharisees were called "strangers" in verse five, "thieves and robbers" in verse eight, "wolves" and "hirelings" in verses twelve and thirteen. In chapter nine, they had shown their true character by casting the poor blind man whom Jesus had healed out of the synagogue.

155

They were exactly like those against whom Ezekiel had prophesied centuries before saying, "Woe be to the shepherds of Israel that do feed themselves! Should not the shepherds feed the flocks? Ye eat the fat, and ye clothe you with the wool, ye kill them that are fed: but ye feed not the flock. The diseased have ye not strengthened, neither have ye healed that which was sick, neither have ye bound up that which was broken, neither have ye brought again that which was driven away, neither have ye sought that which was lost; but with force and with cruelty have ye ruled them" Ezekiel 34:2–4. Thus have the false shepherds acted in every generation.

But Jesus, the Good Shepherd, said, "I know my sheep and am known of mine. . . . I lay down my life for the sheep. . . . And other sheep I have, which are not of this fold: them also I must bring" (John 10:14–16).

Charles E. Fuller

Dear Lord, some sheep of Thine have wandered far
  Into neglect, with no desire
To serve nor feed again upon Thy love,
  Content to sink in sin's deep mire
Until the shadows grow, and night begins
  To creep upon them, dark and cold,
And then they want some shepherd with Thy love,
  To bring them back again into Thy fold.

Dear Lord, such were the sheep that Thou didst seek,
  Enduring loss and earthly lack,
Until, until on Calvary's dreadful cross
  Thy life poured out to bring us back.
Until—dear Lord, until—Oh, give us love,
  Thy love, to go, to pray, to seek
Until we find, until we reach, until
  We bring to Thee, Thine own lost sheep.

Mary Stoner Wine

JUNE 21

Now when He had left speaking, he said unto Simon, Launch out into the deep, and let down your nets for a draught.   *Luke 5:4.*

INTO the commonplace comes the Master and lifts it to the sublime. The rocking boat becomes a pulpit for God; the net, a symbol for divine truth, and a weary fisherman is changed into an awed worshiper with far-away visions.

Chance had no part in directing His steps to the particular spot on the Galilean shore where Simon sat discouraged over a night's fruitless labor. Chance never enters into God's dealings with men. He moves with the unerring certainty of His eternal law and purpose. Hundreds, perhaps thousands, of needy souls surrounded Him, and they were all drawn—in order to be helped—to the boat where the tired Simon sat, because God had prepared for Simon a revolutionizing experience.

And Simon did not miss it! He might have pleaded weariness when told to launch out. He might have been guided by human reason and past experience, but he simply obeyed God, and the blessed consequences of that obedience will throughout time and eternity be multiplied!

ANNA J. LINDGREN

> *Why is thy faith, O child of God, so small?*
> *Why doth thy heart shrink back at duty's call?*
> *Art thou obeying this—"Abide in Me,"*
> *And doth the Master's word abide in thee?*
>
> *Oh, blest assurance from our risen Lord!*
> *Oh, precious comfort breathing from the Word!*
> *How great the promise! could there greater be?*
> *"Ask what thou wilt, it shall be done for thee!"*
>
> *Increase our faith, and clear our vision, Lord;*
> *Help us to take Thee at Thy simple word,*
> *No more with cold distrust to bring Thee grief;*
> *Lord, we believe, help Thou our unbelief.*

W. F. SHERWIN

JUNE 22

The Spirit and the bride say, Come. And let him that heareth say, Come. And let him that is athirst come. And whosoever will, let him take the water of life freely. *Revelation 22:17.*

THE essence of faith is to come to Christ.

This is the first and the last and the surest indication that faith is still alive. A sinner has nothing but sin and distress. The Spirit of God has made that clear to him. And faith manifests itself clearly and plainly when a sinner, instead of fleeing from God and his own responsibility, as he did before, comes into the presence of Christ with all his sin and all his distress. The sinner who does this believes.

It is written, "Him that cometh to me I will in no wise cast out" (John 6:37). "If we confess our sins, He is faithful and righteous to forgive us our sins, and to cleanse us from all unrighteousness" (I John 1:9 R. V.).

That was just what those folk did who came to Christ and heard from Him these words before they departed, "Thy faith hath saved thee." All they did was to come to Jesus and plead their distress before Him, whether it was physical or spiritual or both.

Notice the simple, but unmistakable, mark of a living faith.

Such a faith as this sees its own need, acknowledges its own helplessness, goes to Jesus, tells Him just how bad things are and leaves everything with Him.

You and I can now tell how much faith we need in order to pray. We have faith enough when we in our helplessness turn to Jesus.

This shows us clearly that true prayer is a fruit of helplessness and faith. Helplessness becomes prayer the moment that you go to Jesus and speak candidly and confidently with Him about your needs. This is to believe.

O. HALLESBY

JUNE
23

O how love I Thy law! it is my meditation all the day.   *Psalm 119:97.*

READ the Bible, not as a newspaper, but as a home letter. If a cluster of heavenly fruit hangs within reach, gather it. If a promise lies upon the page as a blank check, cash it. If a prayer is recorded, appropriate it, and launch it as a feathered arrow from the bow of your desire. If an example of holiness gleams before you, ask God to do as much for you. If a truth is revealed in all its intrinsic splendor, entreat that its brilliance may ever irradiate the hemisphere of your life like a star. Entwine the climbing creepers of holy desire about the lattice work of Scripture. So shall you come to say with the Psalmist, "O how love I Thy law! it is my meditation all the day."

It is sometimes well to read over, on our knees, Psalm 119, so full of devout love for the Bible. And if any should chide us for spending so much time upon the Old Testament or the New, let us remind them of the words of Christ, "Man shall not live by bread alone, but by every word that proceedeth out of the mouth of God." The Old Testament must be worth our study since it was our Saviour's Bible, deeply pondered and often quoted. And the New demands it, since it is so full of what He said and did, not only in His earthly life, but through the medium of His holy apostles and prophets.

F. B. MEYER

How blest to brood in holy meditation,
  O'er Thine eternal Word, O Thou Most High,
Enraptured by Thy Spirit's revelation
  Of things invisible to mortal eye!

Away from all earth's clamor and confusion—
  Shut in with Christ, how sweet this trysting place!
How privileged the secret, calm seclusion
  Within the veil, where I may seek His face!

More sweet than honey are Thy words, my Saviour,
  More precious far than gems of purest gold.
The lowliest can know Thy royal favor.
  Sin-burdened hearts can taste Thy love untold.

ANNA HOPPE

JUNE 24

**Watch therefore: for ye know not what hour your
Lord doth come.**   *Matthew 24:42.*

IT IS a solemn thought that every time the Old Fashioned Revival Hour goes out to listeners throughout the world there are several thousand people in the audience who, by the law of averages, will never hear another gospel message. Here is a touching letter from a friend in Oregon telling of such an instance.

"*Dear Mr. Fuller*: I am a widow living all alone. My dear husband has been called yonder. We used to sit and listen to your program every Sunday night. On the night before he was called away he came in from milking and your program began. He invited the boy who was staying with us to listen. I will never forget that Mr. Fuller said, that night, that none of us knew how quick we would be called away. He said, 'There may be some listening tonight who may never hear my voice again.'

"At 11:45 the next night my dear husband was called up yonder. He was so healthy we never could have imagined it would happen so quickly.

"I love to listen to your program. It is the only kind of preaching that satisfies my poor lonesome heart. I can hardly wait from one Sunday to another."

Pray that God may convict many who are soon to be called, of their need of a Saviour. Pray also for those who are bereaved, that Christ may fill the aching void in their hearts. Pray that Mr. Fuller's messages may continue to cause many to find their Saviour before it is too late.

JUNE
25

(He) is able to do exceeding abundantly above all
that we ask or think, according to the power that
worketh in us.   *Ephesians 3:20.*

XCEEDING abundantly." Here Paul coins a word for his own
peculiar use. It seems as though at times the Holy Spirit crowded
such great and radiant revelations into the Apostle's mind and
heart that even the rich vocabulary at his disposal was not sufficient
to express them. But when ordinary language fails Paul employs his
own. There was no superlative at hand which could describe his
sense of the overwhelming ability of God, and so he just constructed
a word of his own, the intensity of which can only be suggested in
our English phrase "exceeding abundantly." The power flows up,
and out, and over! It is a spring, and therefore incalculable.

We can measure the resources of a cistern; we can tell its capacity
to a trifle. We can register the contents of a reservoir; at any moment
we can tell how many gallons it contains. But who can measure the
resources of a spring? It is to this springlike quality in the divine
power, the exceeding abundance, the immeasurable quantity, that the
Apostle refers.

We can bring our little vessels to the spring and take them away
filled to overflowing, and the exceeding abundance remains. The
"doing" of our God is an inexhaustible well.

J. H. JOWETT

JUNE
26

For sin shall not have dominion over you: for ye
are not under the law, but under grace.
                                  Romans 6:14.

IT IS not God's will that sin shall have dominion over any child
of His; all died with Jesus Christ, all were united with Him in
crucifixion, but few enter into the joy of the freedom of the sons
of God, because they will not believe God's Word. Will you not now
bow before God and thank Him that you were crucified with Christ;
begin to thank Him regardless of feeling. It may take a day or a
month, I do not know how long, but I do know that when any child
of God will believe and begin to express that faith in thanksgiving,
day by day thanking Him for the fact which one may not yet have
apprehended, the Holy Spirit will lead that one into a glorious per-

sonal realization of it. Then from the heart he can say, "For the law of the Spirit of life in Christ Jesus hath made me free from the law of sin and death" (Romans 8:2).

L. L. LEGTERS

Not what I am, O Lord, but what Thou art,
That, that alone, can be my soul's true rest;
Thy love, not mine, bids fear and doubt depart,
And stills the tempest of my tossing breast.

Thy name is Love! I hear it from the Cross;
Thy name is Love! I read it in yon tomb;
All meaner love is perishable dross,
But this shall light me through time's thickest gloom.

It blesses now, and shall forever bless;
It saves me now, and shall forever save;
It holds me up in days of helplessness,
It bears me safely o'er each swelling wave.

HORATIUS BONAR

JUNE 27

In my Father's house are many mansions: if it were not so, I would have told you. I go to prepare a place for you. *John 14:2.*

THERE is cure for the troubled heart in the upward look. God caused Noah to build the ark with only one window. That window was in the top of the ark. He did not want Noah to look around at the wild waste of the waters of judgment and death. He gave him the upward look. It is always God's will for us to look at the things above and not the circumstances around us. Paul said, "If ye then be risen with Christ, seek those things which are above" (Colossians 3:1).

When God sent Abraham out of the land of his birth to the land of promise, he was inspired to look for something much higher than the lowlands of Sodom and Gomorrah. He looked for a city which hath foundations, whose builder and maker is God" Hebrews 11:10. He had an eye for eternal things. The injunction of Hebrews 12:2 is, "Looking unto Jesus, the Author and Finisher of our faith."

I want to impress upon you that the things we see around us are all temporal and will soon pass away. God wants us to get our eyes on eternal things. We are told of the wars, pestilences, famines and earthquakes that will characterize the last days, but then we are exhorted to lift up our heads for all these things mean that the day of our redemption is drawing nigh.

161

"If I go . . . I will come again and receive you unto Myself" John 14:3. Heaven is a prepared place for a prepared people and there is only one way to be prepared for that prepared place. That is—to be found in Christ Jesus, "not having your own righteousness which is of the law but that which is through faith in Christ."

Have you put on the robe of His righteousness provided in Christ Jesus? Only so clothed will you be found worthy to attend that great marriage supper of the Lamb.

If God could speak worlds into existence in six days how much more glorious must be the place He is preparing for us in all these years since He went away. He is up there now in glory preparing a place that will go beyond all our comprehension.

When you go into your mansion all the trials of the way, all the testings and heartaches of the pilgrim journey will sink into utter insignificance. Like Paul of old you will say that these light afflictions have worked for you an exceeding and eternal weight of glory.

CHARLES E. FULLER

°o𝕴 JUNE 𝕴o°
28

How fair is thy love, my sister, my spouse! how much better is thy love than wine!
Song of Solomon 4:10.

𝖂E ARE ready enough to take mercies and blessings from the hand of God, and most surely He is ready enough to bestow them. But then we ought to remember that He looks for the loving devotion of our hearts to Him; and if we, in the freshness and ardor of other days, set out to follow Christ, give up all for Him, can we suppose for a moment that He could coldly and indifferently forego His claim upon our heart's affections? Should we like Him to do so? Could we endure the thought of its being a matter of indifference to Him whether we loved Him or not? God forbid! Yea, it should be the joy of our hearts to think that our blessed Lord seeks the loving devotion of our souls to Him; that He will not be satisfied without it; that when we wander hither and thither, He calls us back to Himself, in His own gentle, gracious, touching way.

"When, weary of His rich repast,
I've sought, alas, to rove;
He has recalled His faithless guest,
And showed His banner, Love."

Yes, His banner ever floats, bearing its own inscription upon it to win back our vagrant hearts, and remind us of the original terms. He says to us, in one way or another, as He said to Jacob, "I am the God of Bethel, where thou anointedst the pillar, and where thou vowedst a vow." Thus He deals with us, in the midst of all our wanderings, our haltings, and our stumblings. He makes us to know, that as we cannot do without His love, so neither can He do without ours. It is truly wonderful; yet it is so.

C. H. M.

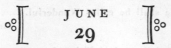

JUNE 29

He that winneth souls is wise.   *Proverbs 11:30.*

ALL who were acquainted with the late General Booth are agreed that the winning of souls was one of the master passions of his life, and that he never lost an opportunity of speaking a word in season. That is borne out by an article which Mrs. Asquith contributed to the "Cornhill Magazine" some time ago, and in which she gives an interesting account of a chance interview she once had in a railway carriage with the founder of the Salvation Army. Very plainly did General Booth speak concerning the things which matter most in life, and after a while they prayed together. Then the General vainly attempted to induce his travelling companion to ride down Rotten Row in one of the Salvation Army bonnets. Before they parted he wrote in Mrs. Asquith's book: "What is life but to walk in harmony with God, to secure that disposition and character which will fit us for the enjoyments and employments and companionships of heaven, and to spend and be spent for the temporal and eternal weal of this suffering world.—William Booth."

The incident is characteristic of the man. He felt he must ever be about his Master's business, and that he must seize every chance to press home the claims of his Lord.

PAGET WILKES

Has someone seen Christ in you today?
Christian, look to your heart, I pray;
The little things you have done or said—
Did they accord with the way you prayed?
Have your thoughts been pure and words been kind?
Have you sought to have the Saviour's mind?
The world with a criticizing view
Has watched; but did it see Christ in you?

Has someone seen Christ in you today?
Christian, look to your life, I pray;
There are aching hearts and blighted souls
Being lost on sin's destructive shoals,
And perhaps of Christ their only view
May be what they see of Him in you.

163

Will they see enough to bring hope and cheer?
Look to your light! does it shine out clear?

J. Danson Smith

JUNE 30

His name shall be called Wonderful. . . .

Isaiah 9:6.

THAT little word "wonderful" has been worn pretty threadbare in these days. We speak of "a wonderful time," "a wonderful person," "a wonderful book," and apply the word to a thousand things entirely unworthy of it. But I would give the word its rightful place as set forth in God's Word. The prophet Isaiah said, concerning the Lord Jesus Christ, "His name shall be called Wonderful."

Truly He was wonderful in the way He fulfilled the many prophecies concerning Himself. "God who at sundry times and in divers manners spake in time past unto the fathers by the prophets" (Hebrews 1:1) spoke to Abraham and provided a nation through which our Lord should come. Then He spoke to Jacob and revealed the chosen tribe of the Saviour's ancestry, the tribe of Judah (Genesis 49:10). There must also be a family, so to Isaiah He made known that it should be of Jesse. To Micah He whispered the name of the birthplace, Bethlehem. Through Daniel He made known the time of Jesus' birth (Daniel 9:25). In Malachi He spoke of the forerunner, John the Baptist, and in Jonah He set forth a picture of our Lord's resurrection. And when the Christ came, He fulfilled to the letter all these predictions. Truly that is wonderful!

Vance Havner

JULY
1

For whom He did foreknow, He also did predesti-
nate to be conformed to the image of His Son,
that he might be the firstborn among many
brethren.   *Romans 8:29.*

PERHAPS the simplest definition of a Christian is "one who is
Christlike." All that is essential to being a Christian is contained in this one law: Be Christlike. But there is a grave danger that we will misunderstand this law; and still graver danger that
we will not interpret it according to the teachings of the Word of God,
or that we will adulterate its significance and meaning. Nevertheless
we believe that when these words are rightly understood they are the
simplest and most adequate definition of a Christian that can be given.

Observe that in the heart of this passage there is set forth, as the
divine ideal for the redeemed, the being "conformed to the image of
His Son."

Man was made in the likeness and image of God. Through sin, he
lost that image; through redemption, it is God's purpose to restore
that image to him. That is why Jesus came into the world—to make
us like Himself. Furthermore, Jesus taught His disciples that they
should be like Him. "Learn of Me," "follow Me," "be like Me"—this
was the heart of His teaching.

Christ came that men might have life, and that they might "have
it more abundantly"—life here and now, as well as hereafter. And
His own life, character, mode of thought and way of living, give to
men a universal example of what they ought to be. It is this person,
this life, which is the distinctive possession of Christianity. A Christian is a Christlike person.

HOWARD W. FERRIN

JULY
2

Be not afraid . . . for I am with thee to deliver
thee, saith the Lord.   *Jeremiah 1:8.*

LIFE is a journey. It is a trip through a strange land where you
have never been before, and you never know a moment ahead
where you are going next. Strange languages, strange scenes,
strange dilemmas; new tangles, new experiences, and some old ones
with new faces so you do not know them. It is just as chock-full of
pleasure and enjoyment as it can be, if you could only make some

provision for the drudgery and hard things that seem to crowd in so thick and fast sometimes, as to make people forget the gladness of it.

Now I have something to tell you that seems too utterly good to be believed, and yet keeps getting better all the way along. It is this: the Master has planned that your life journey shall be a personally conducted one on this ideal plan. He has arranged with His best friend, who is an experienced traveler, to go with you and devote Himself wholly to your interests.

Some of you, I am afraid, will smile, and think that I am just indulging in a fancy sketch—drawing on my imagination. And so I pray our Master to burn into our hearts that it is plain, matter-of-fact truth, for every day life. I would say that it is cold fact were it not that such a fact can never be cold.

S. D. GORDON.

No distant Lord have I, loving afar to be;
Made flesh for me—He cannot rest, until He rests in me.
Brother in joy or pain; Bone of my bone was He,
Now with me closer still—He dwells Himself in me.

I need not journey far this distant Friend to see;
Companionship is always mine, He makes His home with me.
I envy not the twelve; nearer to me is He,
The life He once lived here on earth He lives again in me.

Ascended now to God, my witness there to be;
His witness here am I, because His Spirit dwells in me.
O glorious Son of God! incarnate Deity!
I shall forever be with Thee because Thou art with me.

MALTBIE BABCOCK

JULY 3

Having therefore, brethren, boldness to enter into the holiest by the blood of Jesus, by a new and living way, which He hath consecrated for us, through the veil, that is to say, His flesh . . . let us draw near with a true heart in full assurance of faith.   *Hebrews 10:19-22.*

LUKE the Physician in the beautiful prologue to his Gospel records a gracious declaration of the Spirit. It is that Christ, "the Dayspring from on high, hath visited us . . . to guide our feet into the way of peace" (1:79). It was peace with God that primal man lost at the fall, for enmity as well as sin had entered his heart, and for these he was driven out of Eden. The whole after-revelation from God is mainly occupied with the making again of a

"Way of Peace." This was done by the One who so graphically declared: "I am the Way . . . no man cometh unto the Father but by Me."

Years later as the result of the supreme sacrifice of the Son of God on Calvary, the writer to the Hebrews exhorts us to "draw near" again to God, by a "new and living way" (11:20). Here he is inspired to use a special word only twice found in Scripture. For the word "new" in the text is a translation of the Greek word "prosphatos," which literally means "newly-slain" (Young). Thus it is literally a "newly-slain and living way."

We are therefore to infer, not that this is a way later than Moses' Law, but that it is a newly-slain, and therefore a recently made way. In confirmation of this thought, John peering into heaven (Revelation 5:6) for the Lion of the tribe of Judah, still sees "a Lamb as it had been slain" (sphatto). What a wonderful combination, "a newly-slain yet living way!"

"Newly-slain" brings to mind Luther's delighted exclamation when first the truth of justification by faith was revealed to him. Ascending the Scala Sancta in Rome on his knees to acquire merit, this great truth suddenly burst upon him. Rising to his feet he cried delightedly, in his new-found peace and joy: "Why, Calvary seems as if it were only yesterday!" And that is a profound truth. As an historical event we human beings with our limitations of time and space, date Calvary nineteen hundred years ago and place it upon the Green Hill. Yet as a moral event, it has no date! Actually Christ was slain in the mind and plan of God "before the foundation of the world." Thus morally the event is as near to us as it was to the dying thief.

NORTHCOTE DECK

JULY 4

In that last day, that great day of the feast, Jesus stood and cried, saying, If any man thirst, let him come unto Me, and drink.   *John 7:37.*

UNDERLINE three words and you will have the points of my message. "Thirst." "Come." "Drink." It is so simple that any boy or girl can understand.

The Feast of Tabernacles was about to close. Those who had attended were about to go back to their farms, to their merchandise, to their places of business. It would be the last time that Jesus would look into their faces before His crucifixion. Whereas it was His usual custom to sit and teach; here, because of the urgency of the occasion, we find Him standing. As He stood He cried out this wonderful gospel message. Oh, how the Son of God pleaded with them as He said, "If any man thirst, let him come unto Me and drink."

If any man,—whether high or low, rich or poor, prince or peasant, down in the gutter of sin or up in the four hundred,—has a desire for freedom from the bondage of sin, that desire is the thirst of which Jesus spoke. How tragic it is that many do not seem to "thirst." They seem utterly careless and indifferent. But if a man "thirst" there is hope. Jesus says, "Come to Me; I will quench that thirst."

He is saying to you, today, "Him that cometh unto Me I will in no wise cast out." "Behold, I stand at the door, and knock: if any man hear My voice, and open the door, I will come in to him, and sup with him, and he with Me."

CHARLES E. FULLER

> Into my heart, empty and waiting,
> Over my soul, needy and still,
> Through my whole being, consuming and purging,
> Sweep Thou, until—
> Thou shalt see through my eyes,
> Think through my brain,
> Love through my heart,
> Then, speak through my lips,
> All of my being merging in Thine,
> Holy Spirit divine.
> Now, filled with the source of all beauty and power
> Renewed life is mine,
> Flowing within me each day and hour
> From the Divine.
>
> MIRIAM REED

JULY 5

... stablished in the faith ... abounding therein with thanksgiving. *Colossians* 2:7.

NOT every one is established in the faith. They do have a standing in grace. But standing is not establishment. It has its feet on the rock, but they are not firm. It is based on truth; but the truth is not clearly apprehended and gripped. We must both hold the truth and hold by the truth if we are to be established in the faith. How safe is the man who is so established! No storm can disturb: no enemies vex: no critics of the cross shake his faith. They pass him by as does "the idle wind which he esteems not." "I fear no foe with Thee at hand to bless," says the hymn. And the man that does not fear is the man that best can fight the good fight of faith. He fights in faith, and he fights for more faith. Faith grows as I fight

168

for it and fight in it. I am apprehended of God as I apprehend Him. And His hold of me is firmer than my hold of Him.

When I look at my life and count up my blessings, how many they are! Why am I so favored? Why am I born into a land of such knowledge and light and forward civilization? Why was I not born a Zulu or a Mohammedan?

It is all of grace and not of merit. Lord Jesus, to Thee I owe it. Fill me with gratitude. Help me to abound in thanksgiving.

W. S. BRUCE

> I need not fear, since One is with me
> Who can quiet all alarms;
> I need not fear, for underneath me
> Are "the everlasting arms."
>
> Always the arms are there, outreaching,
> Strong to succor and uphold,
> And, should I fall, would bear me upward,
> In their warm embrace enfold.
>
> What comfort does this thought afford me!
> What assurance, to believe,
> When my frail arms can hold no longer,
> His are waiting to receive!
>
> Eternal God, Thou art my refuge!
> Mine is now the rest of faith,
> For whatsoever can befall me,
> Thy strong arms are underneath.

T. O. CHISHOLM

JULY 6

For they that are after the flesh do mind the things of the flesh; but they that are after the Spirit the things of the Spirit. *Romans 8:5.*

THESE two are deadly enemies. The Cross desires to condemn and put to death "the flesh." "The flesh" desires to cast aside and conquer the Cross. Many, as they hear of the Cross as the indispensable preparation for the fullness of the Holy Spirit, will find out what there is in them which must yet be crucified. We must understand that our entire nature is sentenced to death, and become dead, by the Cross, so that the new life in Christ may come to rule in us. We must obtain such an insight into the fallen condition of our nature and its enmity against God, that we become willing, nay desirous, to be wholly freed from it.

169

We must learn to say with Paul: "In me, that is in my flesh, dwelleth no good thing." "The mind of the flesh is enmity against God: it is not subject to the law of God, neither indeed can be." It is its very essence to hate God and His holy law. This is the wonder of redemption, that Christ has borne on the Cross the judgment and curse of God on "the flesh," and has forever nailed it to the cursed tree. If a man only believes God's Word about this "cursed mind of the flesh," and then longs to be delivered from it, he learns to love the Cross as his deliverer from the power of the enemy.

"Our old man is crucified" with Christ, and our one hope is to receive this by faith, and to hold it fast. "They that are Christ's have crucified the flesh." They have willingly declared that they will daily regard "the flesh" which is in them as the enemy of God, the enemy of Christ, the enemy of their soul's salvation, and will treat it as having received its deserved reward in being nailed to the Cross.

This is one part of the eternal redemption which Christ has brought to us. It is not something which we can grasp with our understanding or accomplish with our strength. It is something which the Lord Jesus Himself will give us if we are willing to abide in His fellowship day by day, and to receive everything from Him. It is something which the Holy Spirit will teach us, and He will impart it to us as an experience, and will show how He can give victory in the power of the Cross over all that is of the flesh.

ANDREW MURRAY

JULY
7

My grace is sufficient for thee: for My strength is
made perfect in weakness.   *2 Corinthians 12:9.*

THE Saviour told the Apostle in effect: "Paul, don't worry about the thorn; don't be distracted by the pain that prods you incessantly. For I have something so glorious that you can forget your bleeding heart and body. I give you My grace, and 'My grace is sufficient for thee.' If you have My grace, nothing else is decisive in life; all problems are solved; all burdens lightened."

How we thank God that it is given to us to repeat for questioning, discouraged men and women across the broad reaches of America this saving pronouncement of Christ: "My grace is sufficient" for you, for every one who comes to that Christ for forgiveness.

As we ask the Holy Spirit of God to implant this pledge from Jesus' own lips on your heart, stop to think of the indescribable riches involved in the short, much-used but often misunderstood word "grace." You can find fifteen definitions for this word in your dictionaries, but when you speak of Jesus Christ and His grace, only one all-inclusive meaning remains: the unmerited love of that Saviour for us despite our sinful hearts and lives; the unending devotion that existed before the foundation of the world and that will exist undiminished after this earth crumbles to pieces; the immeasurable compassion which brought Jesus from the realms of glory and the adoration of the angels to this vice-bound earth so that He might take my place and yours and, bearing our sins in His holy and sinless body, bring us back to God and bless us with the sure seal of our salvation.

This grace of Christ is not a friendly interest, a condescending smile, a tolerant overlooking of human faults and frailties; it is the mightiest power in heaven and earth—the grace of His human birth, the grace of His life of love and service, the grace of His suffering, wounding, bleeding, dying, the grace that promises our souls everything, yet for our salvation demands nothing, that is all Christ's and in no part ours.

WALTER A. MAIER

JULY 8

Behold, now is the accepted time; behold, now is the day of salvation.   *2 Corinthians 6:2.*

To HEAR that people are being deeply convicted of sin by listening to Mr. Fuller's program is no new thing, but to hear of conviction so powerful that sinners seek through the town for someone to pray with them is unusual. God is doing unusual things in these days. The day of miracles is not past. Here is the story of a miracle in Kentucky.

"*Dear Mr. Fuller*: A few months ago a man and his wife near here who had been on a drinking party tuned in on your program after they returned home. As they prepared for bed they had a bottle of whiskey on the bedside table. They listened to your message and came under deep conviction of sin. Finally they dressed again and went to a friend's house to ask him to pray with them. The man was not at home so they came to our church just as we were being dismissed. Our pastor and his brother prayed with them and they accepted Christ. They joined our church the following Sunday."

Doubtless there are many thousands today who are sin-sick and dissatisfied, yet they rarely hear a gospel message because they do not attend church. Radio is about the only means they possess of hearing the Gospel. How important it is that messages like the Old Fashioned Revival Hour continue to go out.

Pray that gospel broadcasting will not be restricted. Pray especially that there will be no lack of means from week to week to keep the message on the air.

JULY 9

If we suffer, we shall also reign with Him.
2 Timothy 2:12.

OUR testimony for Jesus Christ must never depend upon a congenial atmosphere. Eloquence in the prayer-meeting is a poor substitute for dumbness in the workshop. It is where Satan's seat is, where the atmosphere is hot with the breath of blasphemy that our protest against ungodliness is the most vital and effective. Yet how difficult it is to display the badge of Christ in the midst of His most virulent foes!

The insistent temptation which besets us all is to hide our lamp under a bushel, and to seek our own ease by refusing to acknowledge our allegiance to Him. And all the while, in our heart of hearts, we know that that is the shameful coward's course. For such pusillanimity there is only one possible cure. It is in the firm, vigorous, unswerving resolve to follow the Christ, the King; to go straight on, though all hell erects its barricades and seeks to arrest our progress; to shirk no burden, to refuse no battle, but gladly to share the travail which makes His Kingdom come. Take your share of hardship like good soldiers of Jesus Christ. Whether men frown or smile, congratulate or condemn, matters not one jot or tittle. We can live without the applause of men so long as we carry the consciousness of the approbation of the King of kings.

R. Moffat Gautry

Am I a soldier of the cross,
A follower of the Lamb,
And shall I fear to own His cause,
Or blush to speak His name?

Isaac Watts

Then was Jesus led up of the spirit into the wilderness to be tempted of the devil. *Matthew 4:1.*

THE Lord Himself met and foiled Satan after first being filled with the Spirit. And no child of God has ever been victorious over the adversary unless empowered from the same source. Our Lord did not permit His chosen followers to witness a word in His name until endued with power from on high. It is true that before that day they were the "born again" children of the Father and had the witness of the Spirit. But they were not the Lord's efficient co-workers and never could be until Spirit-filled. The divine empowering is for us as well as for them. We, too, may do the works which our Lord did, yea, and greater works.

The Scriptures convey no other meaning to me than that the Lord Jesus Christ planned that the Holy Spirit should continue among us in as mighty manifestation as at Pentecost. One should be able to chase a thousand and two put ten thousand to flight—as of old. Time has not changed the fact that "Jesus Christ is the same yesterday, and today, and forever." "But will it last?" How constantly unbelief puts this question. Of course, the work will last if man is faithful. When the blood-bought servants of Christ yield Him absolute dominion, all the resources of the Godhead are in operation for the glory of the Lamb which was slain.

JONATHAN GOFORTH

Hover o'er me, Holy Spirit;
Bathe my trembling heart and brow;
Fill me with Thy hallowed presence,
Come, oh, come and fill me now.

Thou can'st fill me, gracious Spirit,
Though I cannot tell Thee how;
But I need Thee, greatly need Thee;
Come, oh, come and fill me now.

I am weakness, full of weakness;
At Thy sacred feet I bow:
Blest, divine, eternal Spirit,
Fill with power, and fill me now.

E. H. STOKES

And every man went unto his own house. Jesus
went to the Mount of Olives. *John 7:53; 8:1.*

WONDER if you ever caught the significance of these two verses.
The people to whom He ministered had homes. But He had nowhere to lay His head. He, the Son of God, owned no home down
here. He became the poorest of the poor to make us rich. The Gospels
constantly bring out the contrast of His deity and His humiliation. On
one hand we see His peerless excellency and on the other the depth
of shame to which He descended. He reminds us that "the foxes have
holes and the birds of the air have nests but the Son of Man hath not
where to lay His head" (Matthew 8:20). We see Him by the well at
Samaria, wearied with His journey and thirsty for a drink of water.
He was weary that we might have rest in Him. He was thirsty that He
might bring to the world the Water of Life.

CHARLES E. FULLER

God's bitter cup of righteous wrath,
For sinning souls reserved,
He drank for me—the sinless One—
The cup that I deserved.

That I might take salvation's cup
Now freely offered me,
And thankful drink to thirst no more
Through all eternity.

MAUD E. CRAMER

And this is the blessing, wherewith Moses the man
of God blessed the children of Israel before his
death. *Deuteronomy 33:1.*

MOST men have large undeveloped resources and endowments.
Many of us are one-sided in our development. We are strangers
to the real possible self within, unconscious of some of the
powers with which we are endowed and intrusted. The Holy Spirit,
when given a free hand, works out the fullness of the life that has
been put in. The change will not be in the sort but in the size, and
that not by an addition but by a growth of what is there.

Moses complains that he is slow of speech and of a slow tongue. God does not promise a new tongue but that He will be with him and train his tongue. Listen to him forty years after in the Moab Plains, as with brain fired, and tongue loosened and trained he gives that series of farewell talks fairly burning with eloquence. Students of oratory can find no nobler specimens than Deuteronomy furnishes.

S. D. GORDON

> *I saw a human life ablaze with God,*
> *I felt a power divine*
> *As through an empty vessel of frail clay*
> *I saw God's glory shine.*
> *Then woke I from a dream, and cried aloud:*
> *"My Father give to me*
> *The blessing of a life consumed by God,*
> *That I may live for Thee."*

AUTHOR UNKNOWN

JULY 13

Whatsoever ye shall ask in My name, that will I do, that the Father may be glorified in the Son.
John 14:13.

IN HIS name. In the case of an earthly petitioner there are some pleas more influential in obtaining a boon than others. Jesus speaks of this as forming the key to the heart of God. As David loved the helpless cripple of Saul's house "for Jonathan's sake," so will the Father, by virtue of our covenant relationship to the true Jonathan (lit. "gift of God"), delight in giving us even "exceeding abundantly above all that we can ask or think."

Reader, do you know the blessedness of confiding your every want and every care, your every sorrow and every cross, into the ear of the Saviour? He is the "Wonderful, Counsellor." With an exquisitely tender sympathy He can enter into the innermost depths of your need. That need may be great, but the everlasting arms are underneath it all. Think of Him—at this moment—the great Angel of the Covenant, with the censer full of incense, in which are placed your feeblest aspirations, your most burdened sighs—the odor-breathing clouds ascending with acceptance before the Father's throne. The answer may tarry; these, your supplications, may be kept long on the wing, hovering around the mercy seat. A gracious God sometimes sees it meet thus to test the faith and patience of His people. He delights to hear the music of their importunate pleadings, to see them undeterred by difficulties, unrepelled by apparent forgetfulness and

175

neglect. But He will come at last; the pent-up fountain of love and mercy will at length burst out; the soothing accents will in His own time be heard, "Be it unto thee according to thy word."

J. R. MACDUFF

JULY 14

Jesus wept. *John 11:35.*

How wonderful! The Son of God groaned and wept. Let us never forget it. He, though God over all, blessed forever; though the Resurrection and the Life; though the Quickener of the dead; though the Conqueror of the grave; though on His way to deliver the body of His friend from the grasp of the enemy—sample of what He will soon do for all who belong to Him—yet, so perfectly did He enter into human sorrow, and take in all the terrible consequences of sin, all the misery and desolation of this sin-stricken world, that He groaned and wept! And those tears and groans emanated from the depths of a perfect human heart that felt as only a perfect human heart could feel—felt according to God—for every form of human sorrow and misery. Though perfectly exempt, in His own divine person, from sin and all its consequences—yea, because exempt—He could in perfect grace enter into it all and make it His own as only He could do.

"Jesus wept!" Wondrous, significant fact! He wept not for Himself, but for others. He wept with them. Mary wept. The Jews wept. All this is easily grasped and understood. But that Jesus should weep reveals a mystery which we cannot fathom. It was divine compassion weeping through human eyes over the desolation which sin had caused in this poor world, weeping in sympathy with those whose hearts had been crushed by the inexorable hand of death.

Let all who are in sorrow remember this. Jesus is the same yesterday, today and forever. His circumstances are changed, but His heart is not. His position is different, but His sympathy is the same. "We have not an high priest that can not be touched with the feeling of our infirmities, but was in all points tempted like we are, apart from sin."

C. H. M.

Whose adorning let it not be that outward adorning . . . but let it be the hidden man of the heart.

1 Peter 3:3.

WITH Christ the outward counts for little; the inward counts for much. The first may beautify the person; the second beautifies the personality. The plaiting of the hair is not to be despised for "a woman's glory is in her head." The wearing of gold and goodly apparel may have justification; but the head is more to be thought of than the hair; the clothing of the character with righteousness more than the clothing of the body with fine raiment.

Miss Charlotte Elliot expressed this in words which abide:

> "I want that adorning divine
>   That only my God can bestow;
> I want in those beautiful garments to shine,
>   That mark out Thy Household below."

There can be no ornament so beautiful as that of a meek and quiet spirit. No signet ring can compare with the seal of Christ on the forehead of the Christian. Better far to be clothed with the comeliness of humility than with "garments spotted by the flesh" or of Babylonish make.

If we possess the Indwelling Spirit we shall care little about the house we inhabit or the dress we wear. The one is of primary importance: the other of secondary consideration. The second is merely quantitative; the first is qualitative, and concerns the hidden man of the heart.

The one simply glorifies the body; the other gives glory and value to the soul.

Let us pray for the plenitude of the Spirit within, and think less about plenty in the world without. That will not prevent due attention to our office and our business; it will give uplift and reality to both. The Christian man will be dutiful, careful, attentive, conscientious just because he has learned fidelity to his conscience and justice to his fellowmen. The exterior of life is wholly colored by the interior. Beauty of face in a woman is very charming; but the beauty of holiness is more charming still. The one may endure for life's brief span; the other will endure throughout all the long ages of Eternity.

May the comeliness of Christ be put upon us, and then we shall comply with Isaiah's counsel, "Arise, shine, for thy light is come, and the glory of the Lord has risen upon thee." Lord, make all Thy children to shine.

W. S. BRUCE

When thou wast under the fig tree, I saw thee.

John 1:48.

𝔍 s a w thee." And how much the seeing means! The phrase has infinitely more significance than that of bare recognition. It is not only that Nathaniel was noticed; it means that he was understood. Our Lord's sight is insight. The majority of us see, but only a few perceive. "See ye, indeed, but perceive not." We see a sign, but we cannot give it an interpretation. We see a wrinkle, a grey hair, a tear, a smile, a look of care, a bent back, but we do not perceive their spiritual significance. Our Master not only sees; He "in-sees." When He looked at Nathaniel He understood him. He interpreted his thoughts and fears. He saw him through and through.

The Master knew what was in man. But His seeing implies more than this. It is not only that sight was insight; His perceptions were compassions. He was "touched" with the feelings of men's infirmities. He did not bring to bear upon men the mere dry light of understanding; the light was warm and genial, and sunny with the grace of sympathy. The apostolic word is very beautiful; He was "touched." But the sight means even more than this. The understanding and the sympathy were joined to the ministry of co-operation. The Master not only feels, He works; He not only sympathizes, He serves. When He saw Nathaniel under the fig tree, His understanding, His sympathy, His power, all combined in a ministry of benevolent and beneficent love.

J. H. Jowett

Truly our fellowship is with the Father, and with His Son Jesus Christ.   *1 John 1:3.*

𝔇 o n o t depend upon the fellowship of meetings, happy and blessed as that is. Do not depend upon your busy activity, important as that is. Do not depend upon your "quiet times," though they are absolutely essential. One is coming to see more and more the danger of divorcing good things from the Person of the Lord Jesus Christ Himself.

I would raise the red flag of danger and urge young Christians not to depend upon things, however good in themselves they may be, for the maintenance of their spiritual fullness. It is not in things, which after all are of so little value, but in Him who upholdeth all things by His power.

CAPTAIN REGINALD WALLIS

> LESS, less of self each day,
> And more, my God, of Thee;
> Oh, keep me in Thy way,
> However rough it be!
>
> Less of the flesh each day,
> Less of the world and sin;
> More of Thy love, I pray,
> More of Thyself within.
>
> Riper and riper now,
> Each hour let me become;
> Less fond of things below,
> More fit for such a home.
>
> More moulded to Thy will,
> Lord, let Thy servant be;
> Higher and higher still,
> Nearer and nearer Thee.

AUTHOR UNKNOWN

JULY 18

One thing I know—that I was once blind and that now I can see.   *John 9:25 (Weymouth).*

THIS story of the blind man has all the elements of a good short story: it is right to the point and it is full of human interest. The blind man was unable to see Jesus, but we read that Jesus saw him. He had compassion on him and anointed his eyes with clay, then directed him to go and wash in the pool of Siloam. In a short time he returned, seeing.

Some of you have been wondering how to be saved. This will help you if you will listen carefully. In the thirty-eighth verse we read that the healed blind man said, "Lord, I believe," and worshipped Him. By the way, the key that unlocks John's Gospel is this: "These things are written that ye might believe that Jesus is the Christ, the Son of God; and that believing ye might have life through His name" (John 20:31).

In the healing of the blind man light was communicated to him. Jesus had just been saying, "I am the light of the world." Light dispels darkness. The Pharisees, in chapter eight, rejected the light but the blind man received it and worshipped.

Some of you who read this are no doubt in darkness, unable to see your spiritual condition before God. But Jesus, as of old, is passing by. He sees your condition and knows your spiritual need. He will heal your blindness if you will only believe and obey Him as the blind man did.

God wants you to realize that every man, and that includes you, who has been born into this world, is spiritually blinded. Listen to God's Word for it tells your condition without salvation: "Having the understanding darkened, being alienated from the life of God through the ignorance that is in them, because of the blindness of their heart" (Ephesians 4:18).

The blind man was given direction to do just one thing, wash in the pool of Siloam. He was not told to do twenty or thirty things—just one. Water is a type of the Word. "Ye are clean through the Word."

So, friend of mine, be simple enough to take God at His word today and your blindness will be healed. "Believe on the Lord Jesus Christ, and thou shalt be saved."

CHARLES E. FULLER

JULY
19

Jesus said unto him, If thou canst believe, all things are possible to him that believeth. And straightway the father of the child cried out, and said with tears, Lord, I believe; help Thou mine unbelief.
Mark 9:23, 24.

LISTEN to this, you who are often so helpless that you do not know what to do. At times you do not even know how to pray. Your mind seems full of sin and impurity. Your mind is preoccupied with what the Bible calls "the world." God and eternal and holy things seem so distant and foreign to you that you feel that you add sin to sin by desiring to approach God in such a state of mind. Now and then you must ask yourself the question, "Do I really desire to be set free from the lukewarmness of my heart and my worldly life? Is not my Christian life always lukewarm and half-hearted for the simple reason that deep down in my heart I desire it that way?"

Thus an honest soul struggles against the dishonesty of his own being. He feels himself so helplessly lost that his prayers freeze on his very lips.

Listen, my friend! Your helplessness is your best prayer. It calls from your heart to the heart of God with greater effect than all your uttered pleas. He hears it from the very moment that you are seized with helplessness, and He becomes actively engaged at once in hearing and answering the prayer of your helplessness. He hears today as He heard the helpless and wordless prayer of the man sick with the palsy.

If you are a mother, you will understand very readily this phase of prayer.

Your infant child cannot formulate in words a single petition to you. Yet the little one prays the best way he knows how. All he can do is to cry, but you understand very well his pleading.

Moreover, the little one need not even cry. All you need to do is to see him in all his helpless dependence upon you, and a prayer touches your mother-heart, a prayer which is stronger than the loudest cry.

O. Hallesby

JULY 20

A new heart also will I give you. *Ezekiel 36:26.*

WE HAVE treated the forgiveness of sins, or the purging of the conscience, as being part of the salvation provided for us of God through Christ. Strictly speaking, however, it would be more correct to describe it as the doorway leading thereinto. Salvation itself is the entire renewal of the heart—regeneration—a new creation in Christ Jesus.

When Nicodemus came to Christ, assured that he knew at least something about the Saviour, viz., that He was a teacher, the Lord quickly undeceived him by telling him that in effect He was no such thing. He was a witness in the first place, and a Saviour in the second. A teacher instructs with theory, premise, and syllogism. A witness tells what he has seen and heard. Nicodemus, like all of his kind, was unprepared to take the *ipse dixit* of the witness, or come as a sinner to the Saviour.

In that wonderful conversation that followed, the Lord answered for every seeker, and for all time, the four greatest questions that the human heart can ever ask: What is it to be saved? How can a man be saved? Why can men be saved? Who can be saved?

To these queries the Lord replies in order—Salvation is the New Birth—the work of the Holy Spirit. That is *what* it is. Salvation can only be procured through the Cross—the work of God the Son. That is *how* it is. Salvation is possible only because God so loved the world that He gave His only Son—the work of God the Father. That is *why* it is. Any sinner that will come to the light and believe can be saved. That is the *who* of the matter.

Paget Wilkes

This book of the law shall not depart out of thy mouth; but thou shalt meditate therein day and night, that thou mayest observe to do according to all that is written therein: for then thou shalt make thy way prosperous, and then thou shalt have good success.   *Joshua 1:8.*

IT IS useless to dream of making headway in the knowledge of Scripture unless we are prepared to practice each new and clearly-defined duty which looms out before our view. We are taught, not for our pleasure only, but that we may do. If we will turn each holy precept or command into instant obedience, through the dear grace of Jesus Christ our Lord, God will keep nothing back from us; He will open to us His deepest and sweetest thoughts. But so long as we refuse obedience to even the least command, we shall find that the light will fade from the page of Scripture, and the zest will die down quickly in our own hearts.

F. B. MEYER

I love Thy will, O God!
Thy blessed, perfect will,
In which this once rebellious heart
Lies satisfied and still.

I love Thy will, O God!
It is my joy, my rest;
It glorifies my common task,
It makes each trial blest.

I love Thy will, O God!
The sunshine or the rain;
Some days are bright with praise, and some
Sweet with accepted pain.

I love Thy will, O God!
O hear my earnest plea,
That as Thy will is done in heaven
It may be done in me!

BESSIE PEGG MACLAUGHLIN

The publican . . . smote upon his breast, saying,
God be merciful to me a sinner.   *Luke 18:13.*

ERE is a story of great need—and great conviction. It is typical
of hundreds of letters that are received by Mr. Fuller, who has
gained the trust of many who have been in great sin. Did this
man and his wife really find Christ? We trust so. Salvation for such
needy sinners depends on your prayers as well as the preaching of
the old-time Gospel.

"*Dear Mr. Fuller*: The blunt truth is, I am a sinner. In my
present state I have no hope of heaven or peace of mind in this
world. I know only too well the sin-cursed life I have led for
almost the entire forty-six years of my life. It has included almost
everything—drinking, gambling, and one murder. But for the
prayers of Christian people I would now have two lives to answer
for instead of one.

"My whole life has been cursed and warped by an insane,
uncontrollable temper. Mr. Fuller, believe me, only God can
know how heart-sick and tired I am of this kind of life. I have
heard both you and Mrs. Fuller say so many times that the Lord
can and will forgive—can clean up a life even as wicked as my
own. I have always had a horror of professing to have forgiveness when maybe I haven't it. Surely one will know definitely
when they are truly forgiven.

"I have a wife, Mr. Fuller, that I care for more than anything
in this world. While she is not a Christian girl she is so patient
and understanding. We were talking the other night of how much
more we would be getting out of life if we could just get right
with God. I do so want both of us to live in such a way that we
will have the assurance when death parts us that we will know it
will only be until we meet again over there in the morning.

"I have a mother who is nearly eighty years old. She has spent
many hours in prayer for me, as did my dad. Surely these prayers
will be answered. Please won't you intercede for both my wife and
myself with God."

Pray that God shall raise up a great host of prayer warriors who
will pray prevailingly for these hard cases. Pray that this couple, and
many others like them, may be saved.

As for me and my house, we will serve the Lord.
Joshua 24:15.

AMERICAN fathers particularly must realize that they should be the priests and spiritual leaders of the church in their homes. When scoffing voices are repeatedly raised against fatherhood; when many men nightly seek distraction outside their home, neglect or abuse their wife and children, we must consider that, in the first instance, God has entrusted the direction of the affairs of the home to the father and holds him responsible for its conduct. The Old Testament told the Hebrew father, "When thou buildest a new house, thou shalt make a battlement for thy roof that thou bring not blood upon thine house if any man fall from thence."

It was customary for the Palestinian family to assemble, particularly after sundown, on the flat roof; and in order to protect the members of the family from falling off the roof and bringing blood upon the house, retaining walls had to be erected. With our changed architecture the necessity of these safety provisions is eliminated. Lest fathers bring a far greater loss, the destruction of human souls, upon their conscience; lest they become guilty of driving their own flesh and blood away from Christ, they must erect a high spiritual wall, the protection of God's Word, to keep the members of their household from falling into the destruction of unforgiven sins.

Every father who now hears these words should realize that he needs Christ for himself, for his own family priesthood, for the direction of his home; and as Abraham, the father of the faithful, erected altars and "called upon the name of the Lord" wherever he went, so you fathers must first of all erect the family altar within the four walls of your own home and call "upon the name of the Lord" in the church within your home.

When a demoniac was once healed by the miraculous word of Jesus, the Saviour demanded that he return to his home and there recount the miracle of his healing; and just as soon as any of you have found the Saviour and know with a living, vibrant faith what He means to you, you will not rest until your home becomes a church.

WALTER A. MAIER

It shall be told thee what thou must do. *Acts 9:6.*

O N T H E Damascus road it was that Paul became a child of God by the new birth, and received his call and commission to be God's servant from then on. And in the third sentence he heard that day from heaven there sounded the compelling word of which he was to know so much in all his after life: "It shall be told thee what thou must do." And that same word needs to come much into our lives as well.

This same little peremptory word "must" came early into the Saviour's life. His first recorded sentence contains it: "Wist ye not that I must be about My Father's business?" So He cried to His parents; and this was indeed the truest keynote of His whole earthly life and ministry. For of Him, the Creator of all things, it was truly said, "Even Christ pleased not Himself," but, as He explained, "I do nothing of Myself . . . for I do always those things that please Him." And as "the disciple . . . shall be as his Master," into Paul's Christian life too, there came at once this same commanding word: "What thou must do."

Yet in this lawless, pleasure-seeking age, such a word, such an idea, becomes increasingly unpopular and distasteful; the self in us rebels against any idea of control or compulsion; we do not like to be "under authority," and duty seems dull and intolerable! How much pleasanter to do only what we like, what we want to do! Yet how fatal! For if this tremendous "must" of the will of God has not and does not come early into our lives, to control our actions, and guide our steps, we shall be like rudderless ships, and must make final shipwreck of our lives.

NORTHCOTE DECK

**For the law of the Spirit of life in Christ Jesus
hath made me free from the law of sin and death.**
Romans 8:2.

T H E seventh chapter of Romans shows us the futility of trying to lead a Christian life through our own effort. Paul acknowledged that he was carnal, sold under sin. Notice how many times in this chapter he used the word "I." Paul was saying, "I want to lead a Christian life; I want to do God's will; I want to be fruitful—but I

185

can't do it. I find that there is a law working within me that brings me down when I would rise. I am in bondage when I want to be free." And then he said, "O wretched man that I am, who shall deliver me from the body of this death?"

In contrast, when we get over into the eighth chapter, we find him talking about the Spirit instead of himself. The word "Spirit" occurs twenty-eight times in just a few verses. Here is the secret: "The law of the Spirit of life in Christ Jesus hath made me free from the law of sin and death" (Romans 8:2).

In our physical world the law of gravitation is always at work with its downward pull. But the power of the sun, sweeping over the ocean, pulls the water upward and overcomes the law of gravitation. There are two laws at work, the upward pull of the sun and the downward pull of gravitation.

And so, in the spiritual realm, the moment I fully yield myself and reckon that I am dead unto sin I find that I am instantly made free from the law of sin and death. The lack of this knowledge is the reason why so many church members go on, year in and year out, defeated and discouraged. Notice in the twenty-sixth verse of the eighth chapter how the Spirit helps us in our infirmities and weakness, making intercession for us. "He that searcheth the hearts knoweth what is the mind of the Spirit, because He maketh intercession for the saints according to the will of God" (Romans 8:27).

CHARLES E. FULLER

JULY 26

Commit thy works unto the Lord, and thy thoughts shall be established. *Proverbs 16:3.*

IT IS one thing to work for God; it is another to have God work through us. We are often eager for the former; God is always desirous of doing the latter. One of the important facts in the surrender of the life is that it is the attitude which gives God the chance to work His perfect will through us. For it is God that is working to evangelize the world; it is God who has laid the plans for it; it is God who has the power to successfully execute them. Now the God who is the ruler of the universe does not want us to plan, and worry, and work for Him. For while He appreciates our purposes toward Him, yet they may be all athwart His purposes for and through us. What He wants is not our plans, but our lives, that He may work His plans through us.

JAMES H. McCONKEY

Cease your thinking, troubled Christian,
What avails your anxious cares;

God is ever thinking for you,
Jesus every burden bears.
Casting all your care upon Him,
Sink into His blessed will;
While He folds you to His bosom,
Sweetly whispering, "Peace be still."

How our burdens would be lightened,
Could our hearts at length be taught
At the Master's feet to bury
Every earth-born, anxious thought.
Every doubt and fear would vanish,
Every strife and conflict cease;
Love would sway a boundless empire,
O'er a realm of endless peace.

Jesus knows the way He leads me,
I have but to hold His hand;
Nothing from His thought is hidden,
Why need I to understand?
Let me, like the loved disciple,
Hide my head upon His breast;
Till upon His faithful bosom,
All my cares are hushed to rest.

A. B. SIMPSON

JULY 27

For the flesh lusteth against the Spirit, and the Spirit against the flesh: and these are contrary the one to the other. *Galatians 5:17.*

IT IS so easy to be orthodox in one's beliefs about Him and even earnest in one's labors for Him and yet not really make Him known. Sometimes in advertised places and with much-advertised persons one has expected to see the Lord and has looked in vain for marks of Calvary. Ability, enthusiasm, action, statistics, all these have appeared but flesh uncrucified has spoiled it all. For, no matter how well we know it theoretically, we are ever in danger of forgetting that the way of the cross cuts across every plan and purpose and principle of natural will and wisdom, that success with Him means failure with us, and life with Him death to us. There are many medals but few scars, and seeking our own crowns we miss His.

VANCE HAVNER

"Though He slay me," I would rest
In His sovereign will,
For the joy to feel His arms
Wrapped about me still.

"Though He slay me," I would sing
Alleluia lays;
For the Master's slaying-place
Is the gate of praise.

"Though He slay me," I would cry,
"Lord, our wills are one;
Spare or slay me as Thou wilt;
Let Thy will be done!"

"Though He slay me," yet in Him
All my soul would trust,
Not alone, because it may,
But because it must!

L. A. BENNETT

JULY 28

The natural man receiveth not the things of the
Spirit of God: for they are foolishness unto him:
neither can he know them, because they are spiritually discerned.   *1 Corinthians 2:14.*

HUMAN reasonings are begun, continued, and ended in darkness.
Man reasons about God; reasons about Christ; reasons about
Scripture; reasons about heaven, about hell, about eternity,
about all sorts of things. But all his reasonings are worse, far worse,
than worthless. Men are no more capable of understanding or appreciating the written Word now than they were of understanding or
appreciating the living Word, when He was amongst them. Indeed,
the two things must go together. As the living Word and the written
Word are one, so to know the one we must know the other; but the
natural, the unrenewed, the unconverted man knows neither. He is
totally blind, in utter darkness, dead; and when, without reality, he
makes a religious profession, he is "twice dead"—dead in nature and
dead in religion. What are his thoughts, his reasonings, his conclusions
worth? They are baseless, false, ruinous.

C. H. M.

Take my poor heart and only let me love
The things that always shall abiding prove;
Bind all my heart-strings to the world above,
And lead me in the way everlasting.

Oh, let my work abide the testing day
That shall consume the stubble and the hay;
Oh, build my house upon the rock, I pray,
And lead me in the way everlasting.

A. B. SIMPSON

188

But the day of the Lord will come. *2 Peter 3:10.*

E A R E living in a topsy turvy world. It is a world in which most of the important things and personages are out of place. We cannot expect peace and tranquility until things are put back where they belong.

SATAN is out of place. He is here in the world. He has no right here. He has become the god of this world because men love his reign of darkness rather than God's reign of light. Satan has always wanted to be worshipped as God and he is realizing his desire in greater measure today than ever before. He is at the root of all the hatreds, persecutions, murders, wars, and every form of evil. Yet he has more followers than Christ. Does Satan have a place of his own? Yes, hell is his place. Some day he will go there. Only then will the earth have peace.

MAN is out of place. He has been out of place ever since he lusted for the forbidden fruit and ate it in disobedience to God's command. Disobedience caused his banishment from the Garden. He is out of place because of that disobedience. Only reconciliation with God can bring man back to his rightful place.

CHRIST is out of place. He belongs on the throne of His father, David. God has made a proclamation appointing Christ as the ruler of all things. Listen:—"Wherefore, God hath highly exalted Him and given Him a name which is above every name, that at the name of Jesus every knee should bow" (Philippians 2:9, 10).

Because Jesus is victor over every evil force, upon His return He will put things back in their right place again. The devil will go to the lake of fire; Christ will take His place on the throne; and all men who have chosen to obey Him will be restored to an Eden immeasurably more wonderful than the original Garden.

J. ELWIN WRIGHT

And ye now therefore have sorrow: but I will see you again, and your heart shall rejoice, and your joy no man taketh from you. *John 16:22.*

E M U S T remember that it was to the heart, the affections of His disciples that Christ was speaking on that last night when He spoke of that heavenly home. The shadow of sorrow fell across the table because of the impending separation; but Christ said,

"Let not your heart be troubled. There is a home, a heavenly home, where we shall all meet again."

After the other women had gone away, and after the two disciples had inspected the empty sepulcher and gone back to their home, John tells us that Mary "stood without the sepulcher weeping." There is the one you must answer! There is the sorrow you must meet and assuage, if your doctrine of immortality is to be of any strength or comfort. Mary, standing there, and refusing to be comforted until she saw Christ Himself, is the eternal symbol of human sorrow.

The recollection of departed friends is good; but our hope to meet them again is still better. The sunset glow is good; but better far is the golden light of the radiant morning and the unclouded dawn.

CLARENCE EDWARD MACARTNEY

We wait for the Lord, our Beloved,
Our Comforter, Master and Friend,
The substance of all that we hope for,
Beginning of faith and its end;
We watch for our Saviour and Bridegroom,
Who loved us and made us His own;
For Him we are looking and longing:
For Jesus, and Jesus alone.

ANNIE JOHNSON FLINT

JULY 31

The Lord was not in the wind . . . the Lord was not in the earthquake . . . the Lord was not in the fire . . . after the fire a still small voice.
1 Kings 19:11, 12.

LOVE is not only the finest fruit, but it is the final test of a Christian life. How many splendid men of God seem to lack here. What a giant of faith and strength Elijah was. Such intense indignation over sin! Such fearless denunciation! What tremendous faith gripping the very heavens! What marvelous power in prayer! Yet listen to him criticizing the faithful remnant whom God lovingly defends against his aspersions. There seems to be a serious lack there.

God seemed to understand his need. He asked him to slip down to Horeb for a new vision of the Master. And then He revealed Himself not in whirlwind nor earthquake nor lightning. Elijah doubtless felt at home among these tempestuous outbreaks. They suited his temper. But something startlingly new came to him in that exquisite "sound of gentle stillness," hushing, awing, mellowing, giving a new con-

ception of the dominant heart of his God. Some of us might well drop
things and take a run down to Horeb.

S. D. GORDON

> There is a place where Jesus sheds
> The oil of gladness on our heads;
> A place than all besides more sweet:
> It is the blood-bought mercy seat.
>
> Ah! whither could we flee for aid,
> When tempted, desolate, dismayed;
> Or how the hosts of hell defeat,
> Had suffering saints no mercy seat.

BOEHM

If the Son therefore shall make you free, ye shall
be free indeed. *John 8:36.*

THERE are thousands, and you may be one of them, who are
bound by Satan. They need to be delivered. If this is your condition today you can do no better than face the matter squarely
and listen while I tell you simply and plainly how to be free from this
bondage. It was for this very purpose that Jesus Christ came into the
world. If you will fully yield to Him, He will translate you out of the
kingdom of darkness into the kingdom of His dear Son.

Not so many years ago I was walking upon the broad road to
destruction. I had enjoyed the pleasures of sin for a season. But one
day God spoke to me and brought to me a conviction of my need.
When I cried to Him for mercy a great transformation took place
immediately in my own soul, and I was translated out of Satan's
kingdom into the kingdom of God. At once, because I was now His
child, His exceeding great and precious promises became my portion. What He did for me He can and will do for you if you will
let Him.

CHARLES E. FULLER

Like the sheep of the fold, we have all gone astray,
  But One seeketh for you and for me,
Who would fain bring us back to the fold of His love
  By His grace all-sufficient and free.

Oh, the depth of the riches of infinite grace
  To be found in the Saviour of men!
With His heart of compassion and mercy and love,
  He forgives us again and again.

When His waves and His billows have over us passed,
  And our way is as dark as can be,
Like the sunshine His promise illumines our path,
  "My grace is sufficient for thee."

Christ has died, but is risen, and coming again
  In the rapture His children to meet.
May there be in our hands many trophies of grace
  To lay down at our Lord's pierced feet.

GERTRUDE R. DUGAN

God, who is rich in mercy, for His great love
wherewith He loved us, even when we were dead
in sins, hath quickened us together with Christ,
(by grace ye are saved).   *Ephesians 2:4, 5.*

COULD anything be more gloriously rich in genial and gracious
evangel? All the biggest words in the New Testament are intro-
duced in this one verse of Holy Writ. Here we have "grace,"
and here we have "love," and here we have "mercy," all co-operative
in the ministry of breaking up the winter. Grace is the grand, glorious
goodwill of God. Love is grace on the march toward us, speeding us a
crusade of chivalrous beneficence. Mercy is love arrived, distributing
its gifts to those who are enslaved and winter-bound. Surely, here is
a rich and all-efficient atmosphere, in which even the firmest tyranny
can be melted away! Now watch the ministry of the spring. "Hath
quickened us together with Christ." He hath made us alive again. He
hath released the appalling grip of the despotic master, and the dead-
ened faculties are alive again.

J. H. Jowett

"Son of the Highest," fashioned as a man!
"Incarnate Word" in world's redemptive plan!
Thou "Blest Redeemer" of the human race,
How manifold the riches of Thy grace!

When Thou reveald'st Thyself as Christ divine,
What God-like all-sufficiency was Thine!
Expressed in truths significant and clear
That all who have the ears to hear may hear!

Exemplar Thou of "Truth," abundant "Life,"
A "Resting-place" mid stress of toil and strife,
A "Pilot" to the storm-tossed mariner,
Of things celestial, the "Interpreter."

Thou art the "Way" that leads to heaven's goal,
A "Well of Water" to the thirsty soul,
Unto the hungry, the "Life-giving Bread,"
To all Thy flock the "True and Living Head."

A "Shepherd," Thou, who tends and feeds His sheep,
A "Comforter" to sorrowing ones who weep,
"Bearer of Burdens" for the heavy lade,
A "Friend" to sinners who have erred and strayed.

Harry J. Wright

**Walk in the Spirit, and ye shall not fulfil the lust
of the flesh.** *Galatians 5:16.*

T H E Scripture says that we must be led by the Spirit; that we must
walk by the Spirit. My right relationship to the Holy Spirit is
that I allow myself to be guided and ruled by Him. Obedience
is the great factor in our whole relationship to God. "Obey My voice,
and I will be your God."

Mark how the Lord Jesus, on the last night, when giving His
great promise about the Holy Spirit, lays emphasis on this point. "If
ye love Me, keep My commandments. And I will pray the Father,
and He shall give you another Comforter" (John 14:15, 16). Obedience was essential as a preparation for the reception of the Spirit.
And this thought is often repeated by Him. "He that hath My commandments, and keepeth them, he it is that loveth Me: and he that
loveth Me shall be loved of My Father, and I will love him, and will
manifest Myself to him" (John 14:21). So also in verse 23: "If a
man love Me, he will keep My words: and My Father will love him,
and We will come unto him, and make Our abode with him." "If ye
abide in Me, and My words abide in you, ye shall ask what ye will,
and it shall be done unto you" (15:7). "If ye keep My commandments,
ye shall abide in My love" (verse 14).

Can words more plainly or impressively declare that the whole
life, in the new dispensation, following the resurrection of Christ,
depends on obedience? That is the Spirit of Christ. He lived to do not
His own will, but the will of the Father. And He cannot with His
Spirit make an abiding home in the heart of one who does not surrender himself utterly to a life of obedience.

ANDREW MURRAY

Let the peace of God rule in your hearts.
Colossians 3:15.

T H E peace of God! Think of it for a moment. How wondrous must
be God's peace! With Him there is no frailty, no error, no sin.
With Him there is no past to lament, no future to dread; no
blunders to deplore, no mistakes to fear; no plans to be thwarted; no
purposes to be unmet. No death can overcome, no suffering weaken, no
ideal be unfulfilled, no perfection unattained. Past, present or future;

vanishing time or endless eternity; life or death, hope or fear, storm or calm—naught of these, and naught else within the bounds of the universe can disturb the peace of Him who calls Himself the GOD OF PEACE. And it is this peace that is ours to possess. "The PEACE OF GOD shall keep YOUR hearts and minds." Not a human peace attained by self-struggle or self-discipline, but divine peace—the very peace which God Himself has, yea, is.

This is why Jesus Himself says, "My peace I give unto you." Human, man-made peace, which rises and falls with the vicissitudes of life, is worthless; but the peace of CHRIST, what a gift is this! Mark the surroundings when Christ spake these words, and how wonderful this peace appears! It was just before His death. Before Him is the kiss of the traitor; the hiss of the scourge; the weary blood-stained way to death; the hiding of His Father's face; the thorn-crowned, purple-robed mockery of His kingship; and the awful torture-climax of the cross. If ever a man's soul ought to be torn with agony, burdened with horror, surely this is the hour! But instead of gloom, and fear, and shuddering anticipation, hear His wondrous words, "My PEACE I leave with you!"

JAMES H. McCONKEY

We bless Thee for Thy peace, O God!
  Deep as the soundless sea,
Which falls like sunshine on the road
  Of those who trust in Thee.

We ask not, Father, for repose
  Which comes from outward rest,
If we may have through all life's woes
  Thy peace within our breast.

That peace which suffers and is strong,
  Trusts where it cannot see,
Deems not the trial way too long,
  But leaves the end with Thee.

AUTHOR UNKNOWN

AUGUST 5

We are His witnesses of these things. *Acts 5:32.*

THE natural impulse of one who has received a great gift is to share the news with others. It should be the most natural thing for a new-born Christian to share with others the new-found joy. Our letter tells of such an instance. This young woman is writing on the very day she has accepted Christ and already she feels the urge to win her family to Christ.

"Dear Mr. Fuller: The more I read the book you sent me *(The Old Fashioned Revival Hour, and the Broadcasters)* the more convinced I am that I should take Christ as my personal Saviour. My husband needs Christ, also my mother, my father, my sisters and brothers and all my in-laws. I feel God has chosen me to tell them what a Saviour Christ can be.

As I see what He has done in your life and how He has led you and comforted you and Mrs. Fuller in times of deep trouble I feel I want Him, too. Today is my birthday. I am twenty-four years old and I will always remember that on my birthday I truly accepted Christ. Will you pray for me that my faith may stay strong and that I may be a witness for Christ to everyone I meet?"

Pray for those who read the book, that many may find Christ and be strengthened in the Faith. More than 100,000 copies have been sold and many people have been converted through hearing the story of how Mr. Fuller found Christ and how he came to start the Old Fashioned Revival Hour.*

AUGUST 6

Ye are complete in Him. *Colossians 2:10.*

W H E N you are born again in Him; when in a personal and sincere faith your soul reaches for every precious promise of that Saviour's mercy, then every proud thought of self-sufficiency melts away. You gain humble but heavenly strength when your Saviour whispers to you, as He once did to the Apostle, "My grace is sufficient for thee."

If in penitent pilgrimage your spirit follows Him who was born in a stable, cradled in a manger, rejected by those whom He helped, condemned by those whom He healed, crucified by those whom He had come to save; if over the rumble of Calvary your heart of faith confesses: "He was wounded for our transgressions; He was bruised for our iniquities: the chastisement of our peace was upon Him; and with His stripes we are healed," you have come to completeness, with every obstacle between God and yourselves removed, every barrier on the highroad to salvation swept away, every demand of your conscience met, every claim of divine justice satisfied, every objection of hell overruled, every penny of your ransom paid, every stain of guilt washed away, every sin in your lives atoned.

* See the announcement on the cover of this volume regarding where the Reader may obtain a copy of *The Old Fashioned Revival Hour, and the Broadcasters.*

What immeasurable comfort for our souls we find through this completeness in Christ! For all eternity the haunting fear is dispelled that we ourselves must effect our own salvation, that there yet remains some task that we must accomplish to earn God's recognition, some plans for our own release that we must contrive and construct. In Christ, through Christ, and with Christ we have that sacred assurance of completion by which Jesus went the whole way on that bitter and bleeding path of the world's redemption, by which He removed forever the aggregate of all the guilt that the sin-weighted centuries have heaped. We know in triumphant faith that His red life-blood cleanses not partially but entirely; that His cross in unbroken, undivided, undiminished completeness for all men and forever, shows the unfailing way to a reconciled Father and assured eternity.

WALTER A. MAIER

AUGUST 7

. . . a chosen vessel unto Me, to bear My name . . .   *Acts 9:15.*

THIS great Friend lets you bear His name. Napoleon was a man who had many courtiers but few friends. Indeed, he boasted once that he loved no one living, not even his own brothers. But he was attached in a way to one of his marshals, Duroc. In the battle of Bausten in 1813, Duroc received a fatal wound from a cannon ball. When the army had bivouacked, Napoleon went to see him. The Duke grasped his hand and kissed him. The Emperor, putting his right arm around the Marshal, remained a quarter of an hour, with his head resting on his left hand, and in complete silence.

At length the Marshal said, "Ah, Sire, leave me. Such a sight as this must pain you."

Whereupon the Emperor left, unable to say more than these words, "Goodbye, my friend." He then returned to his tent and admitted no one that night. After the Battle of Waterloo, when he had hoped to find an asylum in England, Napoleon expressed the desire to assume the name of his old friend, and be known merely as General Duroc.

This Friend, your Friend forever, permits you to bear His name, the Name which is above every name, and the Name which God delights to honor.

CLARENCE EDWARD MACARTNEY

There is no Name so sweet on earth,
No Name so sweet in heaven;

197

The Name, before His wondrous birth,
To Christ the Saviour given.

O Jesus! by that matchless Name
Thy grace shall fail us never;
Today, as yesterday, the same,
Thou art the same forever!

E. ROBERTS

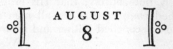

AUGUST 8

I am that bread of life. *John 6:48.*

IN THIS sixth chapter of John, Jesus is presented as the incarnate Son of God—the Son in the place of humiliation. He is the Bread come down from heaven. Notice how Christ presents Himself as the source of Life. "For the bread of God is He which cometh down from heaven and giveth life unto the world" (verse 33). "For I am come down from heaven, not to do Mine own will, but the will of Him that sent Me" (verse 38). "I am the living bread which came down from heaven. If any man eat of this bread he shall live forever" (verse 51).

One who is dead in trespasses and sins has no hunger for the Word of God. But once a soul is made alive, becoming a new creation in Christ Jesus, then there is a hunger for the bread of life, which is in His Word.

How simple, yet how profound, is His statement, "I am the bread of life." Bread is the very staff of life. It is suited to all. Some cannot eat sweets or meats but all can eat bread. Christ is suited to every soul, no matter what its condition. Bread should be the daily food of all. In the Lord's prayer we have that gracious petition, "Give us this day our *daily* bread." How many believers eat that bread only on Sunday and never feast on it during the week. You need God's Word every day.

Bread is a satisfying food. One never tires of bread. One may tire of pastries and other things but not of bread. However, bread cannot sustain you unless you eat it. Someone else cannot eat it for you. You personally must eat it or starve. John 1:12 says, "But as many as received Him (that is, appropriated Him) to them gave He power to become the sons of God."

The essential thing for you to do today is to receive Him as your Bread of Life.

CHARLES E. FULLER

198

Wait on the Lord: be of good courage, and He
shall strengthen thine heart: wait, I say, on the
Lord.   *Psalm 27:14.*

THE favorite word for listening in the Bible is the word waiting.
It is a great word full of simple yet wondrous meaning ... It
means the turning of the face full up to God so as to know by a
look what He would suggest; hearing through the eyes. It is exquisitely
put in the Psalms. God assures us that He is ever keeping His eye
upon us so that by our looking up we can catch His eye and so know
what to do.

It means on our side watching God's slightest movement as
intensely as a slave in those old times watched for the first and least
suggestion of the master's desire. As the watch-guard on night duty
upon the city wall in old Judaea kept his eyes keenly towards the
East to see the first gleam of the coming day that would relieve his
long, lonely vigil—so intensely and keenly we are to look towards
God to get the first inkling of His will. The life is to be lived with its
face always turned to God.

S. D. GORDON

> *When hope deferred brings thy heart nigh to breaking,*
> *With upward looking thine eyes seem to fail;*
> *When thy poor heart has grown weary with aching*
> *And powers of evil thy spirit assail;*
>
> *Still then thy heart for the voice that would guide thee,*
> *Hush every thought that His word you may hear.*
> *Fear not the way for whate'er may betide thee,*
> *He will be with thee to help and to cheer.*
>
> *Be silent to God! Still the voice of thy grieving;*
> *Turn from thy thinking and agonized prayer,*
> *Patiently wait, in His loving hands leaving*
> *All of thy hopes, and thy burdens and care.*

H. D. WINANT

But so did not I, because of the fear of God.
Nehemiah 5:15.

THE brave cupbearer to the King dared to stand alone. He was not afraid of "the sin of singularity." Society does not like it, severely criticises it, and cannot believe there is conscientiousness in it. Yet the men of power have all been singular. They chose their God-given course, and carved their own way to fortune. Dr. Johnson confessed he had to ignore his critics and channel his own path. His strong individuality could do nothing less. Henry Ward Beecher justified his style of preaching by Nehemiah's example. John Wesley, in opposition to friends, said, "I know I am not what I ought to be, nor what I hope to be, but by the Grace of God, I am what I am." Most of us prefer to follow precedents. How have others done? What is customary? Shall I not be thought to be singular?

Yes! but that is not a sin. Only be sure you have conscience on your side. Do not seek for singularity. There may be vanity in that feeling. But when God calls for it, be as brave as Nehemiah.

The true virtue of independence is in the courage which conscientiously does God's bidding. If He calls, dare to be original. The strong man is not capricious, though he will be called so. His path is his own, like that of Luther at Worms, "I cannot do otherwise: so help me God." These words defied the Emperor, and brought about the Reformation.

W. S. Bruce

Before the mountains were brought forth, or ever
Thou hadst formed the earth and the world, even
from everlasting to everlasting, Thou art God.
Psalm 90:2.

NOTHING is more restful to the heart of man than the sense of the eternity of God. The thought is utterly beyond our perfect comprehension, for the mind of man cannot grasp the thought of eternity. The very fact, however, of our inability to do so is the reason for the security we feel when we remember that God is Himself eternal. The secrets of the past, all unknown to us, are ever present to His omniscient mind. Upon the mystery of the future the light of

His perfect knowledge rests; and the problems of today that fret and trouble us are seen by Him in their relation to the past and to the future, and for that reason cease to be to Him perplexing, as they are to us.

In the eternity of God, time has but one significance, it is perpetually and unceasingly "Now." The name by which He revealed Himself to Moses at the burning bush is full of significance. He is the "I AM." Combining this fact with those of His creatorship and His love, we argue at once that the laws He makes for the creatures of His hand and the children of His love, are laws that will take in the sum of things, and so condition the present, that it shall hold within it the power and the promise of the future.

G. Campbell Morgan

> *The God of Abraham praise,*
> *Who reigns enthroned above,*
> *Ancient of everlasting days,*
> *   And God of love!*
> *Jehovah! great I Am!*
> *By earth and heaven confest;*
> *I bow and bless the sacred name,*
> *   Forever blest!*

Thomas Olivers

AUGUST 12

And thou shalt put the mercy seat above upon the ark . . . and there I will meet with thee, and I will commune with thee from above the mercy seat. *Exodus 25:21, 22.*

THERE is the holy and most glorious God who invites us to come to Him, to hold converse with Him, to ask from Him such things as we need, and to experience what a blessing there is in fellowship with Him. He has created us in His own image, and has redeemed us by His own Son, so that in converse with Him we might find our highest glory and salvation.

What use do we make of this heavenly privilege? How many there are who take only five minutes for prayer! They say that they have no time, and that the heart desire for prayer is lacking; they do not know how to spend half an hour with God! It is not that they absolutely do not pray; they pray every day—but they have no joy in prayer, as a token of communion with God which shows that God is everything to them.

Andrew Murray

I spent an hour in the dim sweet wood
With my Beloved, when the morn was new;
And I remembered how His fingers could
And did, make worlds of beauty for my view.

I spent an hour in the crowded shop
With my Beloved, as my trade I plied:
And, pressed with wonder, breathless, I would stop—
Feeling the Carpenter was at my side.

I spent an hour, when the shadows fell,
With my Beloved: and I thought how He,
World-weary too, turned home at dusk to tell
His secrets to the friends at Bethany.
All day with my Beloved I have trod. . . .
My heart is given to the Son of God.

HELEN FRAZEE-BOWER

AUGUST 13

But when ye pray, use not vain repetitions, as the
heathen do: for they think that they shall be heard
for their much speaking.   *Matthew 6:7.*

You have undoubtedly noticed that most of us even change our
tone of voice when we pray. We adopt a peculiar, pleading,
tearful tone of voice. With some it is pure affectation. But this
is certainly not the case with most people. It is with them a naïve,
unaffected, genuine expression of Old Adam's views of God and
prayer: When God hears how great our need is, and how urgent it is
for us to receive that for which we are praying, He will likely be
moved to such an extent that He will yield and let us have it!

A complete revolution with reference to this will take place in our
prayer life as soon as the Spirit has taught us to pray in the name of
Jesus. He will teach us plainly that what we lack in fervency, solicitude, love and faith are not the things which prevent us from being
heard and answered when we pray. These things merely reveal our
helplessness. And helplessness is fundamental in prayer.

When the Spirit shows us the hardness, the slothfulness, and the
indifference of our heart toward prayer, we now become anxious and
confused no longer. Instead, they become added incentives to prayer,
that is, the opening of our heart's door to give Jesus access to all our
distress and all our impotence.

A new and wonderful thing now occurs. Our seasons of prayer
become hours of real rest to our weary souls. They become quiet hours,
hours in which we lie at the feet of Jesus and point to all those things

which we lack and which make our hearts tired and weary. When our prayer chamber thus becomes a resting place, then we begin to long for it and to look forward to it with joy and anticipation from one prayer session to the next.

This again will result in another change. We will begin to accomplish something in prayer. Joyfully and thankfully we will take up the work of prayer. Our secret prayer chamber will become not only a resting place, but a workshop also.

O. HALLESBY

AUGUST 14

I have appeared unto thee . . . to make thee a minister. . . . *Acts 26:16.*

THERE is a wealth of meaning in that word "minister." In the original it is singularly striking, though lack of space forbids my speaking of it here. We are called to "minister the Spirit" of the living God unto men (Gal. 3:5). We are not called merely to preach, teach, and expound, but to cause men to receive the very life of God. What amazing privilege! What an inspiring responsibility!

When the angel visited Cornelius he was able to tell him that his alms and prayers were accepted of God, but added in effect: "I cannot tell you the way of salvation, I cannot communicate to you the gift of eternal life. If you want to know that, you must send to a saved sinner, named Simon Peter."

The angels have no experience of pardoning and regenerating grace. They have never felt rebellion in their hearts; they have never known the mystery of reconciliation; never been plucked from the burning; never been lifted from the slough of sin; never felt the Spirit within, crying "Abba, Father." How, then, shall they speak of these things to men? How shall they be able to communicate eternal life to dead souls?

But to us it is given to be ministers of the grace of God. A friend of mine once observed, "If God gave the command to angels to evangelize the world, heaven would be empty in five minutes." But alas! alas! the eyes of men are withholden from seeing the glory of so divine a commission. We are called, then, to minister, i. e., to cause men to receive. Let this blessed but solemn truth fasten itself upon our hearts till we cry out, "Who is sufficient for these things?" and seek with all our hearts to know the secret of this amazing responsibility.

PAGET WILKES

**Upon the first day of the week let every one of you
lay by him in store, as God hath prospered him.**
1 Corinthians 16:2.

I W A N T to give you a little instruction about giving. Every Christian should give to the Lord of his income. There are three things in our text which I wish to point out as important to you in giving scripturally.

First, give regularly: "Upon the first day of the week." Each and every week of the year you should give to God's work. If we had more of this periodical giving, there would be no place for annual, every-member canvasses and money raising campaigns; no need of concentrated drives and begging for money. The pastor's salary would always be provided; missionary activity would be stimulated; and the widows and fatherless would be cared for, if we gave regularly.

Secondly, give personally: "Every one of you." Every member of the family from the oldest to the youngest should be taught his personal responsibility to God in this matter. Every child should be taught that a portion of his allowance or income belongs to God.

Thirdly, give proportionately: "As God hath prospered." We are not under the law but under grace. We are not commanded in this dispensation to tithe, but I know of no better basis of giving than setting aside the tenth of your income for the Lord. You are not really making an offering to the Lord until *after* you have given your tenth or tithe. And then, in addition to the offering, there is the love offering. If you really love the Lord you will give not only a tithe and an offering but a love offering. We are told in 2 Corinthians 9:7, "The Lord loveth a cheerful giver." That word "cheerful" means, literally, an "hilarious" giver. The Lord loves a giver who "just loves to give." "Out of the abundance of the heart the mouth speaketh" (Matthew 12:34).

When the Children of Israel withheld their tithes and offerings God withheld the rain and the increase of the land and cattle until His people came back to their senses. In Malachi 3:8, we find God asking this question, "Will a man rob God? Yet ye have robbed Me. But ye say, 'Wherein have we robbed Thee?' In tithes and offerings."

But note verse 10: "Bring ye all the tithes into the storehouse, that there may be meat in Mine house, and prove Me now herewith, saith the Lord of hosts, if I will not open you the windows of heaven, and pour you out a blessing, that there shall not be room enough to receive it." So, we see that material blessings were contingent upon giving to the Lord. As they tithed, God blessed—as they withheld the tithes, God's blessing was withheld.

Are you living up to God's standard of when, what, and how a Christian should give?

AUGUST 16

For even Christ pleased not Himself.

Romans 15:3.

THE supreme thought of pleasing His Father was never absent from Jesus' thought. It drove Him to the wilderness, and to Gethsemane, and to Calvary.

Is that the one purpose in your heart in desiring power? He might send some of us out to the far-off foreign mission field. He might send some down to the less enchanted field of the city slums to do salvage service night after night among the awful social wreckage thrown upon the strand there; or possibly it would mean an isolated post out on the frontier, or down in the equally heroic field of the mountains of the South. He might leave some of you just where you are, in a commonplace, humdrum spot, as you think, when your visions had been in other fields. He might make you a seed-sower, like lonely Morrison in China, when you wanted to be a harvester like Moody. Here is the real battlefield. The fighting and agonizing are here. Not with God but with yourself, that the old self in you may be crucified and Jesus crowned in its place.

S. D. GORDON

My Saviour, Thou hast offered rest:
Oh, give it, then, to me;
The rest of ceasing from myself,
To find my all in Thee.

This cruel self, oh, how it strives
And works within my breast,
To come between Thee and my soul,
And keep me back from rest.

How many subtle forms it takes
Of seeming verity,
As if it were not safe to rest
And venture all on Thee.

O Lord, I seek a holy rest,
A victory over sin!
I seek that Thou alone shouldst reign
O'er all without, within.

SIR GEORGE SMART

205

That He would grant you, according to the riches
of His glory, to be strengthened with might by His
Spirit in the inner man; that Christ may dwell in
your hearts by faith; that ye, being rooted and
grounded in love, may be able to comprehend with
all saints what is the breadth, and length, and
depth, and height; and to know the love of Christ
which passeth knowledge, that ye might be filled
with all the fulness of God. *Ephesians 3:16-19.*

How rich and radiant is this passage, and how much beyond the
normal contemplations of the believer! But, is it all an idle
dream? Is it too good to be true? Or are these mere words piled
up by an enthusiast? Can I grasp these riches? Can I be so strengthened in the inner man as to be filled with "all the fulness of God"?
Is there an inner energy which can be communicated to me, by which
I can "live above"?

Well may we ask such questions as these if we look to our own
feeble strength. But the Apostle does not suffer us to do so, for he
directs our attention away from ourselves as he sings: "Now unto
Him that is able to do!" The doxology is occasioned by the thought
of the power which is ours only because it is God's. He can bring
these dreams to reality. He can communicate the power by which we
may live above. His Spirit can work within us until we know "the love
of Christ that passeth knowledge."

Let us look for a moment at the details of the Apostle's triumphant
song: "Now unto Him that is able to do." Who is this One of whom the
Apostle speaks? He is the One, who, in the beginning of His Word,
is seen as coming forth out of eternity—grand and resplendent, the
Ground and Cause of the universe, the Creator of creation. In His
incomprehensible omnipotence He creates and sustains all things. At
the close of His Word, where the new eternal creation breaks upon
our view, we see heavenly creatures and powers cast their crowns
at His feet crying: "Thou art worthy, O Lord, to receive glory and
honour and power: for thou hast created all things, and for thy
pleasure they are and were created" (Revelation 4:11).

HOWARD W. FERRIN

He did not many mighty works there because of
their unbelief.   *Matthew 13:58.*

H E I S still doing mighty works and if He is not doing them in your
life, your church, your community, it is because of your unbelief. The only thing in existence that can limit the power of
the Lord Jesus Christ is our unbelief. He is hindered today by the
same things that have always hindered Him—unbelieving Nazarenes
calling Him the carpenter's son and reducing Him in their thinking
to the stature of a common man, and discouraged Christians letting
the dungeon of circumstances becloud His deity. He is the same as
ever, but He can mean to us only as much as our faith lets Him mean.

The eternal Christ is with us today, and wherever men yield to
Him He works as of old. Men ask, "Is the day of miracles past yet?"
There is no "day" of miracles. Miracles are simply the supernatural
operation of God, and He is timeless—there is no "day" with Him.
He has seen fit to perform different types of miracles to suit His purpose in different periods of earthly time, but His supernatural power
is always the same, and wherever He regenerates and directs a human
heart there you have a miracle. There is abundant evidence all over
the world to a wonder-working God and to a Christ who is the
same today. There are thousands of lives that can be accounted for in
no other way.

VANCE HAVNER

I was in prison, and ye came unto Me.
                    Matthew 25:36.

W H A T an interesting and touching story is this, from a great
prison in California. Your prayers, as well as Mr. Fuller's messages, may be used of God to rescue many such "brands from
the burning."

"Dear Mr. and Mrs. Fuller: I am an inmate of a great California prison. About two thousand of us listen to you every
Sunday night. I am only twenty-four years old. I suppose lots of
people think all of us are bad, but that isn't so, for many of us
have found our Lord. The main thing I wanted to tell you is
that every Sunday night when I am locked in my cell it cheers

me up to hear your services. Whenever you ask everyone to
pray I get down on my knees and pray with you."

Pray for the multitudes of young men who are in prison, that
they may be set free in Christ Jesus.

> *O Lord, in my heart there's a welcome for Thee—*
> *Gladly I now would say*
> *Come in, blessed Saviour, my heart and my life*
> *Henceforth would own Thy sway.*
> *Long hast Thou waited and long knocked in vain*
> *Outside my heart's closed door;*
> *O cleanse me from sin, then, dear Lord, enter in*
> *And dwell there for evermore!*

HILDA M. JARVIS

AUGUST
20

The Lord Jehovah is my strength and my song;
He also is become my salvation. *Isaiah 12:2.*

THE storm is over. Even the distant rumblings have ceased. The
righteous, and yet very tender and pitiful, severity of the Lord
has perfected its ministry and has passed away. The alienated
heart has been constrained by the sharp instrument of suffering to
turn its weary self unto God. And now the sun is shining again, the
birds are singing, the desert is blossoming like the rose! There is a new
heaven and a new earth! "The Lord Jehovah is my strength and my
song: He also is become my salvation."

What does this sweet and joyful singer find in God? "My strength"!
"My song"! "My salvation"! How extraordinarily rich and compre-
hensive! Everything is there! All that a man needs in the battle of life
is enshrined in this most wealthy and ancient word. "My strength";
the very power to fight! "My song"; with my God I can fight to music;
I can march to the war to the accompaniment of the band; I can be a
singing warrior, stepping out to the harmonies of heaven! "My salvation"; with my God I fight to victory, to larger liberty, to ever more
glorious possessions.

I say everything is here, the strength that makes me a warrior,
the song that makes me a happy warrior, the salvation which makes
me a happy warrior fighting unto richer freedom. Here truly is a
perfect equipment for life's battle, and this equipment is absolutely
and entirely found in God.

J. H. JOWETT

Everyone which seeth the Son, and believeth on
Him, may have everlasting life: and I will raise
him up at the last day.   *John 6:40.*

E HAD something very particular to say about us all. And He
said it four times over in the sixth chapter of John, it was so important to us; it was such a glad anticipation to Him. The mo-
mentous fact is that the direction of every believer's life has become
permanently changed from down to up! In fact we are now each one
linked on to Christ; in His upward progress we share in the triumph
of His resurrection from the dead; we are all bound for heaven. This
was the Father's will, the Father's plan, "that every one which seeth
the Son and believeth on Him, may have everlasting life, and I will
raise him up at the last day." He was raised up from the dead, and
just as surely every believer will share in the same mighty miracle
and be raised up.

Meanwhile, what is our prospect, our outlook on this world of
sorrows and alarms? Our outlook must ever be an uplook. "Look up,
and lift up your heads," is as binding on us, and as needful for us, as
many other great and precious promises and commands. It is the divine
prescription for gloom and discouragement. It is just as sorrowful to
the Saviour as it was on the way to Emmaus that we should "walk
and be sad." We have come to the days when, rightly, "Men's hearts
are failing them for fear." Such times have surely begun to come
to pass. Then let us "look up, for our redemption draweth nigh."

Finally "caught up to meet the Lord in the air" (1 Thess. 4:17).
He was "carried up," we are to be "caught up!" Whose are the hands
stretched out now to keep us, then to receive us? Surely the One
whose hands were once nailed to the tree for us. For the Lord's
Christ "having spoiled principalities and powers . . . made a show of
them openly, triumphing over them in it." And in spoiling them He
delivered us, and finally and forever has reversed the downward direction of every believer's heart. So that we, too, are now bound upward,
to be raised up, to be caught up! Wherefore, let us "comfort one
another with these words."

> *"Though the shore we hope to land on,*
>   *Only by report is known,*
> *Yet we freely all abandon,*
>   *Led by that report alone;*
> *And with Jesus,*
>   *Through the trackless deep move on."*
>   NORTHCOTE DECK

209

Be careful for nothing.   *Philippians 4:6.*

THE word careful means "full of care or anxiety." God has promised to throw an impenetrable wall of fire around your heart so
that no enemy can ever successfully reach you. You have a garrison on guard which can never be overcome. Therefore, you have
nothing to worry about. You are not kept by your own power but by
the power of God.

Certainly, your faith will be tried, but "the trial of your faith (is)
much more precious than of gold that perisheth, though it be tried
with fire" (1 Peter 1:7). Take your pen and mark the occurrences of
the word "suffer" or "suffering" in 1 Peter. You will find it fourteen
times. The suffering, the trials, are necessary but not an occasion for
the least anxiety. It is found "unto praise, and honor and glory at the
appearing of Jesus Christ: whom having not seen, ye love; in whom,
though now ye see Him not, yet believing, ye rejoice with joy unspeakable and full of glory."

CHARLES E. FULLER

Nor does He merely sit as a refiner
    Of gold beside the crucible He views;
But walks the furnace with us, our Shekinah,
    With His own might our souls to interfuse.

Ah, yes! I know! Have I not sensed His nearness,
    His soothing touch upon my quivering nerve,
Heard the soft whisper, realized the dearness
    Of that High Presence which still stoops to serve!

Yea, verily, and so I fare, not fearing
    For what I know not now He will unfold.
All's to the good that brings one's footsteps nearer
    To that unveiling where all shall be told.

We know in part: but then swift understanding
    Will flash upon each earthly sigh and groan,
As face to face, unveiled at His commanding,
    We each shall know, as we ourselves are known.

HENRY HOWARD

A man shall be as an hiding place from the wind,
and a covert from the tempest.   *Isaiah 32:2.*

Hail, sovereign love, which first began
The scheme of rescue fallen man!
Hail, matchless, free, eternal grace,
Which gave my soul a Hiding Place.

Against the God that built the sky
I fought with hands uplifted high—
Despised the mention of His grace,
Too proud to seek a Hiding Place!

Enwrapt in thick Egyptian night,
And fond of darkness more than light,
Madly I ran the sinful race,
Secure—without a Hiding Place!

But thus the eternal counsel ran:
Almighty love, arrest that man!
I felt the arrows of distress,
And found I had no Hiding Place!

Indignant Justice stood in view;
To Sinai's fiery mount I flew;
But Justice cried with frowning face,
This mountain is no Hiding Place!

Ere long a heavenly voice I heard,
And mercy's angel soon appeared:
He led me, with a beaming face,
To JESUS as a Hiding Place.

On Him almighty vengeance fell,
Which must have sunk a world to hell!
He bore it for a sinful race,
And thus became their Hiding Place.

Should sevenfold storms of thunder roll,
And shake this globe from pole to pole,
No thunderbolt shall daunt my face,
For Jesus is my Hiding Place.

MAJOR ANDRE
(Shot in the American Revolution as a British spy.)

Among them that are born of women there hath
not risen a greater than John the Baptist.

Matthew 11:11.

STORIES are not uncommon on the mission field of God's messengers passing on their way with the Gospel through some
populous town or tiny village, with a message for the soul and
perhaps with medicines for the body. Some have been allowed of
God to leave such an aroma of Christ behind them, that when, long
after, the Saviour has been described by some later messenger,
previous hearers have mistaken the earlier missionary for his Master and have said: "Oh, yes, we had the One you describe, your
Christ, pass through our town years ago. He was just like you say!"

Oh, may some divine aroma distil from our unworthy lives, as
we pass through the spiritual wilderness which surrounds us! May we
so adorn the doctrine, and so commend the Master, that we may at
least be clearly recognized as belonging to His family and being His
children, with a strong family likeness to Him!

NORTHCOTE DECK

Has some one seen Christ in you today?
Christian, look to your heart, I pray,
The little things you have done or said—
Did they accord with the way you prayed?
Have your thoughts been pure and your words been kind?
Have you sought to have the Saviour's mind?
The world with a criticizing view
Has watched—but did it see Christ in you?

Has some one seen Christ in you today?
Christian, look to your life, I pray,
There are aching and blighted souls
Being lost on sin's destructive shoals,
And perhaps of Christ their only view
May be what of Him they see in you.
Will they see enough to bring hope or cheer?
Look to your light! Does it shine out clear?

AUTHOR UNKNOWN

He staggered not at the promise of God through unbelief.   *Romans 4:20.*

ONTRAST the widow of Sarepta with Elijah the Tishbite. What was the difference between them? Just the difference that ever exists between unbelief and faith. Listen again to the utterance of unbelief. "And she said, As the Lord thy God liveth, I have not a cake, but a handful of meal in a barrel, and a little oil in a cruse; and, behold, I am gathering two sticks, that I may go in and dress it for me and my son, that we may eat it, and die."

Here, truly, is a gloomy picture. An empty barrel, an exhausted cruse, and death! In reality she was out of His presence, and had lost the sense of His all-sufficiency to meet her need and that of her house. Her circumstances excluded God from the vision of her soul. She looked at things that were seen, not at the things which were unseen. She saw not the invisible One; she saw nothing but famine and death.

Not so the man of faith. He looked beyond the barrel and the cruse. He had no thought of dying of hunger. He rested on the word of the Lord. Here was his precious resource. God had said, "I have commanded a widow woman there to sustain thee." This was quite enough for him. He knew that God could multiply the meal and the oil to sustain him and her. Like Caleb and Joshua, he brought God into the scene, and found in Him the happy solution of every difficulty. They saw God above and beyond the walls and the giants. They rested on His eternal word. He had promised to bring His people into the land, and hence, though there were nothing but walls and giants from Dan to Beersheba, He would most surely fulfill His word.

And so with Elijah the Tishbite. He saw the living and almighty God above and beyond the barrel and the cruse. He rested upon that word which is settled forever in heaven, and which never can fail a trusting heart. This tranquilized his spirit, and with this he sought to tranquilize the widow, too. "And he said unto her, Fear not";— precious, soul-stirring utterance of faith!—"go, and do as thou hast said. . . . For thus saith the Lord God of Israel, The barrel of meal shall not waste, neither shall the cruse of oil fail, until the day that the Lord sendeth rain upon the earth."

                                                        C. H. M.

AUGUST
26

If I then, your Lord and Master, have washed your feet; ye also ought to wash one another's feet.

John 13:14.

IN THE first seventeen verses of this thirteenth chapter we are ushered into one of the most sacred scenes ever enacted on this earth, Jesus washing the feet of His disciples. What a glorious scene; the Creator of the universe, the eternal Son of God taking the place of a slave. Herein we see the marvelous grace of the Lord Jesus Christ, that He who was rich for our sakes became poor that we through His poverty might become rich. He came not to be ministered unto but to minister unto others and to give His life a ransom for many.

Why did He wash their feet? Because the feet speak of the believer's walk. "Blessed is he that walketh not in the counsel of the ungodly." The Word has much to say of the believer's walk in this weary, sin-cursed world. We read in Romans 6:4, "Therefore are we buried with Him by baptism into death; that like as Christ was raised up from the dead by the glory of the Father, even so we also should walk in newness of life." And again in 2 Corinthians 5:7, "We walk by faith, not by sight." Galatians 5:16, "Walk in the Spirit and ye shall not fulfill the lust of the flesh." Ephesians 4:1, "Walk worthy of the vocation wherewith ye are called."

In our walk as pilgrims our feet become contaminated with the dust of the way. We need daily cleansing in order that our walk may be pleasing to God.

J. ELWIN WRIGHT

Oh, precious fountain, that saves from sin,
I am so glad I have entered in;
There Jesus saves me and keeps me clean,
Glory to His name.

E. A. HOFFMAN

AUGUST
27

In Thy light shall we see light. *Psalm 36:9.*

WHEN we come to our heavenly Father and meet Him in His Word, a penetrating beam is focused upon us and we see ourselves, not as we think we are, not as we want to be, not as we pretend that we are, not as others believe us to be, but in that unsparing, all-revealing, dazzling brightness without shadow or concealing we

214

see ourselves as we are—poor, helpless, selfish, impure, self-willed.

You have all heard of that mysterious light discovered forty years ago, an invisible X-ray, that penetrates flesh to help reveal, in shadow form, the dark interior of the human body; but the light of God pushes its way to the innermost recesses of the human heart, and not in shadow form, but in clear-cut picture does that flood of light lay the human soul bare and prove this ancient truth, "The heart is deceitful above all things and desperately wicked."

Have you viewed yourself in that light and discovered the sham, the dishonesty, that crowds into our lives? In that blinding light have you learned that "all have sinned and come short of the glory of God"? Not until we stand in that pitiless glare and see ourselves as God sees us, are we prepared for the highest and most blessed revelation of life. That comes when, beholding Jesus Christ and hearing Him twice declare, "I am the Light of the world," we learn our heavenly Father's grace by which we are justified, delivered from the penalty and the power of sin, saved eternally; the grace which seals redemption even for the weakest and most unworthy believer; the mercy which, as it points to the blood-bought forgiveness of our transgressions, forever puts an end to the delusion that our virtues, character, accomplishments, best deeds, are in any way, and even to the slightest degree, the cause of our salvation.

You know of the helpful rays like the ultra-violet. What far greater curing of sin-sick men and their distressed souls emanates from our blessed Saviour and the light of His mercies that guides us from death to life, from despair to hope, from sin to salvation!

WALTER A. MAIER

AUGUST
28

I will seek Him whom my soul loveth.
Song of Solomon 3:2.

THE Spirit desires to have full possession of my life. We pray for more of the Spirit, and we pray well, if alongside this prayer we set the truth that the Spirit wants more of me. The Spirit would possess me entirely. Just as my soul has my whole body for its dwelling-place and service, so the Holy Spirit would have my body and soul as His dwelling-place, entirely under His control.

No one can continue long and earnestly in prayer without beginning to perceive that the Spirit is gently leading to an entirely new consecration, of which previously he knew nothing. "I seek Thee with my whole heart." The Spirit will make such words more and more the motto of our lives. He will cause us to recognize that what remains in

215

us of double-mindedness is truly sinful. He will reveal Christ as the Almighty Deliverer from all sin, who is always near to defend us. He will lead us in this way in prayer, to forget ourselves and make us willing to offer ourselves for training as intercessors, to whom God can entrust the carrying out of His plans, and who day and night cry to Him to avenge His Church of her adversary.

God help us to know the Spirit and to reverence Him as the Spirit of Prayer!

ANDREW MURRAY

AUGUST 29

Wherefore gird up the loins of your mind, be sober, and hope to the end for the grace that is to be brought unto you at the revelation of Jesus Christ.
1 Peter 1:13.

To UNDERSTAND and appreciate this verse you should study the entire chapter. If you do you will be struck with the fact that Peter's mind and heart were running over with feeling for his Lord and Saviour, Jesus Christ. There is hardly a verse without reference to the Lord.

Peter's heart was saturated with memories of his Master. He spoke of His death and His resurrection; but also many times of His return. He hoped, no doubt, that Christ would return while he was yet alive. Some wonder why we still hope for the return of the Lord after nineteen hundred years. Please remember that "one day is with the Lord as a thousand years and a thousand years as one day." "The Lord is not slack concerning His promise."

Peter holds out the fact of the Lord's return as a motive for action, for holiness, and for watchfulness. And so he admonishes those to whom he writes to "gird up their loins," or to be in readiness. Surely this is appropriate for the day in which we live, for these are days of looseness in living, laxity in doctrinal belief and carelessness in religious life. Therefore, gird up your loins: brace yourself, pull yourself together, be firm, be consistent, be determined.

Again he says, "Hope to the end." Certainly the world outlook is dark. According to the signs of the times we are on the brink of the great tribulation period spoken of in God's Word. We have every reason to hope, for we have been begotten from the dead, born unto a living hope. That hope is based upon the fact of Christ's resurrection from the dead. His resurrection is our guaranty of resurrection also.

Listen, beloved, you may not have any place here that you can call your own but in Him you have an inheritance, incorruptible, undefiled and that fadeth not away. This inheritance is for those who are found waiting with loins girded, in readiness to go with Him when He appears.

CHARLES E. FULLER

AUGUST 30

And being made perfect, He became the author of eternal salvation unto all them that obey Him.
Hebrews 5:9.

IF WE would know the good pleasure of God, man must be seen in all his perfection. In Christ we have the revelation of perfect manhood. Think of His perfection of tenderness, His beauty of character, of all the great overwhelming strength which centered in His sacred Person. In beholding Him, behold the "good pleasure of God." "It is God which worketh in you both to will and to do of His good pleasure."

To make us what Jesus was, God works within us; and until that is finally accomplished, the heart of God will never be at rest concerning us: not until that moment dawns, which must come for all who put their trust in Him, when the perfect Son of the living God shall present the many sons whom He brings to glory, in the presence of His Father, without blemish in exceeding joy. That is the intended issue; that is the consummation; that is the crowning and the joy.

G. CAMPBELL MORGAN

Jesus! what a Friend for sinners!
Jesus! Lover of my soul;
Friends may fail me, foes assail me,
He, my Saviour, makes me whole.

Jesus! what a strength in weakness!
Let me hide myself in Him;
Tempted, tried, and sometimes failing,
He, my strength, my victory wins.

J. WILBUR CHAPMAN

AUGUST 31

Our sufficiency is of God.   *2 Corinthians 3:5.*

THERE is that in God which meets every one of our needs. His fulness is sufficient for our emptiness. His life is equal to the supplanting of our death.

How often do we pray as if our pleading must be of the most urgent kind to get the sufficient answer! How often behind our prayers is concealed the thought that grace is limited in its supplies, and is exceeded by our demands! Could there be a larger mistake? In God is all sufficiency. By His command this whole world came into existence, and He never created the end without designing the means. Part fits to part: the effect lies already in the cause. And all are joined into unity by the one Almighty Friend, pervading and sustaining the whole. Nothing is wanting: every necessity is met.

My soul! Thy needs are infinite. Thou needest light to guide, and wisdom to warn, and love to sweeten, and life to supplant the continuous oncoming of death. Seek them not in any other source than in God. Find in Him the Light that never leads astray. Claim the cleansing of His Holy Spirit to make thee fit for His fellowship, and a choice weapon in His hand. Let His will be thy will, and His way thy way, and all thine insufficiency and inaptitudes shall be met by the sufficiency of His grace.

His atonement is sufficient to cancel our guilt. His love is wide enough to cover our many wants. His riches of grace far exceed the poverty of our petitions. Often we think our prayers must be limited lest we ask too much.

No! "Far above all you can ask or think," He can do. Yea, "exceeding abundantly above all."

O my soul live not in poverty and distress, when heaven's wealth is all there to meet thy want. Pray to be saved from the limitation of those mean and mundane horizons. The love of God has an amplitude which is far above thy measurements; it is broader than "all the measures of man's mind." It is high as heaven and long as eternity, and no need of thine can exceed its sufficiency. Be still, my soul—rest calmly in God's all-sufficiency.

W. S. Bruce

Who shall stand in His holy place? He that hath
clean hands, and a pure heart.   *Psalm 24:3, 4.*

A CERTAIN conscientious pastor, who could not bear deceit
in any form, was constantly irritated by the habitual irregularity
of the clock in his church auditorium. His people were ever
commenting on the clock's unreliability, by implication blaming the
"hands" of the time piece. With the thought of teaching an important
lesson, the pastor hung a placard on the wall above the clock reading,
"DON'T BLAME MY HANDS, THE TROUBLE LIES DEEPER."

So with us also when our hands do wrong, or our feet, lips, or even
our thoughts go astray. There is an inner world in which we live a
great portion of our lives—a world of imagination, desire, ambition—
a world that we want to keep ever in the dark. But, Oh, the pleasures
we ofttimes find in entering that world. This inner world may be a
truer index of our character than the outer world in which we live
openly. We like to deny it, say it is not there, but God sees this inner
world more plainly than our neighbors see the outer one.

Yes, the trouble with most of us is that our difficulties lie so deep
that only God's miracle power can deal with them. The beauty of
Jesus was that His inner character was more beautiful than His outer
one. At the transfiguration when His face became as the sun and His
raiment as white as the light, we are given a glimpse of the inward
character of our Saviour without spot or shadow or blemish. God could
turn His Son inside out in the presence of men and not be embarrassed,
but He could not do that with any other son of His.

There is one hopeful thought—sin indeed goes deep but Christ
goes deeper. Not only is He our Substitute in His perfection, but He
is our Indwelling Cleanser of the Temple.

WILLIAM WARD AYER

And as He (Jesus) entered into a certain village,
there met Him ten men that were lepers, which
stood afar off: and they lifted up their voices, and
said, "Jesus, Master, have mercy on us." And when
He saw them, He said unto them, "Go shew yourselves unto the priests." And it came to pass that,
as they went, they were cleansed. And one of them,

when he saw that he was healed, turned back, and
with a loud voice glorified God, and fell down on
his face at His feet, giving Him thanks. And he
was a Samaritan.

And Jesus answering said, "Were there not ten
cleansed? But where are the nine? There are not
found that returned to give glory to God, save this
stranger."   *Luke 17:12-18.*

OUR letter today is from one who was cleansed but who did not
forget his vow to serve God. If he should cross your path today
would he be encouraged on his way by your helpfulness or
would you pass him by "on the other side"?

"*Dear Brother Fuller*: I am writing you once more but, praise
God, I am not writing from the cold gray walls of a prison, this
time. He has spared my life to get out and now I am going to
serve Him. I promised Him that if He would forgive my sins
I would serve Him the rest of my life. It was through your preaching over the radio that I saw my lost and undone condition."

Pray for those who have been saved in prison whose terms are
now expired: that they may find friendly, helping hands as they come
out to take up the duties of life.

> *O blessed Christ, impaled upon the Cross,*
> *Abased, disowned in death's dark agony,*
> *What foes are these that, blind to gain or loss,*
> *Have wrought Thy fall and nailed Thee to a tree?*
> *I know them all:—Indifference! Smugness! Hate!*
> *The guilt is theirs! They pierced Thy tender flesh;*
> *And still they live to scorn and desecrate*
> *Thy selfless gift, and bring Thee wounds afresh.*
> *Alas! O Christ! I too have passed Thee by,*
> *And left Thee hanging lonely on the rood,*
> *Have turned away, have shunned Thy pleading cry*
> *And kept the silence of the multitude.*
> *Forgive! O Christ! Thou hast not died in vain!*
> *Redeeming love shall make me whole again!*
>   ALFRED GRANT WALTON

SEPTEMBER 3

He giveth to all life, and breath, and all things.
Acts 17:25.

MAN needs an atmosphere if he is to reveal his greatness. The tree must have its atmosphere of sunlight and air and water and food, else it cannot live. God is the atmosphere of man. Only in the presence of God, in closest intimacy with Him, under the warm touch of His breath, does he come into his growth. And getting clear in his relation to God simplifies a man's contact with his fellows, and simplifies all of his thinking of life. Simplicity is seeing clearly what is essential and what is detail—non-essential—and being controlled accordingly. So man rises up into the full mastery of himself through his utter dependence upon God.

S. D. GORDON

O heart of God, I hunger still for Thee;
Deeper and yet deeper would I go;
Till my faint heart and Thy great heart agree,
In every throb that from Thy depths doth flow.

Nothing of good hast Thou withheld from me,
Each morning streams of living water flow.
Yet, Lord, my heart is hungry still for Thee:
More of Thy love and passion would I know.

NORMAN LEWIS

SEPTEMBER 4

Like as Christ was raised up from the dead by the glory of the Father, even so we also should walk in newness of life. *Romans 6:4.*

DO NOT play up the negative and hide the positive. We are dead to sin but that we may be alive unto God; crucified that we may live. We magnify our burdens instead of our blessings, our fears instead of faith, and forget that beyond the cross lies the crown. We should yet be in our sins if the Christ of the cross had not also come out of the grave, and we shall be dead in experience if we only die to self and live not in Him.

Thomas knew that our Lord had died. He needed no evidence of that. He wanted to see the cross marks to be sure that He was alive. Thomases today demand to see in us the marks of the cross but not for the sake of the marks; what they are after is to see that He lives in us. Going around with heavy countenance, letting everybody know that you do not play cards, dance or attend the theater is not going to convince Thomas. But if he sees in you a living Christ who so meets your need that the world has lost its charm, he will be constrained to acknowledge Him as Lord and God.

VANCE HAVNER

> Defeat may serve as well as victory
> To shake the soul and let the glory out.
> When the great oak is straining in the wind,
> The boughs drink in new beauty, and the trunk
> Sends down a deeper root on the windward side.
> Only the soul that knows the mighty grief
> Can know the mighty rapture. Sorrows come
> To stretch out spaces in the heart for joy.

EDWIN MARKHAM

SEPTEMBER
5

He came unto His own, and His own received Him not. But as many as received Him, to them gave He power to become the sons of God, even to them that believe on His name: which were born, not of blood, nor of the will of the flesh, nor of the will of man, but of God.   *John 1:11–13.*

THE principal matter in our salvation—that is, how to become a son of God—is faith. Faith is described as receiving the Lord Jesus Christ. Faith is holding your empty cup under the flowing stream and letting it become full; it is the penniless hand held out for alms suddenly becoming filled with riches. Faith in Christ is the connecting link between the impotent and the omnipotent. Faith makes the greatest distinction among men. Note: "He came unto His own and His own received Him not." That is one company. "But as many as received Him to them gave He power." That is the other company. All mankind is divided into two groups, the believer and the unbeliever; the saved and the lost.

In which class are you? Have you received Christ as your personal Saviour? "He that believeth on Him is not condemned: but he that believeth not is condemned already, because he hath not believed in the name of the only begotten Son of God." If you are an unbeliever the wrath of God is literally hanging over your head.

There are many distinctions among men. There are the rich and

222

the poor, the governors and the governed, the teachers and the pupils, the wise and the foolish. But at death all distinctions pass away, except one. The great question will be, "Did you, or did you not, receive Christ as your Saviour while you had the opportunity?"

CHARLES E. FULLER

SEPTEMBER
6

The effectual fervent prayer of a righteous man availeth much. *James 5:16.*

WE LONG for revivals; we speak of revivals; we work for revivals; and we even pray a little for them. But we do not enter upon that labor in prayer which is the essential preparation for every revival.

Many of us misunderstand the work of the Spirit in the unconverted. We think that this work is limited essentially to the time when the awakenings are taking place. We seem to think that the unconverted are not subject to divine influence between times.

This is a complete misunderstanding. The Spirit works without interruption, during awakenings and between awakenings, even though He works differently, and the effect, therefore, also is different in the hearts of men.

The work of the Spirit can be compared to mining. The Spirit's work is to blast to pieces the sinner's hardness of heart and his frivolous opposition to God. The period of the awakening can be likened to the time when the blasts are fired. The time between the awakenings corresponds, on the other hand, to the time when the deep holes are being bored with great effort into the hard rock.

To bore these holes is hard and difficult and a task which tries one's patience. To light the fuse and fire the shot is not only easy but also very interesting work. One sees "results" from such work. It creates interest, too; shots resound, and pieces fly in every direction!

It takes trained workmen to do the boring. Anybody can light the fuse.

This fact sheds a great deal of light upon the history of revivals, a history which is often strange and incomprehensible.

There are many people who would like to light the fuse. Many would like to be evangelistic preachers. And some preachers are even so zealous that they light a fuse before the hole has been bored and explosive matter put in place. The resulting revival becomes, therefore, nothing but a little display of fireworks!

O. HALLESBY

223

Sin, when it is finished bringeth forth death.
James 1:15.

**The blood of Jesus Christ His Son cleanseth us
from all sin.**
1 John 1:7.

THROUGH a great part of the history of the church, leprosy has been taken as a description of sin. There is a good reason for that. Like leprosy, sin is mysterious in its origin. Like leprosy, sin is insidious in its growth. Like leprosy in the body, sin devastates the soul. Like leprosy in the body, sin spreads quickly through a man's whole system. Like leprosy, sin, if not cured, produces death.

The church has always used leprosy to illustrate the power, the devastation and the repulsiveness of sin. That is so. Every sin is repulsive. We sometimes speak of a man as a "moral leper." Remember that is every one of us in our depraved nature, a moral leper, and God sends His Son to touch us. That is what brought the wonder of joy and the doxologies leaping from the lips of those first Christian apostles, the fact that God in Christ could love a sinner! As the great Apostle said, "Scarcely for a righteous man will one die: yet peradventure for a good man some would even dare to die. But God commendeth His love toward us, in that, while we were yet sinners, Christ died for us."

Ah, yes! the love of Christ for a sinner whom no one else will love. Every sin is repulsive, whether it be selfishness or injustice or cruelty or profanity or impurity. It all comes from the same evil fountain. And yet, Christ comes with His healing touch to cleanse us. "The blood of Jesus Christ, His Son, cleanseth us from all sin!"

CLARENCE EDWARD MACARTNEY

*Come, every soul by sin oppressed,
There's mercy with the Lord,
And He will surely give you rest,
By trusting in His Word.*

*For Jesus shed His precious blood
Rich blessings to bestow;
Plunge now into the crimson flood
That washes white as snow.*

J. H. STOCKTON

Now unto Him that is able to do exceeding abundantly above all that we ask or think, according to
the power that worketh in us, Unto Him be glory
in the church by Christ Jesus throughout all ages,
world without end.   *Ephesians 3:20, 21.*

THIS doxology suggests riches beyond compare, and a divine
ability without limit. There is nothing beggarly about these
words; rather, one staggers in the presence of the superlatives
of divine grace there suggested. There can be no question that a
Christian can "live above" if he even half believes this transcending
declaration.

How was this doxology born? What provoked this contemplation
in the Apostle's mind and heart? The answer is to be found, we believe, in his contemplation of the unsearchable riches upon which his
eyes have been feasting. The very language he uses in this Epistle
suggests the inexhaustible resources which are in Christ for the believer. For instance, consider for a moment the very words and phrases
of Ephesians which all speak of the divine wealth at the full disposal
of the Christian. Every one of these words is "gilt-edged"; grace is
used twelve times; glory, eight times; inheritance, four times; riches,
five times; fulness, three times; fill, or filled, four times; and the in-
comparable phrase in Christ, or its equivalent, is used twenty-seven
times. "The riches of His grace" (1:7) and "the riches of His glory"
(3:16) are seen in something of their fulness when we link with
them other words found in the Epistle such as "blessed," "abounded,"
"obtained," "worketh," "give," "know," "saved," "made nigh," "access," "straightened," "filled," "loved," "able to withstand," "able to
quench" and "praying always." These are some of the "current coins,"
writes Ruth Paxon in *The Wealth, Walk and Warfare of the Christian,*
which the Christian may use daily in claiming wealth.

                                        HOWARD W. FERRIN

Teach me Thy way, O Lord; I will walk in Thy
truth.   *Psalm 86:11.*

HERE is George Muller's own statement of how he ascertained
the will of God. It is worthy of our consideration.

1. "I seek at the beginning to get my heart into such a
state that it has no will of its own in regard to a given matter. Nine-

tenths of the trouble with people is just here. Nine-tenths of the difficulties are overcome when our hearts are ready to do the Lord's will, whatever it may be. When one is truly in this state, it is usually but a little way to the knowledge of what His will is.

2. "Having done this, I do not leave the result to feeling or simple impression. If I do so, I make myself liable to great delusions.

3. "I seek the will of the Spirit of God through, or in connection with, the Word of God. The Spirit and the Word must be combined. If I look to the Spirit alone without the Word I lay myself open to great delusions also. If the Holy Ghost guides us at all, He will do it according to the Scriptures and never contrary to them.

4. "Next I take into account providential circumstances. These often plainly indicate God's will in connection with His Word and Spirit.

5. "I ask God in prayer to reveal His will to me aright.

6. "Thus, through prayer to God, the study of the Word, and reflection, I come to a deliberate judgment according to the best of my ability and knowledge, and if my mind is thus at peace, and continues so after two or three more petitions, I proceed accordingly. In trivial matters, and in transactions involving most important issues, I have found this method always effective."

SEPTEMBER 10

Fret not thyself . . .   *Psalm 37:1.*

FRET not thyself." Do not get into a perilous heat about things. And yet, if ever heat were justified, it was surely justified in the circumstances outlined in the Psalm. Evildoers were moving about clothed in purple and fine linen, and faring sumptuously every day. "Workers of iniquity" were climbing into the supreme places of power, and were tyrannizing over their less fortunate brethren. Sinful men and women were stalking through the land in the pride of life, and basking in the light and comfort of great prosperity. And good men were becoming heated and fretful. "Fret not thyself." Do not get unduly heated! Keep cool! Even in a good cause fretfulness is not a wise helpmeet. Fretting only heats the bearings, it does not generate the steam.

J. H. JOWETT

When I'm afraid of times before,
What coming days will bring,
When life's omissions I deplore,
And earth-mists round me cling;
O Lord of love, my weakness see,—
When I'm afraid I'll trust in Thee.

When I'm afraid of wily foes,
  Their flattery and hate,—
Who seek my progress to oppose,—
  My joys to dissipate;
O Lord of hosts, my weakness see,—
When I'm afraid I'll trust in Thee.

When I'm afraid of dangers near,
  Foreboding future ills;
When rocks and shoals and deeps I fear,
  And gloom my spirit fills;
O Lord of might, my weakness see,
When I'm afraid I'll trust in Thee.

When I'm afraid of crushing loss,
  Parting from loved ones dear,
Lest I shall murmur at my cross,
  And yield to faithless fear;
O Lord of peace, my weakness see,
When I'm afaid I'll trust in Thee.

A. GARDNER

SEPTEMBER 11

Now there are various kinds of gifts, but there is
the same Spirit; various kinds of official service,
and yet the same Lord; various kinds of effects,
and yet the same God who produces all the effects
in each person. *1 Corinthians 12:4-6 (Weymouth).*

Two men, absorbed in conversation, stand upon a railroad track,
not noting the approach of a train swiftly bearing down upon
them. Just in time both are snatched, by friendly hands, from
the awful death impending. To both, as they turn away with blanched
faces, the same event has come, namely, rescue from the terrible death
under the wheels of the rushing, roaring train. But mark how differently it affects them. One's eyes fill with tears; his voice trembles with
suppressed emotion; and his heart is quietly uplifted, in profound
gratitude to God. The other, fairly ecstatic in his emotion, leaps for
joy, embraces his rescuers, and exultantly recounts the story of his
deliverance to all whom he meets. The same blessing has come to
both, but the experience manifests itself diversely, because their individual temperament is different.

Just so it is here. Two of God's children yield their lives to Him in
entire surrender. In response to that surrender the same event will
come to them both—a fullness of the Spirit never known, never
thought possible, before. But the manifestation, the experience of that

fullness, will not be the same in both; it will necessarily vary with the individual temperament. For God not only gives the fullness, but He also made the vessels which contain that fullness, and has made them all slightly different. The cup, vase, and goblet of gold, are all full, but the water within them takes shape from the fashioning form of the vessel.

JAMES H. MCCONKEY

Faith adds its amen to God's yea, and then takes its hands off, and leaves God to finish His work. Its language is, "Commit thy way unto the Lord, trust also in Him; and He worketh."

A. B. SIMPSON

SEPTEMBER
12

Come unto Me, all ye that labour and are heavy laden, and I will give you rest. Take My yoke upon you, and learn of Me; for I am meek and lowly in heart: and ye shall find rest unto your souls. For My yoke is easy, and My burden is light. *Matthew 11:28–30.*

NOTICE the three gracious commands in these verses. "Come unto Me . . . take My yoke upon you . . . learn of Me." They will be the subjects of our three messages the rest of this month. Today we will consider the first, "Come unto Me." There are just two persons involved in it: "You" and "Me," that is, man and Christ. The laboring one and the tender, compassionate Saviour who intreats him to come and find rest! There is no one else who can come for you. You must come yourself. No man, no mediator, no minister or teacher, no church, can come in place of you. It is a personal matter.

You may come, no matter who you are, how guilty, how sin-stained, how undone and deep in sin you are. You may come without anyone to plead for you. The peace and rest of heart that you may have in coming to Jesus is worth more than all the riches this old earth can bring. "The wicked are like the troubled sea, when it cannot rest, whose waters cast up mire and dirt. There is no peace, saith my God, to the wicked" (Isaiah 57:20, 21). The most priceless treasure is the peace of heart which comes from the Prince of Peace. This peace or rest of heart cannot be yours until you are free from condemnation. "There is therefore now no condemnation to them which are IN CHRIST JESUS, who walk not after the flesh but after the Spirit" (Romans 8:1). Have you obeyed His command and come to Him? Are you "in Him" today?

CHARLES E. FULLER

228

We may not climb the heavenly steeps,
  To bring the Lord Christ down;
In vain we search the lowest deeps,
  For Him no depths can drown.

But warm, sweet, tender, even yet,
  A present Help is He;
And faith has yet its Olivet,
  And love its Galilee.

The healing of the seamless dress,
  Is by our beds of pain;
We touch Him in life's throng and press,
  And we are whole again.

JOHN GREENLEAF WHITTIER

SEPTEMBER
13

Why . . . is all this befallen us? *Judges 6:13.*

IDEON was soon to learn how God can turn affliction to advantage. Was it not the raiding and plundering by the Midianites that gave him the priceless privilege of seeing God and with his own ears hearing the divine truth? Many know that the God whom they neglected in prosperity came into their hearts with a deepening devotion in adversity. Many who were too busy for Christ, too preoccupied to hear His Word and study His counsel, were brought down on their backs in long sieges of sickness so that they could meet God. Blessed is that suffering and sorrow by which our heavenly Father rescues us from ourselves and saves us for Jesus in those darkened hours of wondering and searching when we ask, "Why . . . is all this befallen us?" and divine wisdom answers, "To bring Christ to you and you to Christ."

Gideon found also an advantage in adversity when that Midianite oppression taught him God's power and removed his doubts. With only three hundred men, and these armed not with bow and spear and sword but with pitchers and trumpets and torches, he was to defeat the vast host of the Midianites and to realize that God always keeps His word and proves His power. Has it not been in the fog of fear that the beacon of God's power has loomed most brightly in your life? When all else gives way, human help founders and men's words flit into thin air, God's words are clearest and answer your question, "Why . . . is all this befallen us?" with the promise, "In order to reveal My power to you, deepen your faith, strengthen your conviction, and remove all your doubt." Again I say, Blessed are the sorrows that shew us the strength of God.

WALTER A. MAIER

229

He has appeared once for all, at the close of the
ages, in order to do away with sin by sacrifice of
Himself.   *Hebrews 9:26 (Weymouth).*

You and I will never hate sin with a perfect hatred until we
look upon Him whom our sins pierced. You and I will never
love holiness with a perfect love until we look up into the face
which was marred more than any man's and with Saint Paul begin
to say, "He loved me, and gave Himself to the death for me." Do not
let us waste our time in cursing Caiaphas and pillorying Pilate and
judging Judas and slandering Simon Peter. We are all involved in the
great tragedy of the cross. We transfixed with nails His blessed hands
and feet. We tore His side with that fierce spear-thrust. It was sin
that slew the Lord of Life—our sins, yours and mine. If the world
had been less defiled Jesus need never have come. If man had not
sinned, the Son of God need not have suffered. "The Son of Man came
to seek and to save that which was lost, and to give His life a ransom
for many."

> *"Bearing shame and scoffing rude,*
> *In my place condemned He stood;*
> *Sealed my pardon with His blood;*
> *Hallelujah! what a Saviour!"*

I know that is old theology, but it is all I have to live by, and one
day it will be all I will dare to die by. I cannot do with one of these
little Christs they have whittled down to something next door to
nothing. A real sinner needs a real Saviour. I need a Christ, big
enough, high enough, holy enough to stoop from heaven's height
down to the level of my ignobility and sin and shame, and lift me out
of the deep abyss. And that is what I have found in Jesus. And from
the fountain which was opened in the house of David for sin and for
uncleanness I received first of all the grace of repentance.

R. Moffat Gautrey

The love of God hath flooded our hearts through
the Holy Spirit given unto us.

Romans 5:5 (Weymouth).

THE all-inclusive result of the infilling of the Holy Spirit is love.
That marvelous tender passion—the love of God—heightless,
depthless, shoreless, shall flood our hearts, making us as gentle
and tender-hearted and self-sacrificing and gracious as He. Every
phase of life will become a phase of love. Peace is love resting. Bible
study is love reading its Lover's letters. Prayer is love keeping tryst.
Conflict with sin is love jealously fighting for its Lover. Hatred of sin
is love shrinking from that which separates from the Lover. Sympathy
is love tenderly feeling. Enthusiasm is love burning. Hope is love ex-
pecting. Patience is love waiting. Faithfulness is love sticking fast.
Humility is love taking its true place. Modesty is love keeping out of
sight. Soul-winning is love pleading.

S. D. GORDON

> The name of my Beloved
> Is sweet as ointment rare;
> The chief among ten thousand,
> The altogether fair.
>
> The voice of my Beloved
> Is sweeter to my ear
> Than earth's divinest music,
> Or voice of friend most dear.
>
> The hand of my Beloved
> Is ever clasped in mine;
> It leads me, heals me, holds me,
> With love and strength divine.
>
> But He, my well Beloved,
> Is more than all to me,
> Himself my joy, my portion,
> Himself my song shall be.

A. B. SIMPSON

He shall call upon me, and I will answer him.
Psalm 91:15.

HERE is a letter which should be a great encouragement to those who have prayed long and earnestly for the salvation of their loved ones, with seemingly no results. Let us learn to persevere in prayer.

"*Dear Brother and Sister Fuller*: Tomorrow will be my husband's fifth birthday in the Lord. Five years ago as he was listening to your broadcast he knelt by the radio and wept his way through to Christ. These have been five happy years serving Him whom to know is life eternal. We are sending an offering which he says he hopes will help to save some other lost, drunken sinner.

"Don't any of you wives give up, who are praying for drunken husbands. I prayed for nineteen long years. God answers prayer. John 14:14 says so and I know it is true."

Pray today for those who have been enslaved by habits which they cannot break without divine aid. Pray for the Pilgrim Hour and the Old Fashioned Revival Hour that the messages, this week, shall result in many conversions.

> *Give me abounding faith, I pray,*
> *That sweeps aside these little things I fear*
> *And pierces through the mist beyond today.*
> *Faith that is sight, that sees Thy Presence near.*
>
> *Give me abiding faith, dear Lord;*
> *Faith in the storm as in the calm;*
> *Faith fed each moment by Thy faithful Word—*
> *My fount of joy—and, through the pain, a balm.*
>
> *Then I shall have a faith that lives,*
> *Not just a doctrine or a passing creed.*
> *But Life—the life of Him who gives*
> *Reward to faith—supply for every need!*
> KENNETH ANDERSON

I have appeared unto thee to make thee a witness of the things wherein thou hast seen Me.

Acts 26:16 (R. V.).

𝕴N ORDER to be a minister, i. e., to have the power of communicating the grace of God to the souls of men, one needs first of all to be a witness—one who has seen, heard, and known.

That great man of God, John Smith, in the early part of the last century once said:—"No man feels the value of the soul of another who has not been made sensible of the worth of his own soul. No man discerns the malignity of sin in the world who has not yet felt its bitterness and terror in his own heart. No man is awake to the peril of the ungodly who has not trembled under the sense of personal danger. No man forms a correct estimate of the value of the atonement who has not had the blood of Christ sprinkled on his own conscience."

Here is a deep secret, and one that is absolutely indispensable for the work of soul-winning. To put it briefly, we may say that the one task that we are called upon to accomplish is to convict men of sin and then to convince them of the love of God in Christ. This we can never do unless we ourselves have had an experience of these very things.

Alas! how many are seeking to avoid any deep conviction of their own sinfulness, not realising that, besides being the very foundation of all true godliness, it is also a priceless asset in the work we are called to do!

We may preach like angels, but unless we have had a deep conviction of sin ourselves we shall never produce it in others; unless we are witnesses of His love we shall never be able to communicate that precious legacy of our dying Lord to those who are in need.

PAGET WILKES

For if through the transgression of one single man the mass of mankind has died, all the more have God's grace, and the gift made through the grace of the one man Jesus Christ, been abundant for the mass of mankind.

Romans 5:15 (Weymouth).

𝔍T GIVES great rest to the heart to know that the One who has undertaken for us, in all our weakness, our need, and the exigencies of our path from first to last, has first of all secured, in every respect, the glory of God. That was His primary object in all things. In the work of redemption, and in all our history, the glory of God has the first place in the heart of that Blessed One with whom we have to do. At all cost to Himself He vindicated and maintained the divine glory. To that end He gave up everything. He laid aside His own glory, humbled, emptied Himself. He surrendered Himself and yielded up His life, in order to lay the imperishable foundation of that glory which now fills all heaven—and shall soon cover the earth and shine through the wide universe forever.

The knowledge and abiding sense of this must give profound repose to the spirit in reference to everything that concerns us, whether it be the salvation of the soul, the forgiveness of sins, or the needs for the daily path. All that could possibly be a matter of exercise to us, for time or for eternity, has been provided for, all secured on the selfsame basis that sustains the divine glory. We are saved and provided for; but the salvation and provision—all praise to our glorious Saviour and Provider!—are inseparably bound up with the glory of God. In all that our Lord Jesus Christ has done for us, in all that He is doing, in all that He will do, the glory of God is fully maintained.

C. H. M.

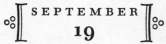

Take My yoke upon you.   *Matthew 11:29.*

𝔗HE yoke of sin is burdensome and heavy, but Christ's yoke is easy. To be in the yoke with Him is to be in fellowship. He becomes your constant companion. Fellowship, or companionship, follows the establishment of this relationship. First, you obey the command to come to Him. After you have come to Him and have been adopted into His family He invites you to the fellowship of service.

There is more to the Christian life than just receiving Christ and becoming a new creation in Him, as blessed as that is. The next step follows naturally. You become His partner in service. There is work to be done. There are burdens to be borne. There is the "fellowship of suffering." But all labor becomes light when He is in the yoke with you. Somehow the joy of His presence and the satisfaction of His companionship make the burden light.

Are you getting the most out of life? Not unless you are in His service. Not if you are living for yourself alone! Not until you have taken upon yourself a concern for others and are willing to become a burden bearer. "Bear ye one another's burdens and so fulfill the law of Christ." "Casting all your care (burden) upon Him, for He careth for you." You take another's burden, making it yours, and then you cast the load on Him. It's a remarkable yoke because only when you are in it with Christ are you free from labor and struggle.

CHARLES E. FULLER

Jesus is calling, is calling to you,
"Haste thee, My child, My work waits for thee.
Lo! In My vineyard there's work yet to do;
Come, labor there with Me!

"White are the fields and the workers are needed.
Shall some be lost while the call goes unheeded?
Forth to the work—it is no time to sleep!
I'll strengthen thee, help thee, My Presence shall keep."
Hark, 'tis the Saviour, He's calling for you,
"Lo! In My vineyard there's work yet to do."

AUTHOR UNKNOWN

SEPTEMBER 20

Set me as a seal upon thine heart, as a seal upon thine arm. *Song of Solomon 8:6.*

GOD's children often think, because they have a guilty conscience, that their Father is frowning upon them, and it keeps them at a distance. This mistrust often leads to mean, unworthy actions towards God. With shame and sorrow I confess, how, when I have sinned and grieved the Holy Spirit of God, I have more than once said to myself, "I will go and visit that old woman, and take her something, and read and pray with her." What for? In order to get myself right with my heavenly Father. And now I am inclined to think that my unworthy plans to re-instate myself in the heart of God must have grieved Him more than the sin which first broke my communion with Him. What I should have done is this: I should at once have gone to my Father, confessed the sin, judged myself for it in His presence, and accepted the forgiveness which was mine according to His Word. (1 John 1:9.)

Christian, never doubt thy Father's love. Never allow any misgiving upon this point to rest upon thy soul. The devil began his foul work by insinuating such a doubt—"Yea, hath God said?" Fling back the doubts and misgivings with which he still would poison thy heart. Look into the face of thy Beloved, and say, "Set me as a seal upon Thy heart." He always loved us; He never ceases to love us, and His love never changes.

J. J. Luce

SEPTEMBER
21

Cast not away therefore your confidence, which hath great recompence of reward. For ye have need of patience, that, after ye have done the will of God, ye might receive the promise.

Hebrews 10:35, 36.

FROM this distance we see how God was moving in the infinite order of His ceaseless love, and what we thought confusion was but the sign of His progress. What light is flung upon the pathway of each day if once this fact is understood. The day is not done with when its sun sets. The deeds of any given hour are not fully comprehended in the passing of its sixty minutes. If the deeds of the days have been those planned by God, then they are days the full blossoming of which will be found in the perfect light of the everlasting day. It has been said that every flower that decks the sod has its root far back in eternity. So also every human life, in the will and purpose of God, is linked to the past and to the future, and His laws for it forget no fact of all the ages.

Need anything further be written to prove the wisdom of abandoning life to His will? See how all other laws fail when placed in comparison with this. The best-loved friend I have cannot compass within the facts of certain knowledge the events of the next hour. They may advise, but their advice is necessarily tentative. They would go this way if—and how much depends upon the *if*. A thousand chances may prove the folly of their wisdom, the shortsightedness of their policy.

This is never so with the soul that has no law save that of the Divine will.

G. Campbell Morgan

236

God Almighty appeared unto me . . . and blessed
me, and said unto me, Behold, I will . . . , I will
. . . , I will. . . .   *Genesis 48:3, 4.*

ᚼACOB had reached the last stage of his earthly pilgrimage. He
had come to a grand old age. But, although his eye-sight had
grown dim and his strength had failed him, these physical infirmities had not impaired the faith of his heart. Long ago, as a young
man, God had met him at a most desperate crisis in his life (Gen. 28),
had blessed him and had promised certain things to him, and although
down through the years many and varied had been his circumstances,
and often wilful his way, the perfume of the meeting, that blessing,
that promise had remained with him. It had served as a beacon light
in the night of sorrow, an urge in the strife of battle; an elixir in the
hour of pain, and a strength in the time of weakness. He had walked
ever with that in view—the PROMISE OF GOD.

He was "going the way of all the earth" now, but still that divine
covenant, made so long before, was as vivid as though it were but
yesterday that it had been given. He knew that God was true and as
good as His word although death might hinder a realization of the
fulfilment of the promise in his time.

Do we have that same faith in the promises of God? Do you have
some special word hidden deep in your heart from the heart of God?
If so, believe God for its fulfilment regardless of all untoward circumstances, even though you may not live to see it. "Let God be true,
but every man a liar!"

PAMEII

When pressed in body, soul, and mind,
When naught of earth brings healing balm,
Then Jesus speaks my spirit calm;
In Him alone true rest I find.

When earth seems but a hateful spot,
And from its scenes I fain would go,
His voice I hear: "Be still, and know
I've prayed for thee that faith fail not."

Life's day swift passes, then comes night—
What shall I do when old age comes?
"I'll ne'er forsake My trusting ones;
At even time it shall be light."

He ever lives and intercedes:
Ah, soul, look up, and grieve Him not,
Nor question more, whate'er thy lot,
His faithfulness who meets thy needs.

EFFIE MAY FOSS

Great peace have they which love Thy law.
Psalm 119:165.

P E A C E is the prize for which a distraught world is eagerly seeking—all because they have not stopped to ponder and believe the truth of this verse, written a thousand years before the Prince of Peace became incarnate in the Babe of Bethlehem. Love of God's law will solve every national problem. It will solve your individual problem today, also. God's law is the law of love but it is first the law of righteousness. His Word says, "Righteousness and peace have kissed" (Psalm 85:10). When? Only when God's righteousness and His love for us in Christ met at Calvary. It was there that He "made peace through the blood of His cross" (Colossians 1:20).

J. ELWIN WRIGHT

"Great peace have they which love Thy law,
And nothing shall offend them";
Thy goodness and Thy mercy, too,
Shall constantly attend them.
They have no fear when swelling tides
Of evil rage around them;
They know in whom they have believed,
And nothing shall confound them.

It is not so with wicked men;
They have no light or vision;
They do not love Thy holy law,
But hold it in derision.
They have no peace, they have no rest—
No help in pain or sorrow;
No God, no hope, for this dark world—
And darker, still, tomorrow!

Though for awhile men give them praise,
Though for awhile they flourish,
They shall be suddenly cut off—
Their very names shall perish!
Lord, write Thy law upon my heart
In letters deeply graven,
So Thy great peace shall e'er be mine,
And greater peace of heaven.

T. O. CHISHOLM

What is man, that Thou art mindful of him.

Psalm 8:4.

WHAT was the attitude of Jesus toward the individual? He "must needs go through Samaria." Note the word of urgency, in order to deal with an individual. He turned aside from the crowd again and again to deal with one soul.

One day He called a man, small of stature, who had climbed a tree out of curiosity, and said, "Make haste and come down, for today I must abide at thy house." Again the note of compulsion, although the multitude murmured saying, "He has gone to be guest with a man that is a sinner." He "must abide" in that house, to make that man and that home forever different. Zacchaeus was "chief among the publicans and . . . rich" and yet, after a day of companionship with our Lord, this rich publican said, "Behold, Lord, the half of my goods I give to the poor, and if I have taken anything from any man by false accusation, I restore him fourfold." What a wonderful change had been wrought in that life!

Our danger today, as Christians zealous for evangelistic effort, is that we will forget the individual in a desire for large totals. What is man, the individual, that thou art mindful of him? Do you see people as crowds, or as lost, dying souls who need the Saviour?

S. MAY WYBURN

The Lord Christ wanted a tongue one day,
To speak a word of cheer,
To a heart that was weary and worn and sad,
And weighed with a mighty fear.
He asked me for mine, but it was busy quite
With my own affairs, from morn till night.

The Lord Christ wanted a hand one day,
To do a loving deed;
He wanted two feet, on an errand for Him,
To run with gladsome speed.
But I had need of my own that day;
To His gentle beseeching I answered, "Nay!"

So that day I used my tongue,
My hands, and my feet as I chose;
I said some hasty, bitter words
That hurt one heart, God knows:
I busied my hands with worthless play,
And my wilful feet went a crooked way.

And the dear Lord Christ—was His work undone
For lack of a willing heart?

239

Only through men does He speak to men?
Dumb must He be apart?
I do not know, but I wish today,
I had let the Lord Christ have His way.

ALICE NICHOLS

SEPTEMBER 25

My God shall supply all your need according to His riches in glory by Christ Jesus.

Philippians 4:19.

ANY of us hedge God around with such limitations, laws, and modes of operation as to practically tie His hands and make it impracticable for Him to do any real supernatural thing in our lives. To really believe in the all-sufficiency of God means to believe that He is actually at liberty to do for us all that we need a God for, and that we have a right to take Him for everything for which we are unequal and insufficient. It means that He has promised all things necessary for life and godliness, that He has provided all things, and that we have a right to come to Him for all things, presenting without question the mighty check on the bank of heaven, "My God shall supply all your need according to His riches in glory by Christ Jesus."

It means that we have a God who is equal to our salvation and the salvation of any sinner, however lost and however long he has resisted the mercy and grace of God. It means that God is equal to your sanctification and the sanctification of any temperament, no matter how impracticable; the counteracting of any habit no matter how confirmed; the overcoming of any defect, infirmity, and sin, no matter how deeply rooted and aggravated; victory over any and every temptation that may come, and a life sanctified through and through and preserved blameless unto the coming of the Lord Jesus Christ.

A. B. SIMPSON

SEPTEMBER 26

Learn of Me.   *Matthew 11:29.*

HIS is linked up with the preceding phrase which we considered last week. "Take My yoke upon you and learn of Me." You can best learn by being with Him constantly. Then you will discover the secret of His power. "I am meek and lowly in heart." All that He was in His earthly life and ministry He wants you to become as His representative and ambassador. He wants you in the yoke so that He may teach you. You will learn to keep in step with Him, not running ahead or lagging behind. You will learn His patience, His gentleness, His forbearance, His stedfastness. He was meek. If you wear the yoke you will learn His meekness, not the meekness of weakness, but of assurance and strength. His meekness led Him to the cross. It will lead you there, too. He was lowly. If you wear the yoke you will walk with Him among the poor, the despised, the outcast, the hopeless, and you will learn to love them as He loved them.

Do you want to learn of Him? Wear the yoke.

CHARLES E. FULLER

Have you walked with the King as your Partner?
Have you taken Him with you each day?
Can you say that your life is much fairer
  Since He is the Guide and the Way?

Have you walked with the King in the garden?
Have you looked on His loveliness there?
Has your soul e'er o'erflowed with His beauty
  As you whispered His name in prayer?

Have you walked with the King in the valley?
When your eyes have been blinded with tears?
Have you felt His kind hand laid upon you
  In sorrowing sympathy dear?

Can you say you've been bought by the Saviour?
Are you saved and redeemed by His blood?
Then love Him, O love Him forever,
  And praise God for His wonderful Word!

MURIEL E. DYHRMAN

SEPTEMBER 27

The law of the Lord is perfect, converting the soul: the testimony of the Lord is sure, making wise the simple. *Psalm 19:7.*

WE FIND no difficulty in distinguishing between the works of God and the works of man. God's works are absolutely perfect; man's are only relatively so. The most perfect needle may be perfect for the work to which it is adapted; but make it a microscopic object and the smooth hole appears ragged and the needle becomes a honeycombed poker. Take, on the contrary, a hair from the leg of a fly, or the dust from a butterfly's wing. Magnify these, and they are seen to be absolutely perfect.

Now there is no more difficulty in distinguishing the Word of God from the word of man than there is in distinguishing the work of God from the work of man. You need the minute examination and the anointed eye that can perceive its beauties which do not lie on the surface. In this way God's Word contains the best evidence of its own inspiration. It could not have been forged or manufactured.

J. HUDSON TAYLOR

Most wondrous Book! Bright candle of the Lord!
Star of eternity! The only star
By which the bark of man could navigate
The sea of life, and gain the coast of bliss.

ROBERT POLLOCK

SEPTEMBER 28

And he repaired the altar of the Lord that was broken down. *1 Kings 18:30.*

WE READ that Elijah began the demonstration of the true God by repairing the altar of the Lord that was broken down. Never was there a revival that did not so begin. And if today God answers from heaven we must begin to repair His broken altars: altars of consecration where once we gave ourselves to God and promised to do His will alone; where we offered Him our talents and time and possessions, ourselves; but with the years we have kept back part of the price and lied unto God until it is a wonder we do not drop dead like Ananias and Sapphira; altars of dedication where we gave our children to God, but later chose our way for them and denied God; family altars where once we gathered to read the Word and commit our way unto the Lord, but now abandon with the silly excuse that since times have changed, it is no longer practical; altars of praise and testimony where once the redeemed of the Lord said so, but sin and worldliness and neglect have closed our lips and stolen our song; altars of service where once we lived only, always, for the King, but have now deserted because we live for self and none beside, just as if Jesus had never lived, just as if He had never died.

Here is our task, to repair these broken altars, and all our pious dodges and clever substitutes to avoid repentance will never avail. Stained-glass windows and robed choirs and anthems and banquets and dramas and eloquence in the pulpit and elegance in the pew have never fooled God. He demands truth in the inward parts, and heaven will keep silent and no fire will ever fall until we approach Him with rebuilt altars in the name of the Lord.

VANCE HAVNER

Whatsoever He saith unto you, do it.   *John 2:5.*

THE Spirit of prayer would teach us that we should disregard the question as to whether the fulfillment of our prayer is hard or easy for God. What we think or do not think about this has no bearing on the hearing and answering of prayer. Not only that; it has a blighting and destructive effect upon our prayer life, because we waste our strength on something which is not our concern, and which our Lord has never asked us to be concerned about.

This secret of prayer became very plain to me once many years ago as I was reading the delightful little account of the wedding in Cana of Galilee (John 2:1–11).

Jesus, His mother, and His disciples were bidden to the wedding. In all likelihood the family was closely related to, or very friendly toward, the family of Jesus. At least, we notice that the host and hostess had acquainted the mother of Jesus with the embarrassing situation which had arisen when the wine had given out.

Whereupon the mother of Jesus reveals herself as a tried and true woman of prayer.

In the first place, she goes to the right place with the need with which she has become acquainted. She goes to Jesus and tells Him everything.

In the next place, notice what she says to Jesus. Just these few, simple words, "They have no wine." Note here what prayer is. To pray is to tell Jesus what we lack. Intercession is to tell Jesus what we see that others lack.

In the third place, let us notice that she did nothing more. When she had told Jesus about the need of her friends, she knew that she did not have to do any more about it. She knew that she did not have to help Him either by suggesting what He should do or anything else. She knew Him and knew that this need had been left in the proper hands. She knew Him. She knew that He Himself knew what He wanted to do.

She knew also that she did not have to influence Him or persuade Him to give these friends a helping hand. No one is so willing to help as He is!

O. HALLESBY

SEPTEMBER
30

From the uttermost part of the earth have we
heard songs.   *Isaiah 24:16.*

THE marvel of radio makes it possible for the whole world to go
to one meeting. The following letter illustrates the world coverage of the Old Fashioned Revival Hour and the Pilgrim Hour.

"*Dear Mr. Fuller*: I have a message for you from far away
North Africa. I have written you about my adopted son, who is
a post commander in an American hospital. His two sisters are
nurses with the American forces abroad. For some time these sisters were 'somewhere in Australia' and, while there, they listened
to the Old Fashioned Revival Hour every Sunday. Later one sister was transferred to Algeria. She listens from there to the Pilgrim Hour from Long Beach.

"Since then all three listen every Sunday, one from eastern
United States, one from New Guinea and one from Algeria. They
say the reception is clear and fine."

Pray today that thousands of doctors, nurses, and wounded in the
hospitals on many fronts may receive and accept God's offer of salvation through the broadcasts by short wave.

Like a river glorious is God's perfect peace,
Over all victorious in its bright increase;
Perfect, yet it floweth fuller every day,
Perfect, yet it groweth deeper all the way.

Stayed upon Jehovah, hearts are fully blest:
Finding, as He promised, perfect peace and rest.
                              FRANCES RIDLEY HAVERGAL

When the enemy shall come in like a flood, the
Spirit of the Lord shall lift up a standard against
him.   *Isaiah 59:19.*

TO EVERY fear the prophet presents a promise; to every sus
picion he offers an assurance. Now, we, too, are exiles returning
to the homeland. We, too, have been in the dark realms of
captivity, and by His redeeming grace our eyes have been lifted toward the better country. And we, too, are full of uncertainties and
fears. There is a desert to traverse, a wilderness to cross, waters to
pass through, mountains to climb, and we know not how we may
safely reach our journey's end. And particularly are we beset by the
enemy, who suddenly and unexpectedly sweeps down upon our path.
But if 'we have the fears, ours, too, are the promises. Between the
enemy and ourselves there shall be erected the standard of the Lord.
"When the enemy shall come in like a flood, the Spirit of the Lord
shall lift up a standard against him."

                                    J. H. JOWETT

> *If I should lose some priceless thing*
> *I loved and treasured long,*
> *Why should I weep? Beneath Thy wing*
> *I sing Redemption's Song!*
> *In GOD HIMSELF I'm fully blest,*
> *For whom have I but THEE?*
> *I know that all is for the best,*
> *And that's enough for me!*
>
> *If dear ones whom I love below*
> *Should leave me here—alone—*
> *The LIVING ONE will never go,*
> *And HE is on the Throne!*
> *Thy love, my God, such sweetness gives,*
> *I'm satisfied with THEE—*
> *I know that my Redeemer lives,*
> *And that's enough for me!*
>
> *So all is well!—Whate'er betide*
> *THE LAMB is on the Throne—*
> *I triumph through the Crucified,*
> *I boast in GOD ALONE!*
> *Now raised by Grace to Heaven above,*
> *I'm seated here with THEE—*
> *I'M LOVED WITH EVERLASTING LOVE*
> *AND THAT'S ENOUGH FOR ME!*

                                    WORTHING

245

My son, give me thine heart.   *Proverbs 23:26.*

How grieved would that true lover be whose betrothed would answer his petition for her heart, herself, by proffering her purse, houses, or lands! How much more must God be grieved by our poor attempts to bribe Him by giving Him everything else except the one thing He wants—ourselves. "My son, give me thine heart." There is a giving which is instead of ourselves; and there is a gift of ourselves. One is the poor bribe of legalism to Love; the other the joyful response of love to Love. So in falling short of giving ourselves to God we fall short of the one supreme gift He desires. For God gave Himself, gave all to us.

If our response to the Lover of our soul falls short of the true-hearted surrender of ourselves, we thereby show that we do not fully trust Him. But the shadow of such distrust haunting the unsurrendered heart is the barrier that keeps it from the fullness of God. For God cannot give fullness of the Spirit to him who does not have such fullness of trust as to yield his life to Him. Wherefore, beloved, knowing that naught but this can bring to your heart His fullness of life, see to it that you omit it not.

JAMES H. McCONKEY

Oh, save me from self-will, dear Lord,
Which claims Thy sacred throne;
Oh, let my will be lost in Thine,
And let Thy will be done.
Oh, keep me from self-confidence,
And self-sufficiency;
Let me exchange my strength for Thine,
And lean alone on Thee.

Oh, save me from self-seeking, Lord,
Let me not be my own;
A living sacrifice I come,
Lord, keep me Thine alone.
From proud vain-glory save me, Lord,
From pride of praise and fame;
To Christ be all the honor given,
The glory to His name.

A. B. SIMPSON

Wilt thou be made whole?   *John 5:6.*

CHRIST was in Jerusalem at the feast. While there He visited the pool of Bethesda. This pool was located by the sheep market which was near the first gate, called the "sheep gate," in the walls of Jerusalem. Please notice this because every detail brought out in God's Word has a meaning. There were five porches at this pool. That, too, is significant. Five is the number of "grace." "Bethesda" means "mercy." This is linked up in this beautiful story with the "sheep gate." All this speaks to us of redemption, for Christ, God's Lamb, is our only approach to God and only God's mercy and grace make our salvation possible.

We are told in the story that a great many impotent folks were lying there at the pool waiting for an angel to trouble the waters, so that the first one to enter the pool afterward might be healed. Jesus came to one of the most helpless of the sufferers and asked him an all-important question: "Wilt thou be made whole?" The reply was, "Sir, I have no man. . . ." Then Jesus said to him, "Rise, take up thy bed and walk." Christ manifested the power of deity, spoke the word of life and immediately the man was healed.

Friend, perhaps you, too, are waiting, as this man waited for thirty-eight long years. He was waiting for healing of body. Perhaps your need is healing for your soul. I am glad to tell you that there is no need to wait longer. Today is the day of God's grace and mercy. There will be no more convenient season. Have you faced your condition frankly? This man at the pool did so. He knew he was in need and helpless. He accepted the help of the One who could heal him. He had "no man" to help him for thirty-eight long years. We have "the Man, Christ Jesus," ready now to bring instant healing to our souls. Will you accept His help?

CHARLES E. FULLER

Always rejoice in the Lord: I will repeat it, rejoice . . . Do not be anxious about anything. . . . So will the peace of God, which surpasses all power of thought, be a garrison to guard your hearts and minds in Christ Jesus.

Philippians 4:4–7 (Weymouth).

THERE is a very depressing brand of mysticism that talks a great deal nowadays in holy phraseology, but gives little evidence of Christian joy and victory. I have observed that those who talk most about being crucified with Christ are often not so dead to self as those who do not have so much to say about it. I recall once in awhile that some of the fine old Christian characters of my boyhood days probably had never read a devotional book and knew little about the different theories of sanctification, but they had a rugged, sturdy, simple faith and a wholesome spirituality that would put most of us to shame.

One becomes a little weary with these inlookers who never can get themselves into just the mood they crave; who emphasize being dead to sin more than being alive to God, and consequently they never seem to become successful corpses; who are always trying to crucify themselves so that they never get around to "Christ liveth in me"; who put their burdens above their blessings, their faith below their fears; who glory in crosses of doubtful make, but wear no crown of rejoicing. These talk much of the "fellowship of His suffering," but we have observed that those who have entered most truly into that, advertise it least. The whole life of such poor souls is shot through and through with such a pallor of artificial saintliness that one recoils from such gloomy piety to say, "Surely this cannot be that hilarious faith of the early church, that new wine of Pentecost, that victory that could cry out from Roman prisons, 'Rejoice in the Lord alway.' "

VANCE HAVNER

OCTOBER
5

**Beware that thou forget not the Lord thy God:
. . . lest when thou hast eaten and art full, and
hast built goodly houses, and hast dwelt therein;
and when thy herds and thy flocks multiply, and
thy silver and thy gold is multiplied, and all that
thou hast is multiplied; then thine heart be lifted
up, and thou forget the Lord thy God; . . . and
thou say in thine heart, My power and the might
of mine hand hath gotten me this wealth.**

Deuteronomy 8:11–17.

A VERY solemn warning that, and yet a warning that is needed
even more than at the time it was given. God knows the temptation to misuse His gifts, and forget Him. Oh, how prone we are
to take advantage of God's wealth for ourselves, instead of investing
it for Him. It is very easy to say, "If only I had money how I would
use it for God!" And yet when wealth does come it is often spent on
self. Better homes are purchased, more luxurious furnishings obtained,
automobiles bought, and thus it is used up, and God's work gets what
is left.

There are very few people who can be trusted with great wealth.
Vast resources mean tremendous responsibility. If God could trust us
He would bless us far more in material things. But would we use them
for Him? What percentage would go for the evangelization of the
world? How much would we keep for ourselves? Would God get the
major portion?

During the lifetime of the sainted George Muller of Bristol, England, there often appeared in the books among other contributions an
entry as follows: "From a servant of the Lord Jesus, who, constrained
by the love of Christ, seeks to lay up treasure in heaven." For years
no one knew who this "servant" was. But after the death of Mr.
Muller it was discovered that the "servant" was none other than
Muller himself. And how much do you think he had given when it
was all totalled up? Over $400,000. What a glorious privilege! But
why did he give so largely? Because God could trust him. He died with
nothing. He gave all. Can He trust you?

OSWALD J. SMITH

And he shall sit as a refiner and purifier.

Malachi 3:3.

THERE is an intensely vivid picture of God's love, its yearningness, and strong patience, and dissatisfaction with less than the best. It is in Malachi's prophecy. The expert workman in refining metals sits patiently over the pot of liquid metal, picking out the dross sent up to the surface by the intense fire, watching keenly for every speck and spot, until by and by his own face is clearly reflected in that over which he is working. Then, the process complete, the metal pure, the fire is withdrawn. Its work is done.

So, we are told, God does. Pain is a fire, sometimes heated seven times hotter than usual. God's love and great ideal for us hold Him steady while the dross is being removed. He is not content until He sees again clearly reflected that great likeness of Himself in which we were originally made. When the likeness is clear and full the fire is withdrawn. And in the after-glory that shall come the pain will seem light, and the time only a moment; yet how impossible that often seems at the time of suffering.

S. D. GORDON

While war its wounds on Time's sad brow is branding,
And earth-born peace from earth departs;
Thy peace, O God, which passes understanding,
Alone can garrison our hearts.

Only in Thee, our Rock and our Salvation,
Anxiety allays in rest;
Only in Thee, our Hope and Consolation,
The living or the dead are blest.

Then keep us, Father, in these days of sadness,
Quiet and confident in Thee;
Save us from fear amid the awful madness
Of ruthless war o'er land and sea.

Above the strife, oh, hear Thy people praying—
Humbled beneath the chast'ning rod;
Above the strife, oh, may we hear Thee saying,
"Be still, and know that I am God."

F. W. PITT

Understanding is a wellspring of life unto him that hath it. *Proverbs 16:22.*

HAT a wealth there is in a wellspring. Climbing a mountain one day, I hit on a bubbling pool of water, amid a mass of green foliage and yellow primroses. What is this? Of course, it was a spring of fresh water bursting out of the mountain's side, pure and perennial. And down it trickled, making one continuous track to the foot of the hill, traceable to my eye by its green ferns and bog willows all the way. What a wealth of greenery is there in a wellspring!

Such riches, too, lie in wise understanding of the ways of God. The wise man is the wealthy man. He knows God and lays claim to all that God is and has. He possesses God's grace, and that makes him gracious; He inherits God's gifts and they make him inherently rich. His heart is a "Wellspring of Joy" which is ever flowing and overflowing. In him are fountains of happy feeling; and they flow all day in streams of solid pleasure. They do not get dry in summer nor "drumly" in winter.

Miss Anna Waring beautifully sings of it. She thanks God that her heart is at "the secret source of every precious thing," that its frail vessel has been so filled, and adds:

"I thirst for springs of heavenly life
And here all day they rise;
I seek the treasure of Thy love
And close at hand it lies.
And a new song is in my mouth,
To much loved music set,
Glory to Thee for all the grace
I have not tasted yet."

Here is a new wellspring of knowledge that very few ever open. The untasted gifts that are to come; the undiscovered fountains that shall meet us on the future road to heaven. Glory be to God for them!

Let us not fail to find every one of these fountains of gladness. Our experience of past mercies should lead us to expect more in the future. We are not half awake to our unnumbered blessings. They have "abounded" far beyond our merits. And through the grace and goodness of God they will abound. Heaven save me from being a discontented growler, the most unchristian being on earth. And heaven grant me the understanding which is a wellspring of life.

W. S. BRUCE

How long wilt thou mourn? . . . Fill thy horn
with oil, and go: I will send thee. . . . I have
provided. . . .   *1 Samuel 16:1.*

Y E S, human sorrow must flow on until the heart finds repose in
the rich resources of the blessed God. The varied blanks which
human events leave in the heart can only be filled up by the
power of faith in the precious word, "I have provided." This really
settles everything. This dries the tear, alleviates the sorrow, fills the
blank. The moment the spirit rests in the provision of God's love,
there is a period put to all repinings. May we all know the power and
varied application of this truth; may we know what it is to have our
tears dried up, and our horn filled by the conviction of our Father's
wise and merciful provision.

                                                C. H. M.

> *The veil is rent:—our souls draw near*
> *Unto a throne of grace;*
> *The merits of the Lord appear,*
> *They fill the holy place.*
>
> *His precious blood has spoken there,*
> *Before and on the throne:*
> *And His own wounds in heaven declare,*
> *The atoning work is done.*
>
> *'Tis finished!—here our souls have rest,*
> *His work can never fail:*
> *By Him, our Sacrifice and Priest,*
> *We pass within the veil.*
>
> *Within the holiest of all,*
> *Cleansed by His precious blood,*
> *Before the throne we prostrate fall,*
> *And worship Thee, O God!*
>
> *Boldly the heart and voice we raise,*
> *His blood, His name, our plea:*
> *Assured our prayers and songs of praise*
> *Ascend, by Christ, to Thee.*
>
>   AUTHOR UNKNOWN

But when a man is tempted, it is his own passions
that carry him away and serve as a bait.
James 1:14 (Weymouth).

HAD we fulness of knowledge, and subtlety of insight, every bit
of pain could be traced clearly, logically, step by step back to
some act of sin. And the tracing would be thought a strangely
interwoven network of sin and that which sin causes. This does not
necessarily mean that the pain is the result of the sin of the man who
suffers the pain. Clearly there is a vast amount of pain on account of
others' acts.

Life is such an intricate network that no man can move or breathe
without affecting somebody else. How terribly selfish sin is. Every act
of sin brings pain to somebody else, to those nearest and most tenderly loved, and those at the farthest reach of influence. Jesus suffered
severest, keenest pain of both body and spirit through sin—the sin of
others. Every bit of pain that came to Him came either through particular acts of sin, or through the whole fog of sin that enveloped His
life as an atmosphere.

S. D. GORDON

What Thou, my Lord, hast suffered,
Was all for sinners' gain;
Mine, mine was the transgression,
But Thine the deadly pain.

Lo, here I fall, my Saviour!
'Tis I deserve Thy place;
Look on me with Thy favor,
Vouchsafe to me Thy grace.

AUTHOR UNKNOWN

And without controversy great is the *mystery* of
godliness: God was manifest in the flesh, justified
in the Spirit, seen of angels, preached unto the
Gentiles, believed on in the world, received up
into glory.   *1 Timothy 3:16.*

THIS is the mystery of the incarnation. The first verse of this
chapter tells us that "in the beginning was the Word, and the
Word was with God, and the Word was God." This "Word,"
who is definitely stated to be God, became flesh. The union of the infinite and the finite in Jesus Christ is the deepest mystery of the

Christian faith. Please bear that in mind when you read of the Virgin Birth of the Lord Jesus Christ in the Bethlehem manger nineteen hundred years ago. There was no room in the inn for God's Son.

The purpose for which He was made flesh is disclosed in 2 Corinthians 8:9: "For ye know the grace of our Lord Jesus Christ, that, though He was rich, yet for your sakes He became poor, that ye through His poverty might be rich." He became the Son of Man without a place to lay His head, that we might become sons of God and heirs of eternal riches.

The Lord Jesus did not lay aside His deity, but it was veiled. On several occasions there was a manifestation of His glory through this veil. We read in connection with the miracle of turning the water into wine, "This beginning of miracles did Jesus in Cana of Galilee, and manifested forth His glory" (John 2:11). Again, when He took His disciples into the mountain apart and was transfigured before them, it is recorded, "His face did shine as the sun and His raiment was white as the light" (Matthew 17:1).

The wonder of it all is that God could compress Himself into a little babe and become flesh. In the flesh He hungered, He was thirsty, He was weary. What does all this mean to us? The Holy Spirit sums it all up by saying, "These things (are) written that ye might believe that Jesus is the Son of God."

CHARLES E. FULLER

OCTOBER 11

. . . that the abundant grace might through the thanksgiving of many redound to the glory of God.
2 Corinthians 4:15.

WHEN the Lord Jesus, full of the Holy Ghost, stood up to speak in the synagogue, it is said the people marvelled at the gracious words that proceeded from His lips. He was full of grace. Fulness of grace is evident by graciousness of address. Some of us have to contend with a naturally ungracious disposition and manner, but the grace of God can change even us. John Wesley was accustomed to observe that he never knew an instance of the grace of God being received and cherished in a man's heart where its transforming power did not soon manifest itself in a change of manners.

Fulness of grace will further manifest itself in our message. Grace always says NOW; grace always has hope for the vilest; grace realizes that salvation is of God, and makes much of His promises and immediate willingness to save. The Lord Jesus is very large in the eyes of one who is full of grace; he loves to think and speak of a Saviour that is always on hand to give and bless. Grace says continually that it is easy for God to bless us. Grace cries, "Today shalt thou be with Me in Paradise." "This day is salvation come to thy house." "This day are these things fulfilled in your ears." "Come, for all things are NOW ready." Yes! it is easy to know if a preacher of the Gospel is "full of grace."

PAGET WILKES

OCTOBER 12

Shew me Thy ways, O Lord; teach me Thy paths. Lead me in Thy truth, and teach me.

Psalm 25:4, 5.

GOD does not show us the whole plan of our life at a burst, but unfolds it to us bit by bit. Each day He gives us the opportunity of weaving a curtain, carving a peg, fashioning the metal. We know not what we do, but at the end of our life the disjointed pieces will suddenly come together, and we shall see the symmetry and beauty of the divine thought. Then we shall be satisfied. In the meantime let us believe that God's love and wisdom are doing the very best for us. In the morning ask God to show you His plan for the day in the unfolding of its events, and to give you grace to do or bear all that He may have prepared. In the midst of the day's engagements, often look up and say, "Father, is this in the plan?" At night, be still, and match your actual with God's ideal, confessing your sins and shortcomings, and asking that His will may be more perfectly done in you, even as in heaven.

F. B. MEYER

His way! I fain would learn it;
His meek and gentle way.
The worldly wise may spurn it,
But teach me, Lord, Thy way.
The meek, they only know it,
They only can be taught.
Oh, gracious, meek One, show it,
To us whom Thou has bought.

We have Thy promise—plead it,
Oh, waiting, longing heart.
Thy teaching, Lord, I need it;
The lesson now impart.
I would be meek and lowly,
So would I learn each day.
Made gentle, true, and holy,
Made wise in Thine own way.

WILLIAM LUFF

255

OCTOBER
13

Behold, I am the Lord, the God of all flesh: is there anything too hard for Me? *Jeremiah 32:27.*

How wonderful is God's power! We see it in creation, we see it in the wonders of redemption recorded in the Old Testament. We see it in the wonderful works of Christ which the Father wrought in Him, and above all in His resurrection from the dead. We are called on to believe in the Son, just as we believe in the Father. Yes, the Lord Jesus who, in His love, is so unspeakably near us, is the Almighty One with whom nothing is impossible. Whatever may be in our hearts or flesh, which will not submit to us, He can and will conquer. Everything that is promised in God's Word, all that is our inheritance as children of the New Covenant, the Almighty Jesus can bestow upon us. If I bow before Him in my Inner Chamber, then I am in contact with the eternal, unchanging power of God. If I commit myself for the day to the Lord Jesus, then I may rest assured that it is His eternal almighty power which has taken me under its protection, and which will accomplish everything for me.

Oh, if we would only take time for the Inner Chamber, so that we might experience in full reality the presence of this Almighty Jesus! What a blessedness would be ours through faith! An unbroken fellowship with an Omnipresent and Almighty Lord.

ANDREW MURRAY

Not a sound invades the stillness,
Not a form invades the scene,
Save the voice of my Beloved,
And the person of my King.

And within those heavenly places,
Calmly hushed in sweet repose,
There I drink, with joy absorbing,
All the love Thou wouldst disclose.

W. JOHNSON

OCTOBER
14

Cast thy burden upon the Lord, and He shall sustain thee. *Psalm 55:22.*

How many people are weighed down with crushing burdens which our Lord longs to carry for them. If these burdens are to be relieved there is something for us to do about it. "Cast thy burden upon the Lord." A part of the ministry of the Old Fashioned Revival Hour is to instruct burdened hearts how to trust

256

the Lord with all their problems and burdens. Here is an example from a listener in Illinois:

"*Dear Mr. Fuller*: I am writing to tell you of the great help your broadcasts have been to me. I have been passing through great trouble and for the past year the burdens have seemed more than I could bear. I had reached a place where neither my Bible nor prayer seemed to help. I felt there was no use to go on.

"I lay on my bed crying with loneliness, one Sunday night, when I reached out and turned on the radio just in time to hear Mr. Fuller say, 'I am much impressed tonight to speak to those that are ready to give up their Christian life.' It was as though the Lord had sent you to meet me face to face with a message. I took your message to my heart and then prayed to God for forgiveness. I carried my burden to Him and was helped in leaving it there. He has been working."

Pray for those who carry heavy burdens. Ask God to make you a faithful witness so that you may lead others to a life of trustfulness.

OCTOBER 15

But we have this treasure in earthen vessels, that the excellency of the power may be of God, and not of us. *2 Corinthians 4:7.*

𝕴T IS our Lord's will that we who have received access to these powers through prayer should go through this world transmitting heavenly power to every corner of a world which needs it sorely. Our lives should be, according to our Lord's plans, quiet but steadily flowing streams of blessing, which through our prayers and intercessions should reach our whole environment.

And it is taken for granted that we, too, like His friends, will "begin in Jerusalem" and then go farther and farther "unto the uttermost part of the earth."

It is His will that we should begin at home. As we go in and out among our dear ones day by day, we should transmit to them by intercessory wireless that supernatural power which will enable them to lead victorious lives and which will put thanksgiving and joy into their hearts and upon their lips, instead of a series of disheartening defeats, bringing discouragement to both body and soul.

We should say to God, as we mingle with our dear ones each day, "God, give them each Thy blessing. They need it, because they live with me, and I am very selfish and unwilling to sacrifice very much for them, although I do love them."

Then there would be a good spirit in our homes. For God hears prayer. Heaven itself would come down to our homes. And even though we who constitute the home all have our imperfections and our failings, our home would, through God's answer to prayer, become a little paradise.

O. HALLESBY

> Before me, just closed doors—Why, I know not!
> He promised to provide, has He forgot?
> I cannot seem to find the proper key;
> Oh God, why do the doors stay locked to me?
> He speaks so soft and low—"Why don't you pray?"
> And in His question, He has shown the way.
> No door is closed when men but intercede;
> And he who prays is he who shall be freed.

AUTHOR UNKNOWN

OCTOBER 16

We also . . . do not cease to pray for you, and to desire that ye might be filled with the knowledge of His will in all wisdom and spiritual understanding. *Colossians 1:9.*

THE will of God touches us at every point in our life, because He is interested in all its details. This is illustrated by some of the most simple and exquisite statements of Scripture.

"Put Thou my tears into Thy bottle."

"The steps of a good man are ordered by the Lord."

"Thou knowest my going out and my coming in."

"Thou knowest my down-sitting and mine uprising."

God among His people gathering up their tears, ordering their steps, knowing their going out, their coming in, their down-sitting, their uprising. Then hear the words of Jesus:

"The very hairs of your head are numbered."

"Not a sparrow falleth to the ground without your Father."

"Take no anxious thought; . . . your Father knoweth that you have need."

If these sentences teach anything, they teach the intense interest of God in the smallest detail of the life of His children, in what we eat, in what we wear, in our recreation, in our homes, in the hidden facts of character. He is so interested that He takes us one by one, and thinks of, and arranges for, every detail of our life. To Him there are no little things. What we call great things are but the perfect union of the small ones, and every small one has the element which makes the greatness of the great ones.

". . . Nothing's small:
No lily-muffled hum of a summer-bee,
But finds some coupling with the spinning stars;
No pebble at your foot, but proves a sphere;
No chaffinch, but implies the cherubim."

G. CAMPBELL MORGAN

OCTOBER 17

Hear, O heavens, and give ear, O earth: for the Lord hath spoken, I have nourished and brought up children, and they have rebelled against Me. The ox knoweth his owner, and the ass his master's crib: but Israel doth not know, my people doth not consider. *Isaiah 1:2, 3.*

WHY does God permit all this present-day bloodshed, distress, destruction, and wholesale slaughter of innocent men, women, and children? Why doesn't He put an end to such terrible loss of life and property? Will the nations ever be at peace? Does the Bible give us light on these questions? Yes, I can say that it does.

Many passages in the Book are devoted to God's dealings with one nation, Israel, and their land, Palestine. Although they were surrounded by larger and more powerful nations, humanly speaking, they had peace and prosperity as long as they followed the precepts and commandments of the Lord. But when Israel forsook God and became disobedient to His Word God permitted these heathen nations to come in and destroy their cities, taking them captive.

One of many instances is in the third chapter of Judges, where we read that the Children of Israel did evil again in the sight of the Lord. The Lord strengthened Eglon, king of Moab. He fought and prevailed against Israel, capturing the city of palm trees. Israel became the servants of Eglon for eighteen years. But when Israel repented and turned away from their sins, God heard their cry and sent a deliverer. Then Israel enjoyed peace again.

God deals the same way with all nations. His principles of government are always the same. If America is involved in war and destruction it is because of sin. There is only one way out: repentance and getting back to God. His offer of mercy is the same now as then. He is saying to America, today, "Come, let us reason together, . . . though your sins be as scarlet, they shall be as white as snow; though they be red like crimson they shall be as wool" (Isaiah 1:18).

CHARLES E. FULLER

Happy is the man that findeth wisdom. . . . She is
more precious than rubies. . . . Her ways are ways
of pleasantness, and all her paths are peace.
Proverbs 3:13–17.

MANY of us are finding out that peace is found in strange paths.
Nevertheless, God's way is always the right way. Believing
this is the foundation of heart rest and abiding peace. And
let it be known that the path is different for each one. Sometimes it
is a shadowed pathway we are to tread. And when the road is dark,
rough, and lonely, and we cannot even see our Guide, let us remember
His promise in Isaiah 30:18–21: "And though the Lord give you the
bread of adversity, and the water of affliction, . . . He will be very
gracious unto thee at the voice of thy cry; when He shall hear it, He
will answer thee."

And sometimes the pathway is difficult, very difficult. "And I will
make all my mountains a way, and my highways shall be exalted"
(Isaiah 49:11). Why? Simply because mountain climbing strengthens
the heart and nerves. We need the mountain atmosphere, the glorious
vision which is the rich reward of the mountain climbers; the ever-
widening spiritual views over far-stretching country which we are to
possess in the name of the Lord Jesus Christ, with the gospel of His
Calvary love. Then, too, God's mountain ways help to lift our confidence and love that they may be strengthened and revitalized for His
praise and glory. And the result? A clear view of God's protecting and
abiding presence!

EVANGELISTIC MESSENGER

God hath His mountains bleak and bare,
Where He doth bid us rest awhile;
Crags where we breathe a purer air,
Lone peaks that catch the day's first smile.

God hath His deserts broad and brown—
A solitude—a sea of sand,
Where He doth let heaven's curtain down,
Unknit by His almighty hand.

AUTHOR UNKNOWN

Glory and honour are in His presence; strength and gladness are in His place. *1 Chronicles 16:27.*

MEN have wondered at the power of George Muller. He had no power of himself; he was simply "THERE," in the place of God's purpose for George Muller. Hudson Taylor said he once thought God was looking for men strong enough to use, but he learned that God was looking for men weak enough to use. The lad who supplied the loaves and fishes for the feeding of the multitude would have been nonplussed if you had told him that morning that he had enough food for several thousand people. He did not know what he had until Jesus took it and broke it and blessed it and passed it around. Nor do you know what you have until you give it to the Lord.

Only when we are "THERE," in the place of His purpose, are we in the place of His power. Samson did a great many remarkable things, but he never was much; he did not stay "THERE." He may have looked better after his haircut but he lost his strength. Too many Christians let the world give them a haircut. One day they carry off the gates of Gaza, but next day they may be in the lap of Delilah; they do not abide in Christ, they do not stay "THERE."

There is no place "just as good" as "THERE," the place of God's purpose. We try to strike bargains with the Lord, offer to do something else, seek a compromise or substitute. We work terribly hard at something that may be fine and lovely, but it is not His choice and inwardly we are rebellious. A minister brother tells of a stubborn youngster in a home who was told by his mother to sit down. He refused twice, and then she made him sit down; but he said, "Mother, I may be sitting down but I'm standing up inside!" So often do we seem to be yielded to God and living "THERE," but there is inward rebellion. And God rates rebellion as a grievous thing: "For rebellion is as the sin of witchcraft and stubbornness is as iniquity and idolatry" (1 Sam. 15:23).

VANCE HAVNER

Now there was leaning on Jesus' bosom one of
His disciples whom Jesus loved.   *John 13:23.*

A FEW Sabbaths since," wrote Fidelia Fiske, the missionary to
Oroomia, Persia, "I went to Geog Tapa, with Mr. Stoddard. It
was afternoon, and I was sitting on a mat seat near the middle
of the church, which had no seats, and only a floor of earth. I had
been to two exercises before, and was weary, and longed for rest; and
with no support, it seemed to me that I could not sit there till the
close of the service. But finding that there was some one directly
behind me, I looked, and there was one of the sisters, who had seated
herself so that I might lean upon her. I objected; but she drew me
back to the firm support she could give, saying, 'If you love me, you
will lean hard.' And then there came the Master's own voice, 'If you
love Me, you will lean hard'; and I leaned on Him, too. I was surprised
to find that I was not at all weary that night, nor in the morning, and
I have rested ever since, remembering the sweet words, 'If you love
Me, lean hard.' "

"*Child of my love, lean hard,
And let me feel the pressure of thy care.
I know thy burden, for I fashioned it—
Poised it in My own hand, and made its weight
Precisely that which I saw best for thee.
And when I placed it on thy shrinking form,
I said, 'I shall be near, and while thou leanest
On Me, this burden shall be Mine, not thine.'
So shall I keep within my circling arms
The child of my own love; here lay it down,
Nor fear to worry Him who made, upholds,
And guides the universe. Yet closer come;
Thou art not near enough. Thy care, thyself,
Lay both on Me, that I may feel My child
Reposing on My heart. Thou lovest Me?
I doubt it not: then, loving Me, LEAN HARD.*"
                                    THE CHRISTIAN

Jesus Himself drew near.   *Luke 24:15.*

"I WILL *never* forsake thee." Sometimes it seems to us, in the hour of trial or bereavement, that He has forgotten His promise. But He has not. The trial is only designed to make us more conscious of our helplessness in order that we may call upon Him. He loves to bear our burdens. "His yoke is easy and His burden is light." He invites us to exchange our yoke for His yoke. Our yoke is irksome; His is restful. But we cannot take His yoke until we give up our own yoke, our own way, and learn to walk in step with Him. If He seems to have gone away it is probably because we are out of step with Him.

J. ELWIN WRIGHT

I prayed for relief from my burden,
Asked the Lord to take it away,
But I grew unsettled and doubtful,
For the burden grew harder each day;
Then I changed the note of my praying,
And asked for the Master alone,
Then turned to take up my burden—
But lo! my burden was gone.

I prayed for more power to witness
The story of Christ's wondrous love,
But no message of might ever came
Though I prayed to our Father above;
So I changed the note of my praying,
Asked Jesus to come in and dwell,
And found to my great satisfaction,
That I the story could tell.

So now, if I'm burdened or doubtful,
Or weary with overmuch care,
I go at once to my Saviour,
Ask Him the burden to share;
And I find Him ever so willing,
For He walks by my side on the road,
Now, wonder of wonders, I'm telling,
He takes from my heart all the load!

AGNES K. KING

The desert shall rejoice, and blossom as the rose.
Isaiah 35:1.

𝕴 KNEW a cobbler who used to sit at his work just where he could catch a glimpse of the green fields! I think that is suggestive of how we ought to sit at our work. So sit as to catch the glory-light! Let the soul be posed toward the Lord, and the light of His countenance will shine upon it; and the light will beam out of the eyes and our work will appear transfigured. "The desert shall rejoice and blossom as the rose."

And surely sometimes our sorrows appear as the desert. We pass into experiences that are dark and cold and lonely, and over which there blows a bitter wind. Surely sorrow is a Black Country to untold multitudes of souls! "Can God furnish a table in the wilderness?" Can He feed us in the season of a sorrow? Let us remember it was in the desert that the miracle of the loaves was wrought, and in the desert of our sorrow a harvest miracle may be wrought today. At His word our desert can abound with lilies and violets and heart's-ease and forget-me-nots. "He will also feed thee with the finest of the wheat." Your sorrow shall be turned into joy. Oh, thou troubled soul, turn to the great Wonder Worker, and thy desert shall blossom as the rose!

J. H. JOWETT

"In pastures green?"—not always. Sometimes He,
Who knoweth best, in kindness leadeth me
In weary ways, where heavy shadows be;
Out of the sunshine warm and soft and bright,
Out of the sunshine into darkest night,
I oft would faint with sorrow and affright,
Only for this—I know He holds my hand;
So whether led in green or desert land,
I trust, although I may not understand.
"And by still waters?"—No, not always so.
Ofttimes the heavy tempests round me blow,
And o'er my soul the waves and billows go.

But when the storms beat loudest, and I cry
Aloud for help, the Master standeth by,
And whispers to my soul, "Lo, it is I."
Above the tempest wild I hear Him say,
"Beyond the darkness lies the perfect day;
In every path of thine I lead the way."
So, whether on the hill-tops high and fair
I dwell, or in the sunless valleys where

The shadows lie—what matter? He is there;
And more than this. Where'er the pathway lead,
He gives to me no helpless, broken reed,
But His own hand, sufficient for my need.

So where He leads me I can safely go;
And in the blest hereafter I shall know
Why in His wisdom He has led me so.

AUTHOR UNKNOWN

OCTOBER 23

Thou in faithfulness hast afflicted me.

Psalm 119:75.

IF SOMETHING has come to you that seems very strange and unexplainable, better hold very quiet and still—God is probably trying to get your ear. He is talking; if you give your attention you will hear something. He needs some help; there is something to be done; He wants you to give Him a hand, a lift, a life-lift. He is trying to attract your attention. If you give it and fall in heartily with His plan, you will understand what He has been doing, and when the thing that hurts has done its work it will likely be taken away.

S. D. GORDON

This moment, Lord, Thy will I choose,
    Nor let me live except for Thee;
My life, my all, I'll gladly lose
    To know Thy perfect victory.

Thy will I choose; I give to Thee
    All of the life Thou gavest me.
Thy will I choose, no life I ask
    Except to do Thy given task.

Never, O Lord, will I reclaim
    The life I lay here at Thy feet;
Thy will shall ever be my aim,
    Obedience, my portion sweet.

No circumstance shall be a wedge
    To sever me from Thee apart.
To Thee, dear Lord, the fullest pledge
    That ever issued from a heart.

265

'Tis settled, Lord, I rest in Thee;
My broken will says only "Yes."
Now, now indeed, my life is free;
Henceforth Thy will it shall express.

NORMAN LEWIS

OCTOBER 24

I lay down my life for the sheep.   *John 10:15.*

NOTICE that four times in this tenth chapter the Lord Jesus speaks of laying down His life for Hi sheep. Verse 11: "The Good Shepherd giveth His life for the sheep." Verse 15: "As the Father knoweth Me, even so know I the Father: and I lay down My life for the sheep." Verse 17: "Therefore doth My Father love Me, because I lay down My life, that I might take it again." Verse 18: "No man taketh it from Me, but I lay it down of Myself."

The love behind this act is beautifully brought out in the Epistle to the Romans, which says, "For when we were yet without strength, in due time Christ died for the ungodly. For scarcely for a righteous man will one die: yet peradventure for a good man some would even dare to die. But God commendeth His love toward us, in that, while we were yet sinners, Christ died for us" (Romans 5: 6–8).

Whenever you find those two words, "But God," in the Scripture, you find an "about face." It is God intervening and changing things. Another example is in Ephesians, the second chapter. First you are given a picture of the state of the unrighteous or unconverted man. He is dead in trespasses and sins. Then God intervenes. "But God, who is rich in mercy, for His great love wherewith He loved us, even when we were dead in sins, hath quickened us (made us alive) together with Christ" (Ephesians 2:4, 5).

Now notice, Christ died *for* us. He did not merely die on behalf of us but instead of us. Yes, Christ died in my place. Nineteen hundred years ago, when God's beloved Son was rich, He became poor that I through His poverty might become rich. I did not deserve such love, "But God." That is the simplicity of the Gospel.

CHARLES E. FULLER

... to open their eyes, and to turn them from darkness to light, and from the power of Satan unto God, that they may receive forgiveness of sins.   *Acts 26:18.*

R EPENTANCE, of course, is not salvation, though absolutely indispensable thereto. The first of these ideas as represented to us is: To turn man from the power of Satan. Behind the depraved desires, the darkened understanding, the seared conscience, and the enslaved will there stands Satan, the arch-enemy of the human soul. It is with him we have to deal. No man has ever yet been a winner of souls who has not known and believed in the devil. Here is one of the sad omissions from the Apostles' Creed: "I believe in the devil." This conviction is absolutely essential; it drives us to prayer and makes us cry, "Avenge us of our adversary." No eloquence, no wisdom, no knowledge of psychology, no clearness of thinking, no simplicity of stating, no depth of feeling, will avail to deliver a seeking soul unless we have first met the enemy on our knees. Men are "taken captive by him at his will." Do we believe it? Have we felt it and faced it? If so, then we shall know that the victory on Calvary and the efficacy of the blood of the Son of God, believed and pleaded in prayer, are the only things that will make him give way and enable us to pluck the prey out of his mighty hand. Only so shall we cause men to repent toward God.

PAGET WILKES

*From prayer that asks that I may be
Sheltered from winds that beat on Thee,
From fearing when I should aspire,
From faltering when I should climb higher,
From silken self, O Captain, free
Thy soldier who would follow Thee.*

*From subtle love of softening things,
From easy choices, weakenings,
(Not thus are spirits fortified,
Not this way went the Crucified)
From all that dims Thy Calvary
O Lamb of God, deliver me.*

*Give me the love that leads the way,
The faith that nothing can dismay,
The hope no disappointments tire,
The passion that will burn like fire;
Let me not sink to be a clod:
Make me Thy fuel, Flame of God.*

AMY WILSON CARMICHAEL

All things are lawful unto me, but all things are
not expedient.   *1 Corinthians 6:12.*

BEWARE of anything which would injure some weaker conscience. This is one of the most important considerations in
Christian living. "All things are lawful unto me, but all things
are not expedient." And why are they not expedient? It is inexpedient
to do things which may be harmless enough in themselves, and which
you may feel able to do with impunity, if in doing them you lead
others to do them also, not because they feel at ease, but simply because they are emboldened by your example, regarding you as further
advanced than themselves in the Christian life, and therefore a
trustworthy guide. Estimate every action, not only as it is in itself, but
as it is likely to be in its influence on others, lest you break down
wholesome barriers, and place others in scenes of temptation which,
however harmless to yourself, are perilous in the extreme to them.

F. B. MEYER

*There's a sweet old story translated for man
But writ in the long, long ago—
The Gospel according to Mark, Luke and John—
Of Christ and His mission below.*

*Men read and admire the Gospel of Christ,
With its love so unfailing and true;
But what do they say, and what do they think
Of the Gospel "according to you"?*

*'Tis a wonderful story, that Gospel of love,
As it shines in the Christ life divine,
And oh, that its truth might be told yet again
In the story of your life and mine.*

*Unselfishness mirrors in every scene,
Love blossoms on every sod,
And back from its vision the heart comes to tell
The wonderful goodness of God.*

*You are writing each day a letter to men,
Take care that the writing is true,
'Tis the only Gospel that some men will read—
That "Gospel according to you."*

AUTHOR UNKNOWN

OCTOBER
27

In every thing give thanks: for this is the will of God in Christ Jesus concerning you.

1 Thessalonians 5:18.

You distress yourself sometimes, poor thing! because amongst those who surround you, there are one or two who worry or annoy you. They do not like you, find fault with everything you do; they meet you with a severe countenance and austere manner. You think they do you harm; you look upon them as obstacles to your doing good. Your life passes away saddened and faded, and gradually you become disheartened. Courage! Instead of vexing yourself, thank God; these very persons are the means of preserving you from humiliating faults, perhaps even greater sins. It is like the blister the doctor applies, to draw out the inflammation that would kill.

God sees that too much joy, too much happiness, procured by those little attentions for which you are so eager, would make you careless and slothful in prayer; too much affection would only enervate, and you would cling too much to earthly things. So, in order to preserve your heart in all its tenderness and simplicity, He plants there a few thorns, and cuts you off from all the pleasures you fancy yours by right. God knows that too much praise would cause pride, and make you less forbearing with others, and so He sends humiliations. Let them be, then, these persons who unconsciously are doing God's work in you. If you cannot love them from sympathy, love them with an effort of the will, and say: "My God grant that without offending Thee, they may work my sanctification. I have need of them."

AMY CARMICHAEL

OCTOBER
28

Whosoever shall call upon the name of the Lord shall be saved. *Romans 10:13.*

Only prevailing prayer backing up the message can avail to rescue these humanly unreachable souls who have gone far on the road to despair and death. The letter given here came from Massachusetts but the same heart-cry is heard from every section of the world in letters received by Mr. Fuller.

"Dear Mr. Fuller: I heard you Sunday night and you said no matter how black your sins are God can save you. Now you do not know how black my sins are. I try to pray but my past is ever before me. Will you please pray for me? I want to be different. I am not doing the things I used to do and I stay at home, but I cannot pray, as I always look at what I might have been and what I am now.

"Mr. Fuller, am I lost? Should I end it all, or what?

"Please let me hear that you are praying for me. (Signed) One Who Can Not Go On."

This letter could not be answered personally as it was not signed. A message of hope was broadcast, however, by Mrs. Fuller, who read it over the air. Doubtless thousands of prayers went up for the salvation of this poor troubled soul. What are you doing to bring these lost ones into the Fold of the Shepherd?

OCTOBER 29

And immediately the spirit driveth Him into the wilderness. *Mark 1:12.*

𝕴T SEEMS a strange proof of divine favor. "Immediately." Immediately after what? After the opened heavens and the dove-like peace and the voice of a Father's blessing: "Thou art my beloved Son, in whom I am well pleased." It is no abnormal experience. Thou, too, hast passed through it, O my soul. Are not the times of thy deepest depressions just the moments that follow thy loftiest flights? Yesterday thou wert soaring far in the firmament and singing in the radiance of the morn; today thy wings are folded and thy song is silent. At noon thou wert basking in the sunshine of a Father's smile; at eve thou art saying in the wilderness, "My way is hid from the Lord." Nay, but, my soul, the very suddenness of the change is a proof that it is not revolutionary. Hast thou weighed the comfort of that word, "Immediately"? Why does it come so soon after the blessing? Just to show that it is the sequel of the blessing. . . . God shines on thee to make thee fit for life's desert places, for its Gethsemanes, for its Calvaries. He lifts thee up that He may give thee strength to go further down; He illuminates thee that He may send thee into the night, that He may make thee a help to the helpless. Not at all times art thou worthy of the wilderness; thou art only worthy of he wilderness after the splendors of Jordan."

GEORGE MATHESON

270

How can a Christian overcome
By sorrow upon sorrow
Rise up again with faith renewed
And wear a smile the morrow?

The love of Christ constraineth us
To live our Lord's command;
With foretaste of the bliss that waits
Us in a sin-free land.

JOAN GEISEL GARDNER

OCTOBER
30

By grace are ye saved, through faith.

Ephesians 2:8.

THE faith that can save men with positive finality is the blessed truth which does not ignore sin, minimize it, but makes sinners contritely confess their own unworthiness, reduces them and exalts God until they are nothing and He is everything; the personal confession, "I know that in me (that is, in my flesh) dwelleth no good thing," and then the confident and complete acceptance of this promise, "By grace are ye saved through faith."

May this day bring a reforming, renewing, revitalizing power into your lives as you contemplate the blessed meaning of these seven one-syllable words, "By grace are ye saved, through faith." Whether you stand before God within the next seven days or the next seven decades, in this faith you have all that you need to claim your prepared place. For Christ's blessed doctrine of sure salvation contains no "perhaps" and "possibly," no "maybe" and "maybe not"; it is no hit-or-miss theory, no pious leap in the dark, no theological random shot. As the unchangeable truth of God, His promise, "Ye are saved," will remain when the earth beneath us is consumed and the firmament above us vanishes, when mountains have crumbled and oceans dried.

As I ask you to behold "the grace of our Lord Jesus Christ," the pardon for which He paid with His own blood, and tell you that in our Saviour there is enough mercy for a myriad of worlds, enough pardon for a race a million times larger than ours, enough grace, though your guilt were a thousand thousand times more terrifying than it is, believe with your hearts that Christ on the cross, in our stead, has done all, suffered all, earned all, acquired all, paid all, completed all that you and I need for the removal of our sins and our restoration to God "by grace . . . through faith."

WALTER A. MAIER

271

Purge out therefore the old leaven, that ye may
be a new lump.   *1 Corinthians 5:7.*

THERE are two distinct classes of people among professed Christians: those who are carnal and those who are spiritual.
Paul, in writing to the Corinthian Church, said, "And I, brethren, could not speak unto you as unto spiritual, but as unto carnal, even as unto babes in Christ. I have fed you with milk, and not with meat: for hitherto ye were not able to bear it, neither yet now are ye able. For ye are yet carnal: for whereas there is among you envying, and strife, and divisions, are ye not carnal, and walk as men?" (1 Corinthians 3:1, 2).

Now I want you to understand the difference between a carnal and a spiritual Christian. All believers have, at conversion, received the gift of the Holy Spirit, for God's Word clearly says, "Now if any man have not the Spirit of Christ, he is none of His" (Romans 8:9). But the spiritual Christian has not only the gift of the Spirit, he is filled with the Spirit.

The carnal Christian lives largely for self. The works of the flesh are predominant; self has not been crucified. The carnal Christian has a good foundation but he builds on it of perishable things, wood, hay, stubble. His carnal works will be burned at the judgment seat of Christ, although he, himself, will be saved.

The spiritually minded Christian has reached that crisis in his experience where he has made a full surrender; he has yielded everything; his all is on the altar. He has obeyed the command in the twelfth chapter of Romans, "Present your bodies a living sacrifice, holy, acceptable unto God, which is your reasonable service."

Can you truthfully say that Christ is all in all to you? Have you made a full consecration of your life to Him? If not, why not?

CHARLES E. FULLER

These that have turned the world upside down are come hither also.   *Acts 17:6.*

EVERY Christian is a contradiction to this old world. He crosses it at every point. He goes against the grain from beginning to end. From the day that he is born again until the day that he goes on to be with the Lord, he must stand against the current of a world always going the other way. God expects him to be "beside himself," "a fool for Christ's sake," "drunk on new wine." If he allows it, men will tone him down, steal the joy of his salvation, and reduce him to the dreary level of the general average. If the devil cannot keep us from being saved, he next endeavors to make average Christians of us, and in this he usually succeeds. He tames the holy recklessness of God's dare-saints until they sink into the drab pattern of most of us, "faultily faultless, icily regular, splendidly null."

The devil does not mind our joining church if we behave like most of those who are already inside. But when a real, wide-awake Christian breezes along, taking the Gospel seriously, the devil grows alarmed and begins plotting his downfall.

VANCE HAVNER

Christ has no hands but our hands to do His work today;
He has no feet but our feet to lead men in His way;
He has no tongue but our tongue to tell men how He died;
He has no help but our help to bring them to His side.

We are the only Bible the careless world will read;
We are the sinner's gospel, we are the scoffer's creed;
We are the Lord's last message, given in deed and word,—
What if the type is crooked? What if the print is blurred?

What if our hands are busy with other work than His?
What if our feet are walking where sin's allurement is?
What if our tongues are speaking of things His lips would spurn?
How can we hope to help Him, and hasten His return?

ANNIE JOHNSON FLINT

Hast thou entered into the treasures of the snow?
Job 38:22.

THROUGH our constant adoration of the Christ-child we also rise from the deadening worries that crowd into this fear-freighted age. Christ may never raise some of us above our restricted income and financial problems. The difficulties of earning our daily bread and retaining our honor and self-respect may increase as the perplexing era marches on; but through Christ we can tower above all fear.

When the snowflakes fall during these November days, remember God's question to Job, "Hast thou entered into the treasures of the snow?" Take one snowflake and examine it under the penetrating lenses of a high-powered microscope. Only a moment will this delicate hexagon linger beneath the human gaze; but what a moment of white majesty and virgin beauty and crystalline symmetry! If you are ever inclined to doubt the providence of God in Christ, if you ever begin to wonder whether life is only a series of haphazard chances, then ask yourself, "Have I 'entered into the treasures of the snow'?" "Can I explain the mysteries of these icy stars that fall from winter's sky, no two patterns alike?" "Must I not, looking to my blessed Saviour and to the radiance of His redemptive love, gain the assurance that my heavenly Father's wisdom, shaping these millions of myriads of frosty patterns, will fashion my life by the cold afflictions into the sacred artistry of holy beauty?"

WALTER A. MAIER

What is faith? Strange answers forth are brought;
  For nimble wit is anxious to be heard.
  With pride of intellect it speaks its word,
The world applauds, and . . . it is soon forgot.
Some search the depths of philosophic thought
  And bring replies with dripping darkness blurred;
  Some weave from ancient falsehoods disinterred
A web of subtle errors deftly wrought.
What is the faith? God's purpose in the Christ
  To save through faith men of a rebel race.
No work of man, but Christ's shed blood sufficed
  To meet God's claim 'gainst man, and, by His grace,
Break sin's harsh chains, dispel its mocking wraith,
And fill with life divine. This is the faith.

EDGAR PUNTENNEY SMITH

NOVEMBER
3

For if by one man's offence death reigned by one;
much more they which receive abundance of grace
and of the gift of righteousness shall reign in life
by one, Jesus Christ.   *Romans 5:17.*

THERE was a little state near ancient Rome that was always being tormented by its warlike neighbors. Again and again they invaded it, and it was perpetually waging war. It was a proud little state, and gloried in its independence and military power. But so strong were the attacks that often it was compelled to call upon the Roman republic to help it. At length the Romans suggested that it should give up its unprofitable independence and become part of the great republic. Eventually it was persuaded to do so, and let go its little armies and executives and became one with the empire which no enemy dared assail. It gave up its little strength, and gained the power of the mightiest state on earth. Even so, we cling for a while to our little faith and power, fight our enemies with our boasted weapons, and ask God to help us out. But there is a way so much better: namely, to give up all our fancied resources and just become one with God, making our cause His own. Then shall all His strength become ours, and we can defy our foes to touch Him. What a solemn responsibility it throws upon us to have such an offer. How severely it condemns all our self-excusing on account of unbelief, and makes our doubts and fears to be evil and malignant sins without one shadow of excuse.

God may well expect confidence from us when He so amply provides for it.

A. B. SIMPSON

The storm had passed me, and I lay
Upon the bosom of Life's ocean, derelict;
Far off the thunder echoed, and beyond
I heard the sullen roar of angry surf
Beating a rock-bound shore, nor hope had I
That ever ray of dawn would pierce the gloom.
At length a star appeared—and through the night
A tender voice I heard: "Fear not, Thou art
Not all bereft. My child, come thou to Me;
When earthly joys take flight true peace is born!"
Then from the deeps of my unmeasured woe,
Stretching my empty hands to Him I cried,—
And when from darkness unto light I turned,—
Lo, it was day.

AUTHOR UNKNOWN

275

Praying always with all prayer and supplication in
the Spirit, and watching thereunto with all perse-
verance and supplication for all saints; and for
me. . . .   *Ephesians 6:18, 19.*

𝔍 MUST know what work I have to do in my secret prayer chamber before I enter into it, what persons and what branches of
the work of the kingdom of God I am to take to God in prayer.
As the Spirit deepens our solicitude and widens our prayer-circle, we
will find many things for which to pray. Such a thing as my occasional
forgetfulness must not be allowed to hinder me from doing this work.
If it is difficult for me to remember every individual person and each
particular cause for which I should pray, I must come to the assistance
of my memory by making a note of them.

Johannes Johnson, a great Norwegian missionary, once told of a
missionary's wife who little by little permitted herself to be trained
in the holy work of prayer. As a result she found more and more things
for which to pray. At last she was unable to remember them all. So
she went to work and resolutely wrote them all down in a note book.

When she was about to pray, she simply took out her little note
book and spoke with God about the one thing after the other which
she had noted down. Thus she continued to pray for a large number of
people and many Christian enterprises. As soon as she was given
something new for which to pray she wrote it down in her little book.
And as the Lord granted her prayers, she crossed out the entries in
her book and wrote in the margin, "Thanks."

I have never had much faith in the old prayerbooks with their
prayer formulas for morning, evening, and special occasions in life,
although they, too, have no doubt been helpful to some people. But
I would recommend most highly prayerbooks of this kind.

O. HALLESBY

And He said unto them, Go ye into all the world,
and preach the Gospel to every creature.
Mark 16:15.

𝔗 HOSE of us who are trying to be winners of souls should take
great comfort from the fact that the Lord has promised us His
own power for the task. The closing verses of Mark's Gospel
present an interesting picture, or rather two pictures. In verse 19,
there is an enthroned Christ; in verse 20, there are His busy servants.

"He" is the key to verse 19, and "they" the center of verse 20. In this double picture, the Lord is in the place of power and the Christian is in the place of service.

Let Him have the throne, and you take the field. How much we need the power of a triumphant Christ for our work and witness! How empty is powerless preaching! How fruitless our powerless attempts to do His work! But how unnecessary when we too may realize "the Lord working with them"! His enthronement does not mean His absence. It rather means power released—all the throne power of Christ brought to bear upon other lives through our yielded lives. May it be so for His Name's sake!

When Robert Morrison was sailing for China alone, the captain of the ship upon hearing his purpose in going to that land asked, "Do you expect to convert China?" "No," was Morrison's reply, "but I expect God to do it."

MOODY MONTHLY

> Faith is a grasping of Almighty power;
> The hand of man laid on the arm of God:
> The grand and blessed hour
> In which the things impossible to me
> Become the possible, O Lord, through Thee.
>
> ANNA E. HAMILTON

NOVEMBER 6

Many waters cannot quench love, neither can the floods drown it.   *Song of Solomon 8:7.*

THERE are, too, some wondrous compensations in that keen pain of having the one who has been by your side, a bit of your very self, slip from your grasp, out of reach, into the other life. To have known love, to have loved and been loved, is to have known the sweetest and most lasting of all life's joys. It makes one the stronger and gentler. The love that has stood the test of time weaves the finest threads into the life web. To love is to live. The life is richer and deeper, finer and more fragrant, for the love that has come in, and that has been drawn out, even though for a time the one loved and loving has slipped from your side upwards.

S. D. GORDON

> Down in the valley, among the sweet lilies,
> Walks my Beloved—His foot-prints I see;
> Haste I to follow Thee, Saviour and Lover,—
> How the winds whisper Thy dear name to me!

Know'st Thou I seek Thee? oh, haste to discover
Where is the place of Thy fragrant retreat!
Where Thou dost rest with Thy flocks at the noon-tide—
Sheltered near fountains unsearched by the heat!

Now I approach Thee, O fairest Redeemer,
Lured by Thy beauty to dwell in Thy love;
Hide not Thy face from the heart that adores Thee!—
Hast Thou not sought me, and called me Thy dove?

Gentler Thy voice than the whisper of angels,
Brighter Thy smile than the sun in the sky;
Gather me tenderly—close to Thy bosom,
Faint with Thy loveliness thus let me die.

H. M. BRADLEY

NOVEMBER 7

He that receiveth Me receiveth Him that sent Me.
John 13:20.

THE grandest of all endowments is to become a son of God. The greatest theme of the Book is the provision that God has made for us to become His sons through faith in Christ Jesus. We are no more servants but sons, joint-heirs with Christ. No wonder the beloved disciple wrote, many years later, under the inspiration of the Holy Spirit, "Behold, what manner of love the Father hath bestowed upon us that we should be called the sons of God: therefore the world knoweth us not, because it knew Him not. Beloved, now are we the sons of God, and it doth not yet appear what we shall be: but we know that when He shall appear we shall be like Him for we shall see Him as He is" (1 John 3:1, 2).

Receiving Christ means that we are born again, made a new creation. Old things pass away. We are made partakers of the divine nature. We enter into the Father-and-son relationship. We are members of the household of faith. All who are in Christ Jesus are brothers and sisters.

There are two great brotherhoods in the world today. One is the brotherhood in the family of God and the other is the brotherhood in the family of Satan. The new birth means being translated out of one family into the other. It means being dead to sin and being made alive in Christ. Every member of the human race is in one brotherhood or the other. Only those who are in the brotherhood of Christ Jesus can pray, "Our Father, which art in heaven," and be heard. The only prayer God will hear from the lips of a sinner is, "God be merciful to me, a sinner."

CHARLES E. FULLER

278

I . . . have poured out my soul before the Lord.
1 Samuel 1:15.

𝕴NTERCESSORY prayer is God's all-powerful agency for the outpouring of the Spirit. No revival has ever yet been given apart from this ministry. Someone has prayed. Go, if you will, to the records of the great awakenings for years past and you will find that the secret, the source, has been prayer. God has burdened a little group here and there, sometimes only two or three in number, but these have so given themselves to intercessory prayer that the result has been a mighty outpouring of the Holy Spirit.

The mystery of the great awakening under D. L. Moody in the church where he preached one Sunday night in England, when hundreds were swept into the Kingdom, for some time remained unsolved, but at last the secret came to light. Two sisters, we are told, lived together. One was an invalid. Some years before she had picked up a newspaper and read an account of the work of the great American evangelist, D. L. Moody. A burden settled down upon her. From that day she began to pray that God would send Moody to England and that he might preach in her church. At last after praying daily her request was granted. Her sister came home one morning and told her that a man by the name of Moody had preached. Under a great burden the invalid shut herself in and refused to be seen. All that afternoon she pled with God, with the result that showers of blessing fell upon the congregation and hundreds were saved at the close of the evening service. That was the beginning of Moody's great work in the British Isles. God had signally set His seal upon the work and it all came about as the result of an invalid's intercession.

OSWALD J. SMITH

NOVEMBER
9

I will not leave you comfortless.   *John 14:18.*

𝕳ERE is One who never fails the heart that leans on Him for repose. Health may fail us but His strength is made perfect in our weakness. Adversity may crash upon us, but He draws nearer than a brother, and whispers, "In the world ye shall have tribulation: but be of good cheer; I have overcome the world." Friends may desert us, so that, like Paul, we may have to say, "No man stood with me." But we may also say with him in the next verse, "Notwithstanding the Lord stood with me" (2 Tim. 4:16, 17). We may have to say with Jeremiah: "The crown is fallen from our head: woe unto us, that we have sinned! For this our heart is faint; for these things our eyes are dim"; but we may also say with him, "Thou, O Lord, remainest forever; Thy throne from generation to generation" (Lam. 5:16, 17, 19). And even when death draws near He assures us, "I am the resurrection and the life" (John 11:25).

> *"My love is ofttimes low;*
> *My joy still ebbs and flows;*
> *But peace with Him remains the same;*
> *No change Jehovah knows.*
> *I change, He changes not;*
> *My Christ can never die;*
> *His love, not mine, the resting place;*
> *His truth, not mine, the tie."*
>
> VANCE HAVNER

NOVEMBER 10

The world passeth away, and the lust thereof: but he that doeth the will of God abideth for ever.

1 John 2:17.

"GOD's will is sweetest to us when it triumphs at our cost."

The restfulness and peace of this attitude of surrender to the divine will lies in the fact that the Eternal God, who in infinite love has created us, has done so for eternal comradeship with Himself; and if He govern the life, He will bring it, notwithstanding all the forces that seem to be against it, to the place of full undying existence. There is no other law of life that will secure this.

"The world passeth way, and the lust thereof, but he that doeth the will of God abideth for ever." From the center of that will man may look out upon change and decay, upon death and destruction, and know that he is perfectly safe from them all; yea, master of every one.

G. CAMPBELL MORGAN

> *Things that once were wild alarms*
> *Cannot now disturb my rest;*
> *Closed in everlasting arms,*
> *Pillowed on the loving breast.*
> *Oh, to lie forever here,*
> *Doubt and care and self resign,*
> *While He whispers in my ear—*
> *I am His, and He is mine!*

His forever, only His;
Who the Lord and me shall part?
Ah, with what a rest of bliss
Christ can fill the loving heart!
Heaven and earth may fade and flee,
First-born light in gloom decline,
But while God and I shall be,
I am His and He is mine.

AUTHOR UNKNOWN

NOVEMBER 11

Workers together with Him.   *2 Corinthians 6:1.*

PASTORS throughout the country have great respect and appreciation for The Old Fashioned Revival Hour. They realize how greatly its message is contributing to their own efforts for the propagation of the Gospel. The following letter from a pastor in South Carolina is typical of the cooperative attitude of those who are preaching the same Gospel which Mr. Fuller loves.

"*Dear Brother Fuller*: Since your broadcast has been reaching us through a local station we have been very happy to announce it in the Sunday evening service and have urged our people to tell all their friends and relatives the great blessing that we are receiving from these services. The response to this announcement has been wonderful. A great many people gather in the homes at 9 o'clock on Sunday evening to hear you. One of our members is printing thousands of slips for distribution that others may know when and where to tune in on the broadcast.

"We are praying that many souls will be saved as a result."

The example of this pastor and his congregation might well be copied by everyone. The stimulation of general interest in the broadcast among the people will inevitably pay big dividends in changed lives and additions to the church.

Is this the time, O Church of Christ, to sound
Retreat? To arm with weapons cheap and blunt
The men and women who have borne the brunt
Of truth's fierce strife and nobly held their ground?

No! Rather strengthen stakes, and lengthen cords.
Enlarge thy plans and gifts, O thou elect,
And to Thy Kingdom come for such a time!
The earth with all its fullness is the Lord's;
Great things attempt for Him, great things expect!
Whose love imperial is, whose power sublime.

CHARLES SUMNER HOYT

He that putteth his trust in Me shall possess the
land, and shall inherit My holy mountain.

Isaiah 57:13.

EVERY act of trust increases your capacity for God. Every time
I trust Him I have more room for Him. He dwells within me in
ever-richer fullness, occupying room after room in my life. That
is a glorious assurance, and one that is filled with infinite comfort.
Let me repeat it again, for it is the very music of the soul; little acts
of trust make larger room for God. In my trifles I can prepare for
emergencies. Along a commonplace road I can get ready for the hill.
In the green pastures and by the still waters I can prepare myself
for the valley of the shadow. For when I reach the hill, the shadow,
the emergency, I shall be God-possessed: He will dwell in me. And
where He dwells He controls. If He lives in my life He will direct my
powers. It will not be I that speak, but my Father that speaketh in
me. He will govern my speech. He will empower my will. He will en-
lighten my mind. He will energize and vitalize my entire life.

J. H. JOWETT

Make thy petition deep, my troubled heart,
God is the same today
As when He bade the clouds of rain depart
And heard Elijah pray.
He who would stem the Red Sea's rolling tides
For Cov'nant Israel,
Still with His own this very day abides.
He is Immanuel!

Make thy petition deep. In sorrow's hour
Doubt not His sovereign might.
He is thy Hiding-place, thy Shield and Tower.
Fear not the shades of night.
His Word reveals His mighty works of old,
And He is still the same.
Like petaled blooms His phophecies unfold.
"Almighty" is His name.

Make thy petition deep. He is a King!
Though princely thy request,
Thy empty vessels to His storehouse bring.
Be with His fullness blest.
Thou art His child, and all He has is thine.
Doubt not thy Father's love.
Stand firmly on His promise, sure, divine—
The Rock that cannot move!

ANNA HOPPE

But we will give ourselves continually to prayer,
and to the ministry of the word.   *Acts 6:4.*

PRAYERLESSNESS circumscribes God's activities. I read in this infallible Word that when Zion travailed she brought forth, and an interceding Christian gives God full place. What mighty things He can do through those who believe, not only in the privilege of prayer but in the power of prayer!

I turn back to the early church and discover that she had power to turn the world upside down. Why? Because of the emphasis placed upon intercession. "We will give ourselves to prayer and to the ministry of the Word." We have reversed the apostolic order. We spend more time in the ministry of the Word than we do in the ministry of prayer. But if we would restore the emphasis regarding prayer, backed by a holy life, then we should experience apostolic results. May there break out in America such a mighty stream of intercession that it will influence the ends of the earth!

A few months ago I was in the city of Edinburgh, Scotland, and lived two doors from the house in which John Knox resided in those far-off days. While there I was reminded of what happened one day in the life of that mighty reformer. He was invited out to his friend's house, and after a while they missed him from the company which had gathered. They sought for him and found him in the garden with his face buried in his hands, and in deep agony of soul, praying, "O God, give me Scotland or I die." And God heard his prayer. God was able to do something through a man like that, and Scotland has never lost the divine impact brought to bear upon it through the intercession of John Knox. No wonder that Bloody Mary said she feared the prayers of John Knox more than an army of soldiers.

HERBERT LOCKYER

Not for myself alone
May my prayer be;
Lift Thou Thy world, O Christ,
Closer to Thee;
Cleanse from its guilt and wrong,
Teach it salvation's song,
Till earth, as heaven, fulfill
God's holy will.

LUCY LARCOM

Be not conformed to this world: but be ye transformed by the renewing of your mind, that ye may
prove what is that good, and acceptable, and perfect, will of God.   *Romans 12:2.*

TODAY, I want to give you a message on practical Christian
living. Christians need to know how to walk worthy of the
vocation to which they are called; how to be fruitful and well
pleasing in God's sight. It should be the earnest heart-cry of every
truly born-again child of God to know His will.

The twelfth chapter of Romans opens with an entreaty to the
brethren, not to sinners, to present their bodies a living sacrifice to
God. This cannot be done until we first are justified freely through
His grace. That is the basis for the message of this chapter. Being
justified we have peace with God. Justification includes not only
pardon but the removal of sin. The moment we accept Christ as our
personal Saviour God puts our sins behind His back and He will never
remember them against us again. Also in justification we are reckoned
righteous in Christ. The sin question is settled once for all.

Now, as believers, we are to yield ourselves unto God. Yielding is
the secret of the abounding, fruitful, victorious life.

Our text directs us not to be conformed to this world—or fashioned according to this age. From the moment of your conversion you
will have a conflict within your heart. The world has a pull which you
must resist. Oh, what joy will be yours if you refuse to be conformed
to the world and become an out-and-out Christian. "Come out . . .
and be ye separate, saith the Lord, and touch not the unclean thing"
(2 Corinthians 6:17). The moment you are saved you become a
stranger and a pilgrim. Your citizenship is not in this world but in
heaven. Therefore, you are to be conformed to heaven and not to this
world. God says, "Love not this world (system), neither the things
that are in the world. If any man love the world the love of the Father
is not in Him" (1 John 2:15).

CHARLES E. FULLER

NOVEMBER
15

For we which live are alway delivered unto death
for Jesus' sake, that the life also of Jesus might
be made manifest in our mortal flesh.

2 Corinthians 3:11.

THE reality and truth of these words is very precious to the one who has been taken from death and placed in life eternal through the grace of God in Jesus Christ. The appropriation of this truth is an ever-growing experience in the life of a Christian as he comes in contact with circumstances and conditions of the journey through this sphere of material life. In Christ we find our all, an answer to every problem, and a possibility for every seeming impossibility, if we but appropriate that wonderful gift of God, which is the life of His Son, true life, sufficient life, satisfying life.

In our meditation upon the Word, we are often convicted of our sinfulness and our unworthiness, and in the face of this truth, we become discouraged and lose hope. But this is only because we look to our own selves for the possibility of following the Word which we have just read. We forget Christ. We forget that He is our life. We forget to appropriate this truth by faith; and as a result, we miss the power which is always present and waiting for our acceptance. Why should we try to accomplish imperfectly what God has accomplished perfectly through Christ? Is Christ your life in reality? Then He is able to do all that which is necessary in your life. Look to Him. Expect great things from Him. Do not hinder Him by your faithlessness. He is doing God's will in and through you by His Spirit which truly dwells within you.

R. G. MARSBACH

NOVEMBER
16

I am in the Father, AND YE IN ME, AND I
IN YOU. *John 14:20.*

THIS means that He, with His whole heart, offers all His divine attributes for our service, and is prepared to impart Himself to us. Christ is the revelation of His love. He is the Son of His love—the gift of His love—the power of His love; and this Jesus, who has sought on the cross to give an overwhelming proof of His love in His death and blood-shedding, so as to make it impossible for us not to believe in that love—this Jesus is He who comes to meet us in the

285

Inner Chamber, and gives the positive assurance that unbroken fellowship with Him is our inheritance, and will, through Him, become our experience. The holy love of God which sacrificed everything to conquer sin and bring it to naught, comes to us in Christ to save us from every sin.

Brethren, take time to think over that word of our Lord: "Ye believe in God, believe also in Me." Believe Me that "I am in the Father, and ye in Me, and I in you." That is the secret of the life of prayer. Take time in the Inner Chamber to bow down and worship; and wait on Him till He unveils Himself, and takes possession of you, and goes out with you to show how a man may live and walk in abiding fellowship with an unseen Lord.

ANDREW MURRAY

NOVEMBER 17

Let your light . . . shine.　　　　*Matthew 5:16.*

BEWARE of any society in which you feel compelled to put a bushel over your testimony. We must shine as lights in the world. The most necessary condition in a lighthouse-lamp is its permanence. If it shines at one time and is hidden at another, now flashing afar over the dark, seething waves, and then standing somber and obscure on the beetling cliff, of what use is it! It is worse than useless. And if we are to be of any real use in this world, our testimony for Jesus must be maintained in season and out of season, in storm and sunshine, always and everywhere. But if, before going into any scene or fellowship, you have to remind yourself that you must not touch on any of those subjects which are dearest to your soul, you may well fear lest you are trespassing on forbidden ground. Go nowhere that you can not take Jesus with you, and ask His blessing before going. "Do all to the glory of God."

F. B. MEYER

> Would I be called a "Christian,"
> 　If everybody knew
> My secret thoughts and feelings,
> 　And everything I do?
> Oh, could they see the likeness
> 　Of Christ in me, each day?
> Oh, could they hear Him speaking,
> 　In every word I say?
>
> Would I be called a "Christian,"
> 　If anyone could know

That I am found in places
  Where Jesus would not go?
Oh, could they hear His echo
  In every song I sing?
In eating, drinking, dressing,
  Could they see Christ, my King?
                              AUTHOR UNKNOWN

NOVEMBER 18

The meek will He guide in judgment: and the meek will He teach His way.   *Psalm 25:9.*

IN OUR younger days, we imagine that we know the possibilities of our being, and are able to plan and arrange the whole line of progress. The years are startling revealers. As they pass, we discover new powers for good and evil that had lain dormant within, and of which we had absolutely no consciousness until some crisis aroused and called forth to action the sleeping forces. How we trembled when we found that there was the power of murder lying hidden in our heart! How we suffered when we came to know of a surety that, in spite of all our earlier boasting, we too had the making of the traitor within, and might have kissed the Master to His death!

Ah, those days of time-tables, and programs, and pledges, and promises, when we proudly said we were masters of ourselves. Through what disappointment, and agonies, and wounds, some of us have come to our first real knowledge, that we are ignorant of ourselves, and cannot therefore govern ourselves.

This drives us to one conclusion. Our demand for perfection can only be met by our living, and moving, and having our being wholly within the will of God. Our neighbor's law fails through the limitation of his knowledge. Our own program collapses because of our ignorance. The will of God moving within the realm of His perfect knowledge leads us on to perfection, and will at last set us in His presence unafraid.

G. CAMPBELL MORGAN

Ye shall receive power. . . . *Acts 1:8.*

JESUS died on the cross to make freedom from sin possible. The Holy Spirit dwells within me to make freedom from sin actual. The Holy Spirit does in me what Jesus did for me. The Lord Jesus makes a deposit in the bank on my account. The Spirit checks the money out and puts it into my hands. Jesus does in me now by His Spirit what He did for me centuries ago on the cross, in His person.

Now these two truths, or two parts of the same truth, go together in God's plan, but, with some exceptions, have not gone together in men's experience. That explains why so many Christian lives are a failure and a reproach. The church of Christ has been gazing so intently upon the hill of the cross with its blood-red message of sin and love, that it has largely lost sight of the Ascension Mount with its legacy of power. We have been so enwrapt with that marvelous scene on Calvary—and that wonder!—that we have allowed ourselves to lose the intense significance of Pentecost. That last victorious shout— "It is finished"—has been crowding out in our ears its counterpart— the equally victorious cry of Olivet—"All power hath been given unto Me."

The Christian's range of vision must always take in two hill-tops— Calvary and Olivet. Calvary—sin conquered through the blood of Jesus, a matter of history. Olivet—sin conquered through the power of Jesus, a matter of experience. When the subject is spoken of, we are apt to say: "Yes, that is correct. I understand that." But do we understand it in our experience? So certainly as I must trust Jesus as my Saviour, so certainly must I constantly yield my life to the control of the Spirit of Jesus if I am to find real the practical power of His salvation.

S. D. GORDON

I've entered the rest of the people of God,
The holy of holies made pure by His blood;
His law is within, I delight in His will,
I've learned how to wait upon God and be still.

I've reckoned myself to be dead unto sin,
And risen with Christ, and now He lives within;
"The life more abundant" He gives unto me,
This overflow life gives me full victory.

JAMES M. KIRK

Yet now, if Thou wilt forgive their sin—; and if not, blot me, I pray Thee, out of Thy book which Thou hast written. *Exodus 32:32.*

For I could wish that myself were accursed from Christ for my brethren, my kinsmen according to the flesh. *Romans 9:3.*

THERE is a remarkable likeness in the heart-cry of these two leaders, Moses and Paul, although they lived so many centuries apart. Perhaps these statements by the greatest leader of Israel and the greatest missionary of the Christian era, give the clue to their greatness. They were outstanding because they loved with a deep passion those to whom they ministered. Both were persecuted and misunderstood by the ones they sought to save, but their love was undiminished. Nothing could quench it. No wonder they occupy the most honored place in God's hall of fame.

Is your heart stirred with compassion for the lost? Have you become an intercessor?

J. ELWIN WRIGHT

Stir me, oh, stir me, Lord—I care not how,
But stir my heart in passion for the world;
Stir me to give, to go, but most to pray;
Stir till the blood-red banner be unfurled
O'er lands that still in heathen darkness lie,
O'er deserts where no cross is lifted high.

Stir me, oh, stir me, Lord, till all my heart
Is filled with strong compassion for these souls,
Till Thy compelling "must" drives me to pray,
Till Thy constraining love reach to the poles.
Far North and South, in burning deep desire,
Till East and West are caught in love's great fire.

Stir me, oh, stir me, Lord, till prayer is pain;
Till prayer is joy; till prayer turns into praise;
Stir me till heart and will and mind, yea, all
Is wholly Thine to use through all the days;
Stir till I learn to pray exceedingly;
Stir till I learn to pray expectantly.

Stir me, oh, stir me, Lord; Thy heart was stirred
By love's intensest fire, till Thou didst give
Thine only Son, Thy best beloved One,
E'en to the dreadful cross, that I might live.
Stir me to give myself so back to Thee,
That Thou canst give Thyself again through me.

Stir me, oh, stir me, Lord, for I can see
  Thy glorious triumph day begin to break;
The dawn already gilds the eastern sky;
  O Church of Christ, awake! awake!
Oh, stir us, Lord, as heralds of that day,
  For night is past—our King is on His way.

AUTHOR UNKNOWN

NOVEMBER
21

Thy words were found, and I did eat them; and
Thy word was unto me the joy and rejoicing of
mine heart.   *Jeremiah 15:16.*

IT IS a tragic thing that so many thousands of people listen to
sermon after sermon and never get to the place of believing God's
Word and appropriating it for themselves. Here is a man who has
studied all about the theory of nutrition. He can tell you in great detail about it. He can take you into the laboratory and show you the
chemical analysis of foods. He can explain the action of these on the
human body. But suppose this man is poor, thin, weak, with sunken
eyes and halting step. You know he has not been practicing what he
knows about nutrition.

Some people are like this regarding spiritual things. They have a
theory about the way of salvation. They love to argue about doctrine.
They understand logic, but it has not occurred to them that they need
to eat the Word themselves. They are weak spiritually because they
talk about it but don't eat it. Eat the Word, friend, and a lot of secondary things will vanish away into thin air. You will grow in grace
and in knowledge of the truth.

How may you eat so that it will really benefit you? You need to
meditate on the Word—or masticate it. Hebrews 4:2, a wonderful
verse, says, "For unto us was the Gospel preached, as well as unto
them: but the Word preached did not profit them, not being mixed
with faith in them that heard it." Many people sit down to dinner
and bolt their food. They are up and gone before others finish their
soup. Listen: they do not masticate—they do not meditate. They get
little benefit. There are people who, when it comes to the Gospel,
grab a verse, then depart and forget about it. When you eat the Word
take plenty of time for meditation. Then it becomes a part of you and
nourishes you.

CHARLES E. FULLER

NOVEMBER
22

Now no chastening for the present seemeth to be joyous, but grievous: nevertheless afterward—
Hebrews 12:11.

GOD seems to love to work by paradoxes and contraries. In the transformations of grace, the bitter is the base of the sweet; night is the mother of day; and death is the gate of life. Many people are wanting power. Now, how is power produced? The other day we passed the great works where the trolley engines are supplied with electricity. We heard the hum and roar of countless wheels, and we asked our friend, "How do they make the power?" "Why," he said, "just by the revolution of those wheels and the friction they produce. The rubbing creates the electric current." It is very simple, and a trifling experiment will prove it to anyone. And so when God wants to bring more power into your life, He brings more pressure. He is generating spiritual force by hard rubbing. Some of us do not like it. Some of us do not understand, and we try to run away from the pressure, instead of getting the power and using it to rise above the painful cause.

A. B. SIMPSON

Little headaches, little heartaches,
Little griefs of every day.
Little trials and vexations,
How they throng around our way!
One great cross, immense and heavy,
So it seems to our weak will,
Might be borne with resignation,
But those many small ones kill.

Yet all life is formed of small things
Little leaves make up the trees,
Many tiny drops of water
Blending, make the mighty seas.
So those many little burdens,
Pressing on our hearts so hard,
All uniting, form a life's work,
Meriting a grand reward.

Let us not then by impatience
Mar the beauty of the whole,
But for love of Jesus bear all
In the silence of our soul.

Asking Him for grace sufficient
To sustain us through each loss,
And to treasure each small offering
As a splinter from His Cross.

GERTRUDE DUGAN

NOVEMBER 23

For ye are His workmanship, created in Christ.
Ephesians 2:10.

THE word which St. Paul uses is "poema." Literally, "Ye are God's poems, written by His own hand. The work was God's and ye are in Ephesus to be God's poetry. The steps of your life are to be stanzas which all may read. Every line is to be glowing literature: so attractive that your neighbors shall be drawn to Christ."

Most suggestive to us today is this word "poem." Have we ever thought of it? Does it not seem such a lofty thing as to be unattainable? In my humble out-of-the-way life, in my poor and commonplace existence, how can I be a poem? My words are not poetic; my soul is not daily soaring to heights of poetry; my thoughts remain low down among the things of sense; and my duties every day drag me down to the shop and the farm, the kitchen and the nursery. I can see no poetry in them. Can God really see it, I wonder? Or was St. Paul himself speaking in a poetic strain?

No! St. Paul uttered a plain and positive truth. A poet is a "maker" —and a poem is what a poet "makes." It is the outcome of a man's deepest thoughts and finest feelings; and into it he throws his whole mind and soul. Dunbar speaks of the Scottish poets of his time as "makers of verse." They were creators of their poems.

Heaven wants to make us like itself. We are to be God's poems, to speak His praise, translate His mind to men, and so create the great and powerful Church of God.

Let us get a sight of our lives in this their true perspective. And heaven save us from being discordant notes in its great harmony! Get every one of your talents keyed to the tune of its grand orchestra and let no function of your body or mind fail to fulfil its part.

I want my will to be one with God's will, and my heart to thrill with the thought of His love. Then I feel sure I shall be a poem of His creation, and give some real though faint expression to the world of the mind of my Maker.

W. S. BRUCE

I am my beloved's, and my beloved is mine.

Song of Solomon 6:3.

THE love which Jesus is loved by is the same that God pours into our hearts. God loves Jesus with an everlasting love, and we share the same love. God loved us in Christ before the foundation of the world. God loves Jesus with a complacent love; He is satisfied in Him, and He says of us, "He will rest in His love, He will joy over thee with singing." No power on earth or in hell shall ever separate Jesus from His Father, and all the powers seen and unseen shall never be able to separate us from the love of God which is in Christ Jesus our Lord.

WILLIAM H. WRIGHTON

Loved with everlasting love,
 Led by grace that love to know;
Spirit, breathing from above,
 Thou has taught me it is so!
Oh, this full and perfect peace!
 Oh, this transport all divine!
In a love which cannot cease,
 I am His, and He is mine.

Heaven above is softer blue,
 Earth around is sweeter green!
Something lives in every hue
 Christless eyes have never seen:
Birds with gladder songs o'erflow,
Flowers with deeper beauties shine,
Since I know, as now I know
 I am His, and He is mine.

Things that once were wild alarms
 Cannot now disturb my rest;
Closed in everlasting arms,
 Pillowed on the loving breast.
Oh, to lie forever here,
 Doubt and care and self resign,
While He whispers in my ear—
 I am His, and He is mine.

His forever, only His;
 Who the Lord and me shall part?
Ah, with what a rest of bliss
 Christ can fill the loving heart!

293

Heaven and earth may fade and flee,
First-born light in gloom decline;
But, while God and I shall be,
I am His, and He is mine.

WADE ROBINSON

NOVEMBER 25

They that have not heard shall understand.
Romans 15:21.

DURING the spring of 1942, Mr. Fuller visited many cities in the United States, conducting great mass meetings in the largest auditoriums available. The writer of the following letter refers to Mr. Fuller's visit to York, Pa., where he addressed seven thousand people at the fair grounds.

"Dear Mr. Fuller: Your sermons are so simple and plain and yet so wonderful. Last evening I had invited a neighbor's boy of fourteen in to listen to your hour. It did him so much good. He said after the broadcast, 'Mr. Fuller tells the story so that anyone can understand.' He will be one of your listeners in the future.

"You have been a wonderful help to me. We were at your service in York, Pa. As a result of it my husband decided to quit selling beer. I have been a Christian for some time and have never stopped praying that my husband would be one, too, and that God would put it into his heart to see the evil of selling beer. Through your message God answered my prayers. The license has been sent back to Harrisburg. My husband is hunting another job.

"I pray for you daily."

During the war, travel restrictions make meetings like the one at York inadvisable, but there are many thousands throughout the country who wait with expectation and longing for the time when they can see, as well as hear, these servants of Christ.

Now if we be dead with Christ, we believe that we
shall also live with Him.   *Romans 6:8.*

L ET us give a hearty assent to what God says about the fact that
we have been crucified with Christ. "I have been crucified
with Christ; and it is no longer I that live, but Christ liveth in
me" (Gal. 2:20). "For if we have become united with Him in the
likeness of His death, we shall be also in the likeness of His resurrection; knowing this, that our old man was crucified with Him" (Rom.
6:5, 6). "For if we died with Him, we shall also live with Him" (2
Tim. 2:11). "If," here, is not the "if" of doubt or uncertainty, but the
"since" of a known fact or condition. "Since" indicates that we died
with Him, hence we are among those who live with Him and have
life. In Romans 6:11, we are commanded to reckon on this fact: "Even
so reckon ye also yourselves to be dead unto sin, but alive unto God
in Christ Jesus." God states the fact that we are united with Christ
Jesus in His death on the cross, regardless of our consciousness of the
matter. There is but one way to translate these truths of God into
life, and that is by believing them regardless of feeling; as we begin
to thank God that they are true, the Holy Spirit works the reality of
these truths into our lives.

L. L. LEGTERS

There's a little word that the Lord has given
For our help in the hour of need,—
Let us reckon ourselves to be dead to sin,
To be dead and dead indeed.

There's another word that the Lord has given,
In the very same verse we read,—
Let us reckon ourselves as alive in Him,
As alive and alive indeed.

While we trust in feeling or inward frames
We shall always be tossed about,—
Let us anchor fast to the Word of God,
And reckon away our doubt.

A. B. SIMPSON

Praise ye the Lord.
Praise God in His sanctuary:
Praise Him in the firmament of His power.
Praise Him for His mighty acts:
Praise Him according to His excellent greatness.
Praise Him with the sound of the trumpet:
Praise Him with the psaltery and harp,
Praise Him with the timbrel and dance:
Praise Him with stringed instruments and organs.
Praise Him upon the loud cymbals:
Praise Him upon the high sounding cymbals.
Let every thing that hath breath praise the Lord.
Praise ye the Lord.   *Psalm 150.*

THE musical rhythmic beat is in all nature and in all life. Were our ears less dulled, and less absorbed in a different sort of thing, we could ever hear the music of God in nature. Through the music of nature as well as its great beauty He speaks to us and reveals Himself. God is musical. Man's love of music, so universal, is evidence of the self-mastery to which he was born. You can't force music. It must go in its own time, or it isn't music. We work best when we work musically, with a fine beat and swing to all our movements; not only best, but do most, and do it most easily.

S. D. GORDON

O for a thousand tongues to sing
  My great Redeemer's praise;
The glories of my God and King,
  The triumphs of His grace!

My gracious Master and my God,
  Assist me to proclaim,
To spread through all the earth abroad,
  The honors of Thy name.

Jesus! the name that charms our fears,
  That bids our sorrows cease;
'Tis music in the sinner's ears,
  'Tis life, and health, and peace.

He breaks the power of canceled sin,
  He sets the prisoner free;
His blood can make the foulest clean;
  His blood availed for me.

CHARLES WESLEY

And ye shall know the truth, and the truth shall make you free.   *John 8:32.*

T H I S section of chapter eight has to do with bondage and liberty. We see here God's estimate of the spiritual condition of the natural, unregenerate heart. This heart is deceitful and desperately wicked. In verses thirty-one and thirty-two, Jesus describes the true disciple as one who continues in the Word. He "shall know the truth, and the truth shall make (him) free."

Those cold, hypocritical Pharisees said, "We be Abraham's seed, and were never in bondage to any man: how sayest thou, Ye shall be made free." They wouldn't admit that their fathers had been in bondage in Egypt and Babylon. Even at the time they spoke they were in bondage to Rome. One of the most difficult things to get across to a self-righteous man is his real condition before God. He is wrapped around with robes of respectability and even religion. He thinks he is free, but he is not.

Beloved brother of mine, if you are not in Christ Jesus you are in great spiritual bondage. Notice that up to the twelfth chapter in Exodus the Children of Israel were in terrible bondage. Then they were free through the shedding of blood.

There are four things that you ought to know about yourself. First, no matter who you are you were born into the world absolutely *destitute of God's standard of righteousness.* "All have sinned and come short of the glory of God." All our righteousness, according to God's Word, is as filthy rags.

Secondly, you are *devoid of God's standard of goodness.* Paul said, "I know that in me, that is, in my flesh, dwelleth no good thing." Therefore, every man is a sinner in God's sight.

Thirdly, the natural man is *destitute of strength.* You cannot pull yourself up spiritually by your own boot straps. Reading the finest literature, keeping the best company will not be enough. God's Word says, "When we were without strength, in due time Christ died for the ungodly."

Fourthly, and this is the point I want to drive home, without Christ you are *destitute of freedom.* You are bound, a captive, a slave in the realm of Satan.

But here is the good news: you may have freedom today by believing in Christ. Isaiah said of Him, "The Lord hath anointed Me to preach good tidings unto the meek; He has sent Me to bind up the broken-hearted, to proclaim liberty to the captives, and the opening of the prison to them that are bound" (Isaiah 61:1).

CHARLES E. FULLER

He thanked God, and took courage. *Acts 28:15.*

IF EVER a man had reason to complain and, from the human point of view, to question the necessity of giving thanks to God, it certainly was Paul, the ambassador of Jesus Christ to the pagan world. Forsaking the successful career which his brilliant endowments seemed to promise, he had left all to follow Christ. What was his reward? The first messenger of God who came to him after his conversion on the Damascus road was sent to show him "how great things he must suffer." From that moment his life-story could have been written in tears, in blood and torture. His own countrymen tried to murder him; the Greeks plotted against his life. He was beaten and stoned, chained and imprisoned. He was fiercely beset by hunger and thirst. Repeatedly he was left naked and homeless. He was cast out of synagogues and into the sea. His audience screamed, "Away with such a fellow!" and literally sought to tear his flesh from his bones. He was banished from his homeland and sent to Rome as a prisoner in irons; yet as he approached the imperial city and met some of his fellow-Christians, he "thanked God"—thanked God that He had brought him to the city where he would be twice imprisoned and finally judged guilty,—the city where the executioner's ax would sever his head from his body!

This was no isolated instance of his gratitude to God. Throughout his entire career for Christ he lived in perpetual praise. They might bind him in black dungeons; but even then in the dark of midnight he sang praise songs to his Saviour. They might hurl jagged rocks at his body; but he could forget all that and exult repeatedly, "I thank God through Jesus Christ, our Lord." He might become, by his own admission, "as the filth of the world"; but listen to his doxology, "Thanks be unto God, which always causeth us to triumph in Christ." They might cite him before the tribunal of Caesar; but he barely touched Roman soil before "he thanked God." They might imprison him; but in his bonds and in that Roman jail he writes in one of his last letters, "I thank Christ Jesus, our Lord . . . that He counted me faithful." Even when his head dropped to the ground, surely his soul rejoiced in the faith by which he had previously exulted, "O death, where is thy sting? O grave, where is thy victory? . . . Thanks be to God, which giveth us the victory through our Lord Jesus Christ."

WALTER A. MAIER

In every thing give thanks: for this is the will of
God in Christ Jesus concerning you.

1 Thessalonians 5:18.

IT FOLLOWS, necessarily, that where life is governed only within the will of God, every date and every event become links in the chain of a perfect whole. All contribute to a finality. It is impossible here and now for us to discover the relation of the present moment either to past or to future. But that relation is always present to the mind of God. We are permitted occasional gleams of light upon this truth as the years of our life pass on. The light falls in the act of retrospection. Looking back today to the events of years that have passed, we begin to discover their meaning. They are seen to be part of the divine mosaic. The keen disappointment, the whelming sorrow, came after all as a necessity out of the past, and hold within themselves the elements that make the present, and color all the future. The present place of service and of blessing could not have been but for the events that seem to create confusion.

G. CAMPBELL MORGAN

I walked with God this morning along a country lane,
And suddenly, I knew that I would never walk again
On any path that took me from His side;
For by His footprints flowers bloomed that I was sure had died,
And every dusty blade of grass, and every drooping tree
Lifted its head, and as He passed strange immortality
Clothed all the world within my wondering view—
Making that old familiar scene beautiful, bright and new.

I walked with God this morning along that country lane
That I had always thought to be so commonplace and plain:
I wonder if old friends will see in me such radiance
As His presence shed upon that drooping tree!

MURIEL WRIGHT EVANS

For it was not an enemy that reproached me;
then I could have borne it: . . . But it was thou, a
man mine equal, my guide, and mine acquaintance.
We took sweet counsel together, and walked unto
the house of God in company. *Psalm 55:12–14.*

THERE is no painful road on which He has not walked; He is
always further on the road than we have gone: "They laid to
my charge things that I knew not." Our roughest storm appears
a zephyr when we think of the hurricanes that beat upon Him. Even
the grief of seeing the staff whereon we leaned snap under sudden
strain; even the shock of finding one whom we had thought flint
turned to a man of straw, and the twist of pain that wrings out the
cry, "It was not an enemy . . . ; then I could have borne it. . . . But it
was thou!" even that poignant grief He knew to the uttermost.

"Ah, but the treason of friends, their shiftiness, their suspicion,
their doubt, their withdrawal!—therein lies real suffering. Those who
have never felt that have felt nothing, have never suffered even a
scratch," wrote the discredited Didon. The Sinless One walked that
road. "Consider Him who endured." The word has a tranquilizing
power. The endurance which "remains under," does not try to slip
from under, or to float over and so escape from the trial—that is
what we see when we consider our Lord, so marred, more than any
man. . . . But if we are to "remain under" and triumph in our lesser
trials, so that in the end we shall sing, "O my soul, thou hast trodden
down strength," we must make fortitude a settled habit.

AMY CARMICHAEL

All we like sheep have gone astray; we have turned
every one to his own way; and the Lord hath laid
on Him the iniquity of us all. *Isaiah 53:6.*

THE story is told of one under deep conviction of sin. Finding
no relief, he called on an earnest Christian friend, who, being
very busy and having no time at his disposal to give to the
anxious enquirer, hearing briefly of his trouble, replied: "Go home,
open your Bible at Isaiah 53:6, go in at the first ALL, and come out at
the second."

With that he bade him farewell and went on his way. The heavy-

laden sinner at first thought that his friend was jesting, and went home
somewhat ruffled. Turning, however, to the Book, he read: "All we
like sheep have gone astray; we have turned every one to his own
way." "Well," said he, "that is true of me: I can certainly go in at
that ALL." "But the Lord hath laid upon Him the iniquity of us all."
"If that is true, then, I can also go out at the second, and I am saved."
Faith conquered, and he was free.

PAGET WILKES

> Herein is love!
> A cross whose outstretched arms
> Stood stark against a low'ring sky;
> A form divine—God's own immortal Son—hung helpless there;
> And from His lips there issued in the dark
>   A strange, an awful cry!
>
> Herein is love!
> Not in our love for God, whose Son,
> So well-beloved, hung between the earth and sky—
> But in His willingness to see—for us—
>   That loved Son die.
>
> Herein is love!
> God's love—His Son the channel for its flow;
> A love by sacrifice made perfect in His sight;
> Glowing throughout eternal, endless years,
>   A holy, radiant Light!

ANNABEL LEE CRUMLY

DECEMBER 3

**Likewise the Spirit also helpeth our infirmities:
for we know not what we should pray for as we
ought: but the Spirit itself maketh intercession for
us with groanings which cannot be uttered.**

Romans 8:26.

NOTICE how graciously prayer has been designed.
To pray is nothing more involved than to let Jesus into
our needs. To pray is to give Jesus permission to employ His
powers in the alleviation of our distress. To pray is to let Jesus glorify
His name in the midst of our needs.

The results of prayer are, therefore, not dependent upon the
powers of the one who prays. His intense will, his fervent emotions, or
his clear comprehension of what he is praying for are not the reasons

why his prayers will be heard and answered. Nay, God be praised, the results of prayer are not dependent upon these things!

To pray is nothing more involved than to open the door, giving Jesus access to our needs and permitting Him to exercise His own power in dealing with them.

He who gave us the privilege of prayer knows us very well. He knows our frame; He remembers that we are dust.

That is why He designed prayer in such a way that the most impotent can make use of it. For to pray is to open the door unto Jesus. And that requires no strength. It is only a question of our wills. Will we give Jesus access to our needs? That is the one great and fundamental question in connection with prayer.

O. HALLESBY

Prayer is the soul's sincere desire,
Uttered, or unexpressed;
The motion of a hidden fire
That trembles in the breast.

Prayer is the burden of a sigh,
The falling of a tear,
The upward glancing of an eye,
When none but God is near.

Prayer is the simplest form of speech
That infant lips can try;
Prayer the sublimest strains that reach
The Majesty on high.

JAMES MONTGOMERY

DECEMBER 4

If any man will do HIS will, HE SHALL KNOW. . . . *John 7:17.*

To the soul new-born the will of God is revealed again, not as a perfect and final program of life, but in a claim demanding immediate obedience, and then by successive revelations concerning the pathway of life. So that a man may say, as he steps out upon his new life,

"One step I see before me,
'Tis all I need to see."

When Saul of Tarsus was apprehended of Jesus Christ, he was not told that he was to become the apostle to the Gentiles, the mightiest missionary of the Cross, the greatest theologian of the Church. Jesus said to him, "Rise, enter into the city, and it shall be told thee what thou must do." The next step was marked. Taking this, another was revealed; and so ever on, until at last, saying, "I have fought a good fight; I have finished my course; I have kept the faith"—he passed to the place of perfect light and perfect life.

G. Campbell Morgan

I choose Thee, blessed will of God!
In Thee alone, my heart can rest,
The current of Thy love, I know
Can only bear me to Thy breast.

I choose Thee, blessed will of God!
The sweetest thing my heart hath known;
A chariot my God hath sent
To bear me upward to His throne.

I choose Thee, blessed will of God!
For in the circling of Thine arms,
The gladdest Spring of Joy I find;
Outside Thee fears and strange alarms.

May Agnew Stephens

DECEMBER 5

Now the Spirit speaketh expressly, that in the latter times some shall depart from the faith.

1 Timothy 4:1.

HERE we are given a warning that is especially needed in the day in which we live, "the latter times," the day of the near coming of the Lord. We are told that it will be a day of apostasy. Therefore we may expect to see people "giving heed to seducing spirits and doctrines of demons, speaking lies and hypocrisy, having their conscience seared with a hot iron, forbidding to marry, commanding to abstain from meats" and departing from the Word. For this reason Paul exhorted his son Timothy to "preach the Word; be instant in season, out of season; reprove, rebuke, exhort with all longsuffering and doctrine" (2 Timothy 4:2).

The day in which we live is, more than any other time in all history, one of isms and schisms. It is a day when multitudes are following a bloodless, Christless, social gospel which only leads to destruction. Paul, in writing to the Galatian Church, said, "If any man preach any other gospel than that ye have received, let him be accursed" (Galatians 1:9). Now that is strong language but it is God's Word.

God's judgments must inevitably follow when the people depart from His Word.

In Isaiah we find a sentence recurring five times which is of great significance, "For all this His anger is not turned away, but His hand is stretched out still" (Isaiah 5:25; 9:12; 9:17; 9:21; 10:4). Read carefully the indictment against Israel. The conditions were remarkably similar to those of today. The trouble then as now was that the people were following false teachers and leaving God out of the picture. One thing only will bring us out of our trouble. We must turn away from evil and seek God. A world-wide revival is the only thing that can save the situation.

CHARLES E. FULLER

DECEMBER 6

I am come that they might have life, and that they might have it more abundantly.   *John 10:10.*

OUR Lord spoke this word concerning the more abundant life when He said that He had come to give His life for His sheep.

A man may have life, and yet, through lack of nourishment, or through illness, there may be no abundance of life or power. This was the distinction between the Old Testament and the New. In the former there was indeed life, under the Law, but not the abundance of grace of the New Testament. Christ had given life to His disciples, but they could receive the abundant life only through His resurrection and the gift of the Holy Spirit.

All true Christians have received life from Christ. The greater portion of them, however, know nothing about the more abundant life which He is willing to bestow. Paul speaks constantly of this. He says about himself that the grace of God was "exceeding abundant": "I can do all things through Christ who strengtheneth me." "Thanks be unto God, who always causeth us to triumph in Christ." "We are more than conquerors through Him that loved us."

It is of the utmost importance for us so to understand this more abundant life, that we may clearly see that for a true life of prayer nothing less is necessary than that we should walk in an ever increasing experience of that overflowing life.

What is it, then, which peculiarly constitutes this abundant life? We cannot too often repeat, or in different ways too often set it forth —the abundant life is nothing less than the full Jesus having the full mastery over our entire being, through the power of the Holy Spirit.

ANDREW MURRAY

**That which is born of the flesh is flesh; and that
which is born of the Spirit is spirit.   *John 3:6.***

JUST as it is impossible for a living organism to live the life of
a horse before it actually becomes a horse, or to live the life of
a flower before it becomes a flower, so it is impossible for any
human being to live the divine life, which is but another name for
the Christian life, until he has received the life that is divine—the
life that is from above. Now we begin to see why our Lord said to the
most sincere, earnest and devoutly religious man, Nicodemus: "Except
a man be born from above, he cannot see the kingdom of God," for
the life in that kingdom is God-life. As we are familiar with the
mineral, vegetable and animal kingdoms and the characteristics of
each, so the life of the divine kingdom has certain characteristics
which are known only through vital union with Christ, the only One
by whom the divine life can be and is communicated to the soul
of man.

Furthermore, such a conception of the Christian life makes clear
those startling and hard-to-be-believed words of our Lord: "Without
Me ye can do nothing." What! must I admit that, endowed as I am
with these marvelous faculties of spirit, mind and body, I am incapable
of doing anything that will be acceptable to God? Yes, indeed, that is
exactly what our Lord intended to teach. Beneath His words lies the
fundamental truth which we so easily lose sight of, namely, that man
is not an independent creature, but in every sense dependent, and
never adequate to fulfill the righteous and life-producing moral and
spiritual laws of God which completely surround him until and unless
he casts himself utterly on God. We must ever remember that "the
just shall live by faith."

HOWARD W. FERRIN

**The Lord gave, and the Lord hath taken away;
blessed be the name of the Lord.   *Job 1:21.***

WAS not Job mistaken? Should he not have said, "The Lord gave,
and Satan hath taken away?" No, there was no mistake. The
same grace which had enabled him unharmed to receive
blessing from the hand of God, enabled him to discern the hand of
God in the calamities which had befallen him. Satan himself did not

presume to ask of God to be allowed himself to afflict Job. In the eleventh verse of the first chapter he says, "Put forth Thine hand now, and touch all that he hath, and he will curse Thee to Thy face"; and in the second chapter and the fifth verse, "Put forth Thine hand now, and touch his bone and his flesh, and he will curse Thee to Thy face." Satan knew that none but God could touch Job; and when Satan was permitted to afflict him, Job was quite right in recognizing the Lord Himself as the doer of those things which He permitted to be done.

Oftentimes shall we be helped and blessed if we bear this in mind —that Satan is servant, and not master, and that he, and wicked men incited by him, are permitted only to do that which God by His determinate counsel and foreknowledge has before determined shall be done. Come joy, or come sorrow, we may always take it from the hand of God. Judas betrayed his Master with a kiss. Our Lord did not stop short at Judas, nor did He even stop at the great enemy who filled Judas' heart to do this thing; but He said, "The cup which My Father hath given Me, shall I not drink it?"

J. Hudson Taylor

"Thou wilt keep him in perfect peace
Whose mind is stayed on Thee."
I read the dear old promise o'er,
And ask, "Is this for me?"
When troubles throng without surcease,
Can God keep me in perfect peace?

"In perfect peace," when seas run high,
When loud the cutting blast?
When laid upon a bed of pain?
When tears are falling fast?
If Satan all his pow'r release,
Can God still keep in perfect peace?

Yet I recall that far-off night,
Upon a storm-swept sea,
When urgent cries for succor came
From men in jeopardy,—
How, instantly, the waves were still
In swift obedience to His will.

O mighty Master of the sea,
Thou art my Master, too!
And Thou, all things unto Thyself
Art able to subdue—
Thou biddest inner tumult cease;
Thou keepest me "in perfect peace."

T. O. Chisholm

DECEMBER
9

**The Lord is nigh unto them that are of a broken
heart; and saveth such as be of a contrite spirit.**

Psalm 34:18.

FROM a California prison comes this letter. What a testimony
to the power of the Gospel!

"*Dear Mr. Fuller*: Your program has just gone off the air.
I received such a blessing from it that I feel I should write to
you. I am on condemned row in ——— prison. Only God can
prevent my being executed, but if it is His will that I die in that
manner I can only rejoice that I will be in heaven that much
sooner.

"I was first saved in 1934 but backslid into the worldly life
again. I have just recently come back to Jesus. The Old Fashioned
Revival Hour is a source of much pleasure to me and my Bible is
a gold mine of joy. Several of us fellows have a sort of Bible
class during part of our recreation period every day and are wonderfully blessed, as it helps us understand God's Word more
thoroughly.

"I wish you would ask your radio audience to pray for the
men up here and for all the other condemned men, because if
there ever were men who need God it is we who are in this
situation."

Shall we not all pray today especially for these poor souls who
have gone astray? God is able and willing to save them if they will
turn to Him. How wonderful that hundreds like this man have an
opportunity to know the love of God as they listen in on Sunday
evenings. For many it will be the last message before they meet
their Maker.

DECEMBER
10

**But they that wait upon the Lord . . . shall mount
up with wings as eagles.** *Isaiah 40:31.*

LIFE with wing-power is characterized by loftiness. "They shall
mount up!" You know how we speak of the men and women
endowed with wings. We speak of a "lofty character," as op-
posed to one who is low or mean. There are men with low motives,

and they move along the low way. There are men with mean affections which do not comprehend a brother. Now, it is the glorious characteristic of the Christian religion that it claims to give loftiness to life.

There is no feature that the Bible loves more to proclaim than just this feature of "aboveness." It distinguishes the disciples of Christ. See how the ambitions of the Book run:—"Seek the things that are above"; "Set your mind on things above." It speaks also of dwelling "with Christ in the heavenly places." All this describes the life that looks at everything from lofty standpoints and approaches everything with high ambition. We know these men when they appear. How often one has observed the power of their presence in public meetings! Other speakers have addressed the assembly, and the thought and life of the meeting have grovelled along a mean and questionable way. And then the wing-man comes! He lays hold of the subject, and what happens? Everybody says, "How he lifted it up!" A pure atmosphere came round about the assembly; everybody felt the inrush of a purer air and a finer light. We had mounted up with wings as eagles.

J. H. JOWETT

DECEMBER 11

Call ye on the name of your gods, and I will call on the name of the Lord: and the God that answereth by fire, let Him be God.   *1 Kings 18:24.*

ND let it never be forgotten that here is the real test: "The God that answereth by fire, let Him be God." Men have made finances and figures the test, and the church with most statistics in its favor has been adjudged most favored of God. Fame has been made the criterion and publicity has created much that God never approved from heaven. And their number is legion who, in their Christian experiences, would have it read, "The God who answereth by feelings, let Him be God." But the test is FIRE, supernatural fire, not the strange fire of Nadab and Abihu, but the heavenly flame of Pentecost.

Too many of our meetings can be accounted for on purely natural grounds: we meet and sing and talk and pray and nothing happens that cannot be explained. We need some meetings that cannot be accounted for nor be explained away, where men must shake their heads and say, "We have seen strange things today." Some may attribute it to new wine, but it was that sort of meeting that added three thousand souls to the church in a day.

The infidel who stood at a burning church and explained his presence there by saying, "I never saw this church on fire before," would be found multiplied by thousands if spiritually our assemblies caught on fire from above. Even fundamentalists do not escape here, for all too often they have the facts but still lack the Flame. God is not revealed so much in correct theology; heads may be right and hearts still be wrong. Painted fire may even be added to touch up the doctrine, but painted fire is not Pentecost fire; it will not burn.

VANCE HAVNER

ᵒ₈[DECEMBER]₈ᵒ
12

Except a man be born again, he cannot see the kingdom of God. *John 3:3.*

𝔍N THE first eight verses of the third chapter of John we find recorded one of the most important conferences ever held by two persons. One of the persons was the Lord Jesus Christ, God's well-beloved Son. The other was Nicodemus, a highly educated man, a teacher in Israel, a member of the highest court. The outcome of this conference changed the eternal destiny of one man. Nicodemus, before the conference, although religiously educated, moral, upright —a man among men—was lost, dead in trespasses and sins, without hope. After the conference he was a new creation in Christ Jesus, born again and on the road to heaven.

Nicodemus came to Jesus by night for fear of the Jews. He acknowledged that Jesus was a great teacher and that God was with Him. Perhaps he had heard of the miracle of changing the water into wine which is recorded in chapter two. Jesus said to him, "Verily, verily, I say unto thee, Except a man be born again, he cannot see the kingdom of God" (John 3:3). It was difficult for Nicodemus to understand how this could be but Jesus told him that He was speaking of a spiritual birth. "That which is born of the flesh is flesh; and that which is born of the Spirit is spirit."

I want you to see the importance of the new birth. It is significant that this teaching comes first in the Gospel of John. This discourse is not on how men are to live but on how they are to be made alive spiritually. Jesus' use of "verily, verily," denotes something very important, something which demands closest attention. Then the importance of the new birth is brought out by the statement that without it no one can see the kingdom of God. The natural man, or one who has not been born again, cannot receive the things of the Spirit of God for they are foolishness unto him. To be born again involves new understanding, new desires, new relationships, new plans. How need-

309

ful it is that we check these matters to discover whether we are really transformed by the miracle of the new birth. As with Nicodemus, it is a life and death matter to know that we have passed from death unto life.

CHARLES E. FULLER

DECEMBER 13

I will put my Spirit within you, and cause you to walk in my statutes, and ye shall keep My judgments, and do them. *Ezekiel 36:27.*

T H E highest spiritual condition is one where life is spontaneous and flows without effort, like the deep floods of Ezekiel's river, where the struggles of the swimmer ceased, and he was borne by the current's resistless force. So God leads us into spiritual conditions and habits which become the spontaneous impulses of our being, and we live and move in the fulness of the divine life.

But these spiritual habits are not the outcome of some transitory impulse, but are often slowly acquired and established. They begin, like every true habit, in a definite act of the will, and they are confirmed by the repetition of that act until it becomes a habit. The first stages always involve effort and choice. We have to take a stand and hold it steadily, and after we have done so a certain time, it becomes second nature, and carries us by its own force. The Holy Spirit is willing to form such habits in every direction in our Christian life; and if we will but obey Him in the first steppings of faith, we shall soon become established in the attitude of obedience, and duty will be delight.

A. B. SIMPSON

This crystal spring beneath the linden tree
Has quenched the thirst of toilers on the land;
And travelers have come from afar to see
Its waters surging up through sunflecked sand.
Its overflow has made a ferny track
Of sweet, perpetual beauty down the hill—
Earth's dark and hidden waters given back
To joyous living in a singing rill.
Here I have mused in wonder and in awe
Upon the deeper mysteries that cling
To nature's picturing forth the higher law
In the simple teaching of a wayside spring—
A symbol of that Living Water's store
Of which all men may drink and thirst no more.

AGNES BARDEN DUSTIN

310

No man that warreth entangleth himself with the
affairs of this life; that he may please him who hath
chosen him to be a soldier.   *2 Timothy 2:4.*

THIS is the sum and substance of the "officer's" message in
Deuteronomy 20:5–7, "No man that warreth entangleth himself." He demands, on the part of God's warriors, a disentangled
heart. It is not a question of salvation, of being a child of God, of
being a true Israelite; it is simply a question of ability to wage an
effectual warfare; and, clearly, a man cannot fight well if his heart is
entangled with a "house," "a vineyard," or "a wife." Nor was it a
question of having such things. By no means. Thousands of those who
went forth to tread the battlefields and gather the spoils of victory, had
houses, and lands, and domestic ties. The officers had no quarrel with
the possessors of these things; the only point was, not to be entangled
with them.

The Apostle does not say, "No man that warreth engages in the
affairs of this life." The grand point is to keep the heart disentangled.
God's warriors must have free hearts, and the only way to be free is
to cast all our care upon Him who careth for us. I can stand in the
battlefield with a free heart when I have placed my house, my vineyard, and my wife, in the divine keeping. But, further, God's warriors
must have courageous hearts as well as free hearts. "The fearful and
the faint-hearted" can never stand in the battle, nor wear the laurel
of victory. Our hearts must be disentangled from the world, and bold
by reason of our artless confidence in God.

J. GREGORY MANTLE

THE MINISTER

There is a human touch about his hand,
A ring of human kindness in his tone;
Yet he who meets his eye will understand
How many are the hours he spends alone.
Far from the crowd that throngs the city street,
The crowd whose burdens he cannot forget,
But for whose sake he slips away to meet
The Father on some silent Olivet.

Life's jewels oft he gathers from the dust,
He makes the mending of marred lives an art.
The children come to him in trust,
And sinners hide their stories in his heart.
The high and low who chance his way to plod,
Grow strangely conscious of the touch of God.

CLARENCE EDWIN FLYNN

And thine ears shall hear a word behind thee,
saying, This is the way, walk ye in it, when ye
turn to the right hand, and when ye turn to the
left.   *Isaiah 30:21.*

THERE is a tender awe in knowing that there is Someone at
your side guiding every step, restraining here, leading on there.
He knows the way better than the oldest Swiss guide knows the
mountain trail. He has love's concern that all shall go well with you.
There is a great peace for us in that, and with it a tender awe to think
who He is, and that He is close by your side. When you come to the
splitting of the road into two, with a third path forking off from the
others, there is peace in just holding steady and very quiet while you
put out your hand and say, "Jesus, Master, guide here." And then to
hear a Voice so soft that only in great quiet is it heard, softer than
faintest breath on your cheek, or slightest touch on your arm, telling
the way in fewest words or syllables—that makes the peace unspeakable.

S. D. GORDON

My plans were made, I thought my path all bright and clear,
My heart with song o'erflowed, the world seemed full of cheer.
My Lord I wished to serve, to take Him for my Guide,
To keep so close that I could feel Him by my side,
 And so I traveled on.

But suddenly, in skies so clear and full of light,
The clouds fell thick and fast, the days seemed changed to night;
Instead of paths so clear and full of things so sweet,
Rough things and thorns and stones seemed all about my feet,
 I scarce could travel on.

I bowed my head and wondered why this change should come,
And murmured—"Lord, is this because of aught I've done?
Has not the past been full enough of pain and care?
Why should my path again be changed to dark despair?"
 But still I travel on.

I listened—quiet and still, there came a voice—
"The path is Mine, not thine, I made the choice;
Dear child, this service will be best for thee and Me,
If thou wilt simply trust and leave the end to Me."
 And so we traveled on.

GRIT STORY SECTION

Now I Nebuchadnezzar praise and extol and honor
the King of heaven, all whose works are truth,
and His ways judgment.   *Daniel 4:37.*

SOMETIMES our minds are so taken up with the proud "lights"
of fad and fancy that the heavenly glories are lost to our spiritual vision. In mercy God places us in some dark room where
the shades of gloom and despair are pulled down so tight against the
lower window sash that we are well nigh overwhelmed. In dismay
we cry, "Why, oh why, this darkness?" Perhaps we can find the answer
very finely put in the following excerpt taken from the S. S. World:

A man was invited by an artist to come to his house to see a
picture which he had just finished. When the visitor arrived, he was
shown into a room which was pitch dark, and there he was left for a
quarter of an hour alone. Not unnaturally, when the artist came to him,
he expressed some surprise at the reception that had been given to
him.

"Surprised, were you?" said the artist. "Well, I knew if you came
to the studio with the glare of the street in your eyes, you would never
be able to appreciate the fine coloring of my picture, and so I left
you in the dark until the glare had worn away from your eyes."

Is not that the secret of many an hour in which God leaves His
children in the darkness? When we are dazzled by the pleasures and
successes of this present life, though in themselves they may be innocent and happy, we cannot see the things that are unseen, and an
interval is necessary in the darkness until the glare has worn away
from our eyes."

PAMEII

"Jesus only," 'midst the shadows,
    That within the valley lie;
He it is who calls us onward,
    To the glory of the sky.
He it is who points us upward,
    Far above the mountain height—
Far above the valley shadows,
    To the radiant glory light.

"Jesus only," when the sunbeams
    Gleam around our pilgrim way;
When no shadows seem to darken,
    Throughout all the long bright day;
Then He comes and walks beside us,
    Whispering words of tenderest love,

Tells us of the light and glory,
Of the sunny land above.

AUTHOR UNKNOWN

DECEMBER 17

But if the Spirit of Him that raised up Jesus from the dead dwell in you, He that raised up Christ from the dead shall also quicken your mortal bodies by His Spirit that dwelleth in you. *Romans 8:11.*

THE Scripture frequently mentions the resurrection in connection with the wonder-working power of God, by which Christ was raised from the dead; and from which comes the assurance of "the exceeding greatness of His power to us-ward who believe, according to the working of His mighty power, which He wrought in Christ, when He raised Him from the dead" (Eph. 1:19, 20). Do not pass hastily from these words. Turn back and read them once more, and learn the great lesson that, however powerless and weak you feel, the omnipotence of God is working in you and, if you only believe, will give you in daily life a share in the resurrection of His Son.

Yes, the Holy Spirit can fill you with the joy and victory of the resurrection of Christ, as the power of your daily life, here in the midst of the trials and temptations of this world. Let the cross humble you to death. God will work out the heavenly life in you through His Spirit. Ah, how little have we understood that it is entirely the work of the Holy Spirit to make us partakers of the Crucified and Risen Christ, and to conform us to His life and death!

ANDREW MURRAY

Sing with all the sons of glory,
Sing the resurrection song!
Death and sorrow, earth's dark story,
To the "former days" belong.
Even now the dawn is breaking,
Soon the night of time shall cease,
And, in God's own likeness waking,
Man shall know eternal peace.

"Life eternal!" heav'n rejoices,
Jesus lives who once was dead;
Join, O man, the deathless voices,
Child of God, lift up thy head.
Patriarchs from distant ages,
Saints all longing for their heav'n,
Prophets, psalmists, seers and sages,
All await the glory given.

WILLIAM J. IRONS

314

For verily I say unto you, If you have faith as a grain of mustard seed, ye shall say unto this mountain, Remove hence to yonder place; and it shall remove; and nothing shall be impossible unto you.

Matthew 17:20.

ONE of those who had had the opportunity to make use of this equipment throughout a whole lifetime of work and sacrifice says of it, "In nothing be anxious; but in everything by prayer and supplication with thanksgiving let your requests be made known unto God" (Philippians 4:6).

He who had sent them knew that this weapon, this piece of equipment, would make them invincible. "Nothing shall be impossible unto you," were His words.

When at His ascension He took leave of His friends, as far as His physical presence was concerned, He extended His almighty arm so far down that we insignificant and sinful men can reach it every time we bend our knees in prayer.

Whenever we touch His almighty arm, some of His omnipotence streams in upon us, into our souls and into our bodies. And not only that, but, through us, it streams out to others.

This power is so rich and so mobile that all we have to do when we pray is point to the persons or things to which we desire to have this power applied, and He, the Lord of this power, will direct the necessary power to the desired place at once.

This power is entirely independent of time and space. In the very moment that we bend our knees and pray for our brethren and sisters in Zulu, Madagascar, Santalistan, China, or the Sudan, in that same instant this power is transmitted to these people. Here is an example of wireless transmission of power which transcends the dreams of the boldest inventor.

O. HALLESBY

Name of Jesus! living tide!
Days of drought for me are past:
How much more than satisfied
Are the thirsty lips at last!

Name of Jesus! dearest Name!
Bread of Heaven, and balm of love;
Oil of gladness, surest claim
To the treasures stored above.

GERHARDT TERSTEEGEN

315

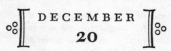

DECEMBER
19

And he brought him to Jesus. *John 1:42.*

I WANT you to underline these six words in your Bible. There are four instances of conversion recorded in this chapter. Andrew, Peter, Philip, and Nathaniel. It is interesting to note that these men were not saved in the same way. No two conversions, it seems, are alike. The first, Andrew, heard the Spirit-filled message of John the Baptist, "Behold, the Lamb of God, that taketh away the sin of the world." Peter and Nathaniel were brought to the Lord by the personal work of a believer. Philip was won directly by the Lord. No human instrumentality, as far as I can find, was used.

It is interesting to note the different personalities of these men. Andrew had a practical, calculating mind. No sooner had he come to Christ than he went at once to find Peter. Peter was a hot-headed man, full of zeal and impulsiveness. Philip was sceptical and materialistic. Nathaniel was meditative and retiring. In spite of all these differences of temperament they all found satisfaction in Christ. He is the only One who can satisfy the deep hunger of the human heart.

Andrew became a soul-winner at once. He quickly found his brother and brought him to Jesus. We can learn valuable lessons from him. To be a soul-winner one must first himself be a follower of Jesus. Men who have never seen the beauties of the Lord are not fit to tell others about Him. One of the surest signs that you are born again is your desire to see others saved. Andrew does not appear to have been brilliant. He was just a man of ordinary capacities. He was just a young convert. But he was able to win a soul. Your ability to be a soul-winner does not depend upon whether you have a college education—it depends upon your love for Christ and your fellow-men. God loves to take the weak things of the world and confound the wise. He can use your talents today if you really love Him.

CHARLES E. FULLER

DECEMBER
20

The night is far spent, the day is at hand. . . .
Romans 13:12.

A CURRENT newspaper carried the advertisement of a large concern, now transforming its gigantic plant from the making of heating equipment to the making of gun parts. This was headed, "We're in the army now—and the time is short!" As we read the

316

phrase, our heart said, "Yes, we are in the army, the army of the Lord, and the time is short!"

I wonder, if, as Christians, we appreciate to the full the fact that each one of us is a soldier, waging a battle as vital as any on the world's battlefronts (although our weapons are spiritual not carnal) and that the time is short—"the day is at hand." Have we put on the whole armor of God? Are we able to stand, and having done all, TO STAND? Are we fully prepared for whatever assault the enemy may make upon us? Do we spend much time in prayer and meditation?

Soldiers leave behind them the comforts, conveniences, problems, and pleasures of civilian life, and gird themselves for one purpose— to fight. Are we willing to "lay aside every weight" (and the sin that is in good standing with church members!) in order to fight the enemy of souls wherever we meet him? What is our tendency in life? Paul wrote, "Whether we live, we live unto . . ." Fill in the answer. We live unto money? We live unto pleasure? We live unto ease? We live unto fame? We live unto indifference? "Let us therefore cast off the works of darkness, and let us put on the armor of light."

GEORGE PALMER

Faint not amid the battle smoke,
Nor falter in the fight;
Press on until the foe gives way,
Walk in the Saviour's might.
Thy breastplate, helmet, and thy sword,
Take up, and ne'er lay down;
He that endureth to the end,
The same shall wear a crown.

Then sound the battle cry of faith,
Catch and repeat the strain,
Till every heart shall be inspired,
And swell the glad refrain.
Endure all hardness for His sake,
Like soldiers overcome,
E'en till from labor to reward,
The hosts are marshalled home.

E. GRACE UPDEGRAFF

**His delight is in the law of the Lord; and in His
law doth he meditate day and night.** *Psalm 1:2.*

THE Bible seldom speaks, and certainly never its deepest, sweetest words, to those who always read it in a hurry. Nature can only tell her secrets to such as will sit still in her sacred temple till their eyes lose the glare of earthly glory, and their ears are attuned to her voice. And shall Revelation do what Nature cannot? Never. The man who shall win the blessedness of hearing her must watch daily at her gates and wait at the posts of her doors. There is no chance for a lad to grow, who only gets an occasional mouthful of food and always swallows that in a hurry!

F. B. MEYER

Lord, I have shut the door;
Speak now the word
Which in the din and throng
Could not be heard.
Hushed now my inner heart,
Whisper Thy will,
While I have come apart,
While all is still.

In this blest quietness
Clamorings cease;
Here in Thy presence dwells
Infinite peace;
Yonder the strife and cry,
Yonder the sin:
Lord, I have shut the door,
Thou art within.

Lord, I have shut the door,
Strengthen my heart;
Yonder awaits the task—
I share a part.
Only through grace bestowed
May I be true;
Here, while alone with Thee,
My strength renew.

WILLIAM M. RUNYAN

DECEMBER 22

**Whether therefore ye eat, or drink, or whatsoever
ye do, do all to the glory of God.**

1 Corinthians 10:31.

THE Bible does not specifically name modern amusements. It
does, however, have much to say about purity of heart and the
danger of worldliness. The Word of God may be applied to all
men in all times and in all places. The devices of Satan change with
the times; the penalty of sin remains the same in all ages. The Gospel
of Christ is intended to make a good heart, a clean character, and a
conscience void of offense. By reading the Word of God, any Christian
can determine what is right and what is wrong in the world of amusements. Every question should be settled by the Word of God, which
gives us adequate and specific tests for our amusements.

Test your amusements by the following:

1. Does the amusement in which you engage tend to enslave you?
"All things are lawful . . . but all things are not expedient . . . I
will not be brought under the power of any" (1 Corinthians 6:12).

2. Does the amusement help in building up your body, your mind,
and your spirit? "All things are lawful, but all things edify not" (1
Corinthians 10:23).

3. Does the amusement cause others to stumble over you? "But
when ye sin so against the brethren, and wound their weak conscience,
ye sin against Christ. Wherefore, if meat make my brother to offend,
I will eat no flesh while the world standeth, lest I make my brother
to offend" (1 Corinthians 8:12, 13).

4. Does the amusement glorify God? "Whether therefore ye eat,
or drink, or whatsoever ye do, do all to the glory of God" (1 Corinthians 10:31).

JOHN BUNYAN SMITH

DECEMBER 23

**Give unto the Lord the glory due unto His name:
bring an offering, and come before Him: worship
the Lord in the beauty of holiness.**

1 Chronicles 16:29.

IN SPITE of the great number of letters received by Mr. and Mrs.
Fuller, special thought and prayer are given to all those that
express needs. Here is a letter from California, typical of many
which tell of return to faith, answered prayer and gratitude to God for
the radio ministry.

"Dear Brother Fuller: We received the book, *The Old Fashioned Revival Hour* and have almost finished reading it. It is wonderful. Now we understand why we were so blest when we started helping a little with the broadcast.

"We are a large family, much larger than the average. My husband was working on a job that furnished us a bare living, in fact we had many bills that we could not pay. He commenced to listen to the Old Fashioned Revival Hour and was earnestly trying to live a Christian life, after having been backslidden for several years. I would not listen, for the sermon troubled me. I was bitter and resentful because of financial reverses and losses, as well as a great sorrow in the family.

"My husband was taken suddenly and desperately ill. He was taken to a large hospital where I was not allowed to see him. It seemed to me that this was the last straw. Something prompted me to write you, as it was through you that my husband was again believing and trusting God. I felt surely the prayers of God's people would save his life. I received a nice reply from you which I carry in my purse.

"Well, my husband was remarkably healed. He remained several days in the hospital but gained rapidly. When he returned home, we were never before so badly off financially. However, when he got his first pay check he suggested that we send a dollar to the Revival Hour. We then sent a dollar every month. Before long we were able to pay our bills."

It would have been justifiable, seemingly, for these people to have neglected giving to God's work until they were out of debt, but robbing God is not the way to financial prosperity. God will honor those who obey His injunctions about tithes and gifts.

DECEMBER 24

Thanks be unto God for His unspeakable gift.
2 Corinthians 9:15.

WHEN St. Paul calls Christ God's "unspeakable Gift," he is not toying with exaggerating superlatives, polishing his style with impressive phraseology. The blessing of the Saviour's Gospel was as inexplicable to him as it must be to us. The Apostle uses a term here which means: one "cannot bring out" or "express" the blessing, the fulness, the glory, the riches, the value, of this divine gift. If St. Paul, acknowledged even by the Christless world as a master of logic, expression, and rhetoric, asserts that God's Christmas-gift to the world defies all description, where will we find words or pictures, poetry or painting, that can reproduce in full majesty the limitless love of our Lord Jesus?

No sacred oratorio, not even the unforgettable strains of Handel's "Messiah" and its climax in the stirring "Hallelujah Chorus" or the artistry of Bach's "Christmas Oratorio," can be classed with the angel chorus reechoing over Bethlehem; and even those angel voices could not sing the full glory of Christ.

All the hands of genius painting nativity scenes, the fifty-six madonnas of Raphael, or an art gallery graced with the masterpieces of the ages that have depicted the Christ-child can truly delineate the personal blessings of Bethlehem. No poetry, not even the sacred lines of our hymnals, the measured stateliness of any nativity ode, not even the ancient psalms of inspired prophecy, can fully express the height and depth of God's love in Christ. The heart of Christmas remains unspeakable in its beauty, immeasurable in its power, unutterable in its glory.

WALTER A. MAIER

DECEMBER 25

Behold, a virgin shall conceive and bear a son, and shall call His name Immanuel. *Isaiah 7:14.*

THIS day is a day of remembrance, for it is the focal point of all the ages. Everything in human history, from the day of man's tragic fall to the birth of God's only begotten son in Bethlehem's manger, hinged upon His coming to redeem the world. Without that birth there would be no ray of hope for those whom God created in His own image. When God said to Satan, "I will put enmity between thee and the woman, and between thy seed and her seed; it shall bruise thy head and thou shalt bruise His heel," He was giving to unborn generations the promise of deliverance from bondage to the arch enemy of mankind. Wrapped up in that statement is the whole plan of redemption: warfare between Satan and mankind with God working in man's behalf; the birth of One who would be the deliverer (stronger than Satan although born of woman, and therefore both human and divine); One who in the process of accomplishing redemption would suffer ("thou shalt bruise His heel"); but One who should conquer (He "shall bruise thy head").

"Unto us a Child is born, unto us a Son is given: and the government shall be upon His shoulder: and His name shall be called Wonderful, Counsellor, The Mighty God, the Everlasting Father, The Prince of Peace" (Isaiah 9:6).

J. ELWIN WRIGHT

321

And did the lovely mother visualize
The nailprints in those tiny hands that morn,
And through a halo did she see a thorn?
At dawning twilight did she realize
The truth? Did joy and grief then agonize:
"The Man of sorrows unto me was born
This day"? And was the heart within her torn
To see the shadow of a cross arise?
"Good tidings of great joy," the angels sang,
Re-echoing through the world with one accord;
And over all their glory songs there rang
One voice, "My soul doth magnify the Lord."

Tonight the star of Bethlehem shines again,
The Prince of Peace is born and love shall reign.

BEATRICE E. LEEK

DECEMBER 26

(He) dwelt among us. *John 1:14.*

WHAT condescension! What voluntary humiliation! The Son of God, creator of the universe, left heaven—not for a few days, but to dwell among men for thirty-three years. He shared our burdens, bore our diseases, was subject to all the pain of body, loneliness of spirit, weariness, poverty, and heart-break that any human being may know, because He loved us. He had no place to call His own. He said to one who professed to want to follow Him, "Foxes have holes, and the birds of the air have nests, but the Son of Man hath not where to lay His head."

The word "dwell" in the original carries the thought of "tabernacling." He "tabernacled" among us. Instantly our thoughts go back to the tabernacle of Exodus, when the Israelites journeyed from Egypt to Canaan. We are told in Exodus 25, "The Lord spake unto Moses, saying, Let them make Me a sanctuary that I may dwell among them." That tabernacle was God's dwelling place in the midst of Israel's camp. Everything about its construction speaks of Christ. There was only one door to the outer court. Christ is *our* only door. Inside the door stood the brazen altar upon which the sacrifices were made continually. No man could go into the tabernacle until the sacrifice was made. Next was the laver where his hands and feet must be cleansed—signifying the cleansing of the Word. But the place of communion and fellowship was reached only in the holy of holies, where the blood was sprinkled on the mercy seat of the ark of the covenant. This was the dwelling place of God in the midst of His people.

When the Son of God was crucified, the veil of the temple was rent in twain and this place of communion was open to all who accept the finished work of Christ. So He who came to dwell with us becomes our dwelling place. He says, "Abide in Me" (John 15:4).

CHARLES E. FULLER

DECEMBER 27

They that wait upon the Lord shall renew their strength; they shall mount up with wings as eagles; they shall run, and not be weary; and they shall walk, and not faint. *Isaiah 40:31.*

THEY shall mount up with wings as eagles." Who shall? "They that wait upon the Lord." And waiting upon the Lord is not merely a passing call but a permanent abiding in His presence. He that waits upon the Lord shall be endowed with resources he has never before known. Nor is this passing strange, for when we consider the One upon whom we may wait, with faith and expectation, it would be great wonder indeed if we were not strengthened by His magnificent power.

"When do you get your wings?" is a question quite familiar to young air pilots in these days. More and more we are "taking to the air." It is unquestionably true that, following the war, there will be more travel by air than ever before. But though we may soar above in airplanes, we may still be living our spiritual life on an earthly plane. So we would ask: "Have you got your wings?" that is, the wings of which the prophet here speaks—eagle's wings, if you please—by which you can mount up to the highest levels of spiritual living? "They that wait upon the Lord" obtain their wings, that is, they obtain resources which endow them with a power of detachment, a power of elevation, a power of soaring on high in order that they may approach all problems from above. Such a life gains new power, extraordinary capacity in a sense of buoyant strength which is not known by those who remain on the earth. Wing-power is essential to higher living.

HOWARD W. FERRIN

*. . . the God of all comfort; who comforteth us in
all our tribulation, that we may be able to comfort
them which are in any trouble.*

2 Corinthians 1:3, 4.

HE God of all comfort." What music there is about the word!
It means more than tenderness: it is strength in tenderness, and
it is tenderness in strength. It is not a mere palliative, but a
curative. It does not merely soothe, it heals. Its ministry is not only
consolation but restoration. "Comfort" is "mercy" at work, it is Sa-
maritanism busy with its oil and wine. And again let us mark that
whenever we find this busy goodness among the children of men, ex-
ercising itself among the broken limbs and broken hearts of the race,
the Lord is the fountain of it. He is "the God of all comfort," of every
form and kind and aspect. Again I say, how boldly the Apostle plants
the Lord's flag, and claims the gracious kingdom of kindly ministries
for our God!

J. H. JOWETT

What can it mean? Is it ought to Him
That the days are long, and the nights are dim?
Can He be touched by the griefs I bear,
Which sadden the heart and whiten the hair?
About His throne are eternal calms,
And strong glad music of happy psalms,
And bliss unruffled by any strife—
How can He care for my little life?

When shadows hang o'er the whole day long,
And my spirit is bowed with shame and wrong,
And I am not good, and the bitter shade
Of conscious sin makes my soul afraid;
And the busy world has too much to do
To stay in its courses and help me through;
And I long for a Saviour—can it be
That the God of the universe CARES FOR ME?

Let all who are sad take heart again;
We are not alone in our hours of pain:
Our Father looks from His throne above
To soothe and comfort us with His love.
He leaves us not when the storms are high,
And we have safety, for He is nigh;
Can that be trouble which He doth share?
Oh, rest in peace, for the Lord DOES CARE!

HUGH MILLER

But, beloved, be not ignorant of this one thing,
that one day is with the Lord as a thousand years,
and a thousand years as one day.   *2 Peter 3:8.*

I SUPPOSE the insects at our feet, if they could think, would
probably think our movements very slow. How long it must seem
that a man's foot stays on the ground when he is walking, even
walking fast. The ant down there can scurry along several times its
own length while that foot remains unmoved. But the length of the
foot's stay on one spot tells of the size of the body it is holding up
and swinging forward.

God's movements seem so slow to us. His march through history,
the coming of justice to the weak and oppressed, the shining of light in
the dark places—all this has so often been called slow. God is so big,
so great. He is moving steadily on. The apparent slowness only spells
out the greatness of His size and of His plans. It takes time to swing
great things forward. Time is but a hyphen between two eternities.
God lives and moves in eternity. He breathes in the atmosphere of
greatness.

S. D. GORDON

I know not if we long must wait
The summer of His smile;
I only know that hope doth sweep
With thrilling touch my heart strings deep,
And sings "a little while."
I know not on this glorious theme
Why lips so oft are dumb;
I only know the saddened earth
Will flush with beauty and with mirth
At sound of "Lo, I come."

AUTHOR UNKNOWN

Thou crownest the year with Thy goodness; and
Thy paths drop fatness.   *Psalm 65:11.*

H APPY New Year!" we say. And the old one was happy, too.
All our years, with Him, are happy years. True, some of the
days were dark, and some of the nights brought pain, but even
the darkest day had its showers of blessing, and through the darkest
night shone the star of hope.

"I love you, good Old Year!
Not that your days unclouded came and went;
Not that the light was sweet,
But that darkness drew us close to Christ
In following His feet.
Hallowed by fires of pain—God's proof of love,
Pure, infinite, and free—
You helped us gauge the cost and weigh the worth
Of human sympathy."

So when I watch you dip below the horizon of time into the shoreless sea of eternity my heart is stirred to gratitude, for I remember the rich gifts of friendship, kindness, beauty, and truth you brought, and I know that increased happiness awaits me in the future, if I bring into it the wisdom you gave.

ANNA J. LINDGREN

Another new year now awaits us,
A page that is spotless and white;
New grace, our dear Lord, wilt Thou give us,
To watch each new day what we write;
For Thine all-seeing eye is upon us,
Thine ear hears the words which we speak,
And Thy heart knows the impulse which moves us,
Thy mind knows the object we seek.

Thy Word is the light which shall lead us,
Thy Word is a lamp to our feet;
We seek and believe it, and hold it,
The source of Thy blessings replete.
The days Thou shalt give us in mercy,
We promise to spend to Thy praise;
And may honor, and power and glory
Be Thine, O Thou Ancient of Days!

AUTHOR UNKNOWN

DECEMBER 31

Forgetting those things which are behind, and reaching forth unto those things which are before, I press toward the mark for the prize of the high calling of God in Christ Jesus. *Philippians 3:13, 14.*

THE record of the year that is past has been written. We may not go back over the pages to re-write them to our liking, however much we desire to do so. There may have been pages soiled with our sins. Others are stained with our scalding tears that fell in moments of sorrow or remorse. But there is one great consolation. In so far as the record is blemished or its writing is against us, we may ask the help of One who is able to blot it all out and remember it no more against us forever. In this comforting assurance we may turn our faces resolutely to the dawn of the new day in a New Year and forget the things that are behind while we press on toward the mark.

J. ELWIN WRIGHT

To the veiled portal of another year
  With softened tread I come, for none can show
Its secrets perfectly to me, and yet—
  Some things I know:

Though o'er a trackless wild the pathway lead,
  Where hidden dangers lurk on every side,
I may walk safely, undismayed, with Thee,
  My faithful Guide.

The wilderness for me no food may yield,
  Barren and waste the desert pathway trod;
I cannot hunger as on Thee I feed,
  O Bread of God.

Earth's cisterns would invite but to deceive
  If, thirsting, I to them for drink should go;
But pure, abundant, living waters from
  The Rock shall flow.

And if, to stay my heavenward journeying,
  The adversary come with dire intent;
Unharmed, I pass, for all his darts upon
  My Shield are spent.

Thus right courageously I fare me forth;
  With Thee so near, no fears my soul appall,
Naught shall I need that Thou wilt not supply,
  My All in All.

K. F. S.